A TRAILS BOOKS GUIDE

BIKING IOWA

50 GREAT ROAD TRIPS AND TRAIL RIDES

BOB MORGAN

Trails Books
Madison, Wisconsin

Library of Congress Control Number: 2005908956
ISBN: 1-931599-63-7

Editor: Mark Knickelbine
Graphic Designer: Kathie Campbell
Photographs: Bob Morgan
Maps: Magellan Mapping Co.
Cover photo: Jerry Luterman

Printed in the United States of America by Sheridan Books
11 10 09 08 07 06   6 5 4 3 2 1

Trails Books, a division of Big Earth Publishing
923 Williamson Street
Madison, WI 53703
www.trailsbooks.com

This book is dedicated to Linda—my wife, lover, partner, and stoker—
who encouraged me to take it on, rode with me while I researched it,
and put up with me while I wrote it.

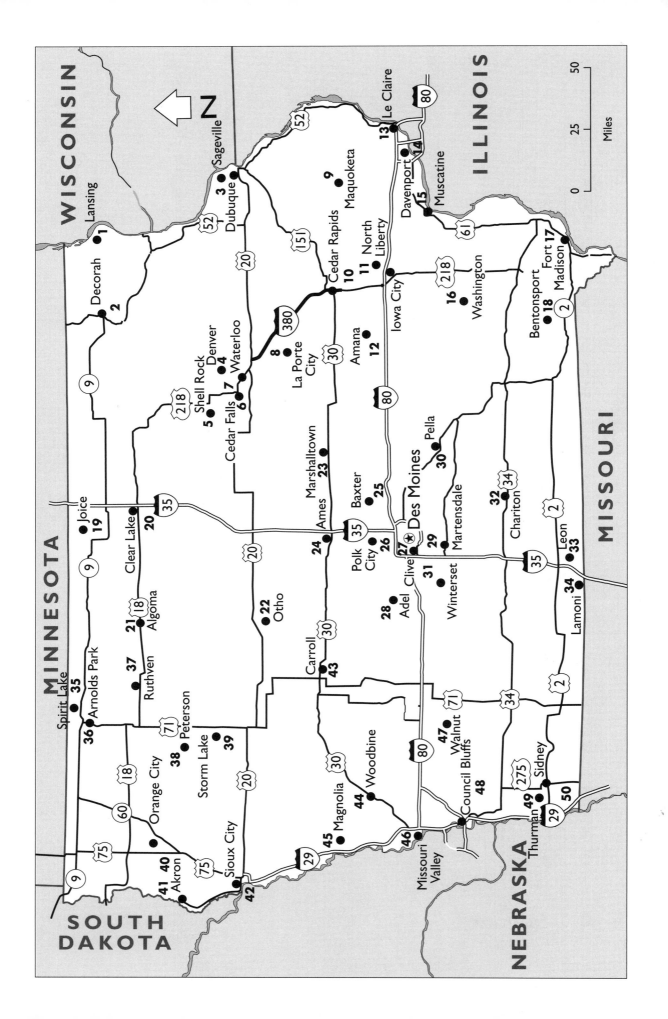

CONTENTS

RIDES IN WESTERN IOWA

PREFACE

A bicycle is the perfect vehicle for exploration.

On a bicycle, you *experience* places. There's nothing between you and the world, no glass and steel cage to distort or constrict your view, block the sun and wind, muffle the world's sound, or disguise its scent.

What you only glimpse from a speeding car, you can appreciate at a bicycle's pace. No wayside flowers escape your notice. You can count the turtles basking on a half-sunken log in a pond. Absent the rush of wind, the thrum of traffic, and the racket of a radio, you can hear the land's voices: birds and insects, leaves rustling in the wind, varmints skittering in the underbrush, water burbling over a shallow creek bed. You can smell rain on the wind and new-mown hay in the fields.

Iowa is best explored on a bicycle. Before I moved to Iowa in 1990, I'd driven across the state a couple of times on Interstate 80, heading from one coast to the other. Iowa looked to me like the oft-cited "nice place to visit," with its green and gold landscape under blue skies and its smallish, litter-free cities. Yeah, I thought, good old Middle America, and I crossed Iowa as swiftly as I thought I could without getting a ticket.

Pedaling a bike along Iowa's sparsely traveled county roads and away-from-it-all trails, however, I've discovered much more than I ever suspected as I sped over the Interstate. What looked from I-80 like an unvarying landscape of gentle slopes and flatlands was revealed as a rich variety of sweeping, un-dulating, rolling, steep, even precipitous hills; of dips and depressions, hollows and valleys. There are level areas, of course, but Iowa is certainly *not* flat.

From the interstate, Iowa looked like an unending field of corn and soybeans. Seen from a bicycle, those fields are interspersed with grasslands and patches of prairie, savannahs and groves, thickly forested slopes and floodplains. The roadsides are alive with flowers: purple vetch and bird's foot trefoil, clover and coneflowers, prairie sunflowers and Indian paintbrush, a dozen varieties of daisies, black-eyed Susans, asters in astonishing arrays, chicory, Queen Anne's lace, Canada lilies, irises, flowering thistles, prairie roses, and many more.

And the birds! The air is alive with winged creatures: startlingly yellow goldfinches, territorial redwing blackbirds, indigo buntings, orioles, bluebirds, cardinals, sparrows by the flock, crows and ravens and starlings, soaring hawks and osprey, turkey vultures, owls, Canada geese and white pelicans and swans, herons and egrets, a dozen varieties of ducks, pheasant and quail and wild turkeys.

On a bicycle's whispering wheels, you surprise deer as you round a bend in a trail, startle woodchucks and ground squirrels along county roads, spy a sly fox slipping through the tall grasses, spot the coyote loping across a slope, scare up rabbits by the dozen.

When you bicycle through Iowa, the dots on your roadmap become small towns with tree-lined streets, neatly kept homes and trimmed lawns, carefully tended gardens, and fresh laundry waving from backyard clotheslines. Grain bins and elevators cast their shadows down Main Streets where people look you in the face as they nod and smile a greeting.

And perhaps those people are the best part of exploring Iowa by bicycle. The chance encounters, common courtesies, and surprising kindnesses I've met as I've pedaled through and around this state are dearer to me than the rides themselves. In a small town in western Iowa, I asked a businessman where I could find a pay phone and he directed me to his office, told me to tell the receptionist that Dean said I could make some calls. On an August evening in the center of the state, Julie delayed closing a county park's swimming beach so I could take a dip after a hot day of cycling. Pete, a young farmhand in southern Iowa, put my bike into the back of his truck and drove twenty miles out of his way to a hardware store with bicycle tires to replace the one I'd shredded. The list could go on and on.

Iowa's beauty is of many colors and dimensions, and it's a shame that so many people only see it through the windows of a motor vehicle. This book offers guidance to *experience* the land and its denizens from the saddle of a bicycle. It's an experience you'll cherish.

I wish you tailwinds on all your rides.

INTRODUCTION

A BICYCLIST'S PERSPECTIVE ON IOWA

Welcome to Iowa. In the following pages, you'll find descriptions of fifty excellent bike rides. Frankly, they just scratch the surface of great bicycling in this state.

Unbeknownst to most outsiders, Iowa has a wide variety of terrain for cycling. You want to cruise the flats? Got 'em. Gently swelling hills? Got them too. Roller coaster rides? Plenty of them around. Challenging climbs and ripping descents? No problem. All those types of terrain in a loop you can ride in an afternoon? You've come to the right state.

The land and how it got this way

Like most of the Midwest, the Iowa landscape was formed largely by the continental glaciers that advanced and retreated repeatedly during the Pleistocene ice ages that began about 1.6 million years ago. The glaciers pretty much played bulldozer over Iowa, leveling out the land and, together with the winds, spreading a thick layer of pulverized soil over it—the incredibly fertile topsoil that made Iowa a dream come true for the farmers who swarmed into the state in the 19th century.

Most people think Iowa's flat, and they're half-right. The last ice age, the Wisconsinan Event, sent a land-leveling blanket of ice called the Des Moines Lobe down the center of the state, all the way to Des Moines (hence its name). Permafrost conditions of both sides of this lobe left behind the basically flat Iowan Surface on the east and the even-flatter Northwest Iowa Plains on the west.

This is land where you can get into a comfortable gear and pedaling cadence and cruise along for miles. Catch a tailwind, and you'll think you're sailing, but a headwind makes it feel like you're climbing a mountain.

Don't get the idea that bicycling in Iowa is like riding over a pool table. As the glaciers melted, they left hummocks and moraines, accumulations of the soil, rocks, and detritus the ice had been hauling around. For a cyclist, these relatively gentle humps become great rollers—gear up to gain speed on the down slopes, rocket across the saddle, and gear down to spin up the next hummock, then repeat.

Iowa also has its share of serious hills that will get your heart rate up and make you glad you've got that third chain ring. In the northeast corner of the state is the Paleozoic Plateau, the "Driftless Area" that the glaciers missed completely. Here are high, steep, rugged hills—we're talking thigh-burning grades over eight percent—that extend south from the Minnesota border to just below Dubuque, and

west from the Mississippi River through Allamakee and Winneshiek Counties. The steepest railroad in the United States is in Dubuque, Iowa, climbing a 60-degree incline. (At just 296 feet in length, it's also the shortest railroad in the nation.)

The northeast isn't the only hilly area in Iowa: you'll find plenty of long climbs and fast descents in the Southern Drift Plain, which covers the entire southern half of the state. The Wisconsinan glaciers didn't reach this far, but their melt water certainly did. A million or so years of wind and water carved deep valleys and hollows, creating a wonderfully rolling landscape that will give your gears—and legs—a workout.

Along the western edge of the state, parallel to the Missouri River, winds pushed the loess soil into the ramparts of the Loess Hills. Composed of some of Earth's most fertile soil, this narrow band of rugged hills rises two hundred and more feet above the Missouri River's valley and offers some of Iowa's most beautiful—and challenging—terrain for bicycling.

The Prairie Farmer Trail runs through farm country between Ridgeway and Calmar.

A gloriously green country

Iowa is 332 miles long from east to west and 214 miles tall north to south, encompassing 56,276 square miles. About 93 percent of that land is in farms. Only Nebraska has a larger percentage of its land in agriculture.

It's wide-open country, blanketed in green under an enormous sky. Most of Iowa used to be a tall-grass prairie, but now you'll see tall corn instead. A fifth of all the corn grown in the United States grows in Iowa. Right behind corn in production are soybeans, Iowa's second-largest crop. Third on the list is hay.

Iowa's farmers like to say that they feed the world, but mainly they feed livestock. Only about seven percent of the nation's food supply comes from Iowa, and it's mostly meat. One out of four hogs produced in the United States comes from Iowa, and the state produces a sizeable percentage of the country's beef and dairy cattle as well. Iowa is also the nation's top egg-producing state.

Instead of oceans, Iowa has a sea of corn, with tree-shaded farmsteads dotting the far vistas like the islands of an archipelago. In mid-to-late summer,

The Heritage Trail follows the Little Maquoketa River through the bluffs.

the sun glints and sparkles off the wind-waving corn very much as it does off ocean swells.

While much of Iowa is shade-deprived, as you might imagine, it's not as treeless as it was when the land was covered by prairies. Prairie fires doomed most tree seedlings to short lives, but farmers put an end to those land-sweeping conflagrations and now trees thrive wherever crops aren't planted. Cottonwood, box elder, silver maple, poplar, mulberry, willow, and other shade trees line the watercourses, streams, and river floodplains. The steep slopes of the Driftless Area, the Southern Drift Plain, and the Loess Hills are largely wooded with oak, ash, sugar maple, linden, hickory, and other species. Evergreens, however—pines, spruce, cedar, and their like—are in short supply.

Good roads started with Iowa bicyclists

It's true: the Good Roads Movement of the late 1800s was started by bicyclists in Iowa. The rich soil that covers most of the state soaks up moisture like a sponge and turns into deep, sucking mud in wet weather, which all but immobilized wheeled vehicles dependent on dirt roads. Cyclists banded together to lobby state, county, and local governments to pave the roads—a movement that was resisted by farmers, who didn't want to pay more taxes so those townspeople with bicycles or the new-fangled automobiles could have a good road. The farmers came around eventually—possibly because their wives were sick of being trapped at home for months every spring when the dirt road into town turned into a quagmire—and now the state is crisscrossed by an excellent system of two-lane county roads.

Paved road shoulders are rare in Iowa right now, but that will change. The Iowa Department of Transportation has recently adopted a policy of putting paved shoulders on all state highways. That sounds better for bikes than it actually is: DOT policy also calls for carving rumble strips into all the shoulders, which, except when the shoulder is six feet wide, will leave cyclists only a two-foot-wide strip of pavement outside the travel lane.

The county roads, however, are unlikely to get paved shoulders much before hell freezes over. But that's okay—most of the county roads have so little traffic that a paved shoulder is superfluous to cyclists.

In addition to good roads, Iowa has over 1,300 miles of trails suitable for bicycling. Many of these are paved with asphalt or concrete; others have a crushed-limestone surface. Twenty-eight of the rides included in this book use trails as part or all of their routes.

Best of all,
Iowans are bike-friendly people

Iowa is home to RAGBRAI, the (Des Moines) Register's Annual Great Bike Ride Across Iowa. It's the largest (8,500 registered riders and as many as 15,000 day-trippers and unregistered hangers-on when the ride goes through metropolitan areas like Des Moines) and oldest (the first one was in 1973) cross-state ride in the United States.

RAGBRAI has had a tremendous influence on bicycling in Iowa. Every July, for more than three decades, a horde of bicyclists have pedaled across the state. The route is always west to east, from the Missouri River to the Mississippi, but its specifics change every year. RAGBRAI has gone through a *lot* of Iowa's towns, providing great entertainment—and dropping lots of cash on food, drink, and entertainment—to the people of those towns. This has convinced Iowans that cyclists are basically decent people (though somewhat crazy), and has created a high level of tolerance and courtesy among Iowa motorists for cyclists on the roads. You'll encounter lots of smiles and friendly waves as you bicycle around Iowa.

Iowa is a land of small towns. The biggest city in the state, Des Moines, has only about 200,000 people, and there are only nine cities in Iowa with populations above 50,000. Forty percent of Iowa's 2.9 million people live in rural areas, ten percent of them on farms. Say what you like about small towns, the people in them are darned hospitable, helpful, and courteous, and particularly pleased when someone comes to visit.

Every bicycle tourist has encountered a "road angel" or two—complete strangers who've gone out of their way to be helpful or generous to a bicyclist in need. Don't be surprised if complete strangers look at you and your bicycle and ask where you're from and where you're headed. (Their second question will probably be "Have you done RAGBRAI?") Don't be amazed when someone you never saw before and will probably never see again offers you help when you're fixing a flat or staring, bewildered, at a map. And don't be shy about saying hi, or asking questions of the people you meet in Iowa. Iowa, you'll find, has an ample supply of road angels.

A good variety of terrain, beautiful country, good roads and trails, and friendly people—you're going to love bicycling Iowa!

The Great River Road skirts the Mississippi River bluffs south of Lansing.

BICYCLING SAFELY IN IOWA

Bicycling is not a dangerous sport. In terms of fatalities per mile of travel, bicycling is much safer than swimming, for instance; in terms of fatalities per hour of activity, bicycling is almost twice as safe as driving a car.

Still, bicycle crashes happen. The vast majority of them are simple falls that result in minor scrapes and bruises, and are never reported. But, let's face it: The bicycle crashes we worry about the most are ones that involve motor vehicles. Or, more precisely, the ones where cars hit bicycles. Particularly *our* bicycles.

Relax. Cars are not the major hazard to bicyclists. Car-bike crashes actually account for only about one in ten of *reported* bicycle crashes. And of all bicycle crashes resulting in injuries severe enough to require hospital visits, fewer than 20 percent involve motor vehicles.

However, over half (55 percent) of car-bike crashes are *the bicyclist's fault!* And many of the rest could have been avoided if the bicyclist had been more alert and ready to take evasive action.

Ride the roads the same way you drive them

Bicyclists have the right to use all roads in Iowa except the interstate highways. Along with that right, however, comes responsibilities. The laws that pertain to motor vehicles on the roads pertain to bicyclists as well. In general, you should drive your bicycle the same way you drive your car, obeying the same laws and rules of the road. *Never* ride against traffic. Fully one third of all bicycle fatalities involve wrong-way cyclists. *Do not* blow through stop signs and traffic lights. Nearly 75 percent of bicycle-car crashes occur at intersections.

The three commandments for bicycling safely on the roads are: Thou Shalt Pay Attention, Thou Shalt Be Visible, and Thou Shalt Be Predictable.

THOU SHALT PAY ATTENTION. Your driver's ed instructor surely told you to drive defensively. That goes double for driving a bicycle. Be alert to your surroundings, especially the motor vehicles sharing the roads with you. Be particularly attentive at intersections, where most car-bike crashes occur: Don't assume a driver is going to stop at a stop sign until you see him slow down, and even then expect him to do a rolling stop. Watch for the other person to make a mistake.

The most common car-bike crash happens when a car turns left across a bicyclist's path. The second most common crash type is the "right hook," where a car turns right across a same-direction bicyclist's path. The third-most common car-bike crash involves a car exiting a driveway or running a stop sign.

Be alert to road hazards—loose gravel, broken glass, storm drain grates, rocks, potholes, and pavement cracks running in your travel direction. Be careful on railroad crossings; try to cross them at as close to a 90-degree angle as possible to avoid getting a tire caught. In wet weather, remember that painted pavement is likely to be slick.

THOU SHALT BE VISIBLE. The most frequently heard words from a motorist who's just hit a bicyclist are "I didn't see him!" even when the cyclist is a six-foot-tall, two-hundred-pound object clothed in neon yellow.

Car drivers don't deliberately run into things they can see, so make sure they can see *you.* This goes beyond wearing high-visibility clothing, reflective tape, safety triangles, or flags.

Being visible means being where other road users are looking for traffic. Don't hug the curb. Motorists generally watch the area right in front of them: the traffic lane. A cyclist next to the curb or the pavement's edge escapes their attention or gets lost among parked cars and the landscape. This is especially true at intersections—a turning motorist is watching for traffic in the lanes, not at the edge of the road.

The best place to be is where drivers are looking. Ride three feet from the edge of the pavement, in the cars' right wheel track, where a motorist can't help but see you. If the lane is wide enough to share safely, you can move closer to the pavement edge as an act of courtesy, once you're sure the overtaking driver is aware of you. If the lane is too narrow to accommodate both you and the motor vehicle, *take the lane* by moving into the middle of it. Hit-from-behind crashes are the *least* common type of car-bike conflict, accounting for just 0.2 percent of serious bike crashes. Unless they're homicidal maniacs, overtaking drivers will wait until it's safe for them to cross the centerline to pass you.

At traffic lights and four-way stop signs, when you "filter forward" on the right of stopped traffic, proceed slowly and watch for cars preparing to turn right. *Do not* go to the head of the line—stop behind the lead car. The driver may be planning to turn right, and forgot to signal the turn. The driver will be watching for traffic from the left, not looking to see if a bicycle has come up on the right.

Iowa law requires bicyclists to have a headlight and rear reflector when traveling at night. Go beyond the law: put a taillight on your bike, too. Though a mere seven percent of bicycle trips occur at night, they account for nearly a third of all car-bike fatalities. *Only fools with suicidal tendencies ride in the dark without lights!*

THOU SHALT BE PREDICTABLE. Drivers expect other drivers to act in a predictable manner; it's the sudden, unexpected moves that cause problems. When you maintain a straight line, other drivers can "predict" that you'll continue to do so, and it helps them decide when it's safe to pass you.

In urban settings, if you cut in close to the curb when there's no car parked at it, then swerve back into the lane to get around a stopped vehicle, the effect on overtaking drivers is the same as if you were popping into their path from out of nowhere. It's much safer—and more *predictable*—if you hold to a steady line that keeps you *at least* three feet to the left of parked vehicles, out of the "door zone."

Try to make eye contact with drivers whose paths you intend to cross; if they don't look at you, assume that they haven't seen you. When you approach an intersection and there's a car waiting to cross in front of you, keep your pedals turning so the driver knows you're not going to yield your right-of-way, but keep your hands on your brake levers just in case.

Rearview mirrors are handy, but don't depend on them. When you look back over your shoulder, you give overtaking drivers an indication that you may be planning to move into their path, or, at the very least, you tell them you're aware of them.

Make your intentions obvious to motorists; use hand signals to indicate that you're turning or slowing down. It helps if you actually point to the place you're going. Make your left turns in stages: from your position on the right side of the lane, look back and signal a left turn, then move to the left side of the lane; before the intersection, look back and signal again before you make the turn. On multi-lane roads, treat each lane change as a left turn—look back and signal your moves.

Trails are car-free, not care-free

Too many bicyclists seem to turn off their brains when they get on a bike trail. Since there are no motor vehicles on trails, cyclists often assume that they're safer than roads. Bicycle crash statistics, however, don't support this assumption. In fact,

The Waverly Rail Trail crosses the Cedar River on a spectacular, 23′-wide bridge.

studies indicate that bicyclists are more than twice as likely to crash on trails as they are on the roads. The only type of crash that a trail eliminates is the "hit-from-behind" collision, the least common type of car/bike conflict.

To put it as bluntly as possible: The vast majority of bicycle crashes happen because the cyclist isn't paying attention to bicycling.

Don't let your attention wander when you're on a bike trail; keep your mind on your driving and your eyes on the path. Trails are considerably narrower than roads and usually have no shoulders. A moment's inattention is plenty of time for you to swerve off a trail and into a tree or other fixed object, the most common type of crash on a trail.

Ride to the right on a trail, but don't assume that all other trail users will be doing the same. Other trail users—pedestrians, joggers, in-line skaters, dog walkers, equestrians, and other bicyclists— are considerably less predictable than motor traffic. You never know when a pedestrian might suddenly change direction and step into your path. Call the warning, "Passing on your left," or ring your bell when you're overtaking other trail users.

Statistically, a cyclist is *more than four times* as likely to have a crash at the intersection of a trail and a road as at the intersection of two roads. Motorists are generally unaware of intersecting trails—they're not looking for traffic to come out of nowhere and cross in front of them. Approach road crossings with caution and be prepared to stop quickly.

Be especially alert on side paths

A trail that runs right next to a road—a "side path"—is the most hazardous type of trail. Motorists generally don't watch for traffic on the side path and are apt to turn across it without looking for traffic. When you ride on a side path, you must be particularly cautious at every driveway or road intersection. Check behind you for overtaking traffic that might turn across the path. Don't assume that drivers on the intersecting roads see you; their attention is on the road, not on the side path.

Most side paths are bi-directional, so you may be riding against the flow of traffic in the adjacent road lane. This calls for heightened caution on your part. A car driver approaching an intersection looks first to his left, for traffic in the first lane he'll cross. When he looks to the right, his attention is on the far side of the road. He'll probably never see you approaching from the wrong direction on the side path.

Safety is *your* responsibility, whether you're on the road or on a trail. Iowa's motorists are uncommonly courteous to other road users, but they're no less apt to make mistakes than anyone else. Make it easy for them to see you, predict your movements, and avoid running into you. Obey the traffic laws, use common sense, and, above all, stay alert.

The views are wide open from the Rolling Prairie Trail.

GETTING READY TO RIDE

The rides described in this book are suitable for any type of bicycle, but will probably be most enjoyable on a road bike with a triple chain ring and multiple rear gears. A hybrid or mountain bike is okay too, but knobby tires are definitely overkill.

Before you start out, make sure your bike is in good working condition. While most of these rides are in areas where there are bike shops, the shop may be a long way from you if you break down. Do the "ABC Quick Check" at the beginning of every ride:

A IS FOR AIR. Check your tires. The most common cause of flat tires is underinflation: you hit a pothole or rock and the tube gets pinched between the rim and tire, causing the familiar "snake bite" holes. Don't rely on pinching the tire between your fingers to tell if there's enough air in it—put a pressure gauge on and make sure the tire is inflated to its recommended pressure.

B IS FOR BRAKES. Squeeze your rear brake lever and try to roll your bike forward. If the rear wheel rolls, you need to adjust your brakes or get new brake pads. Do the same with your front brake. You should be able to lock up the wheels without having to put a death grip on the brake levers.

C IS FOR CRANK. Holding the bike upright, take hold of a pedal and try to pull it away from the bike. There shouldn't be any play at all in the crank.

QUICK IS FOR WHEELS. If you have quick-release wheels, make sure they're secure. It should take a considerable amount of pressure to pull the lever to the release position.

CHECK YOUR BIKE OVER. Make sure all the bolts holding your bottle cages and racks on are tight. Look your tires over to be sure there are no obviously worn or cracked spots. Are your water bottles filled? Okay, you're ready to ride.

A few words about clothing and equipment

Cycling shorts, jerseys, gloves, and bike shoes have all been developed to make bicycling more comfortable. They accomplish that, but none of them are necessary to bicycling. Wear whatever you like.

For wet weather, it's wise to carry rain gear. A poncho or rain cape has some advantages over a rain jacket—you can drape the front of the poncho over the handlebars, and the back is long enough to tuck under your butt and sit on, which keeps you drier.

Iowa weather can be capricious, particularly in the spring and fall. During those seasons, it's a good idea to carry an extra layer—a sweatshirt or jacket—just in case of a sudden change in temperature.

There is no law requiring you to wear a helmet while bicycling in Iowa, but an ANSI-approved helmet, properly fitted and worn, can prevent some head injuries in case of a fall.

When you're riding on trails, a bell is very handy. With it, you can alert other trail users that you're approaching. The ring of a bell seems to cut through the sound from a jogger's headphones better than your voice.

If you plan to ride in the pre-dawn, twilight, or nighttime hours, you need a good headlight and taillight, in addition to reflectors.

Finally, it's a good idea to carry an Iowa road map, or the *Iowa Transportation Map for Bicyclists*. Despite your best intentions, you may make a wrong turn and suddenly discover that you're off the route described in this book, or even off the map that accompanies that description. Maps are available from the Iowa Department of Transportation (www.dot.state.ia.us) or the Iowa Tourism Office (www.traveliowa.com). *The Bike Map* shows a few more roads than the regular road map, and is color-coded to indicate traffic volumes. It also shows the major bicycle trails.

How to use this book

The following rides are arranged by geographic area: Eastern Iowa, Central Iowa, and Western Iowa. Within each of those three sections, the rides are arranged from north to south. If you're looking for rides in a particular area, check Appendix C, where the rides are listed by town and by county.

It's a good idea to read the ride description before you embark, to familiarize yourself with the route and any hazards that have been noted. You'll also have a good idea of attractions, historical sites and interesting stuff to watch for as you ride.

In Appendix A, you'll find suggestions for linking some of these rides together into longer rides, including multi-day tours.

One of the nicest things about bicycling is that it doesn't require a lot of equipment or preparation: all you really need is a bicycle, decent weather, and a good route to follow. You've got your bike. Iowa's climate affords a comfortable bicycling season that runs from mid-April to mid-November, and days even in the winter months when you can get out on your bike without having to bundle up too heavily. And there are fifty great bicycling routes in the pages that follow.

Enjoy the rides—and have a great time Biking Iowa!

EASTERN IOWA

RIDE 1
Mississippi Bluffs Butt Buster

LOCATION: County and state roads between Lansing and Harpers Ferry
DISTANCE: 29.3-mile loop
SURFACE: Paved roads
TERRAIN: Steep climbs and descents, flat along river
DIFFICULTY: Strenuous
SERVICES:
Restrooms: Restaurants and convenience stores in Lansing and Harpers Ferry
Water: Same
Food: Same
Camping: Red Barn Resort and Campground, Lansing; Andy Mountain Campground, Harpers Ferry
Lodging: Motels, hotel, and a bed and breakfast in Lansing; motel in Harpers Ferry; motels in DeSoto and Ferryville, Wisconsin, across the river from Lansing
Bike Shop: None nearby
STARTING POINT: T.J. Hunter's Pub and Grill on Main Street (State Highway 9) in Lansing, two blocks west of the river, on the south side of the street

The Driftless Area

The glaciers that smothered most of the Midwestern landscape missed a large area of southwest Wisconsin and northeast Iowa. Outcrops of solid bedrock, mostly limestone, are very common and form the bluffs along the Mississippi River. Known as the Paleozoic Plateau, or, more commonly, the Driftless Area, this jumble of high, steep hills in Iowa's northeast corner offers some of the most challenging and scenic cycling in the state.

In the 19th century, logging was a major industry here: trees from this region became buildings on flatter ground. The cleared land atop the hills and in the narrow valleys became farmland, but the steeps have been reclaimed by the forest.

It's country that will test your thighs and make you glad you have that granny gear in the triple chain ring on your bike. The hills will also test your brakes: You can hit 40+ mph without moving your pedals on some of the descents.

The Mississippi River and its tributaries carved the limestone into cliffs that now soar hundreds of feet above the water. On Ride 1: Mississippi Bluffs Butt Buster, you'll have great views of those cliffs—and challenging climbs up the bluffs. Ride 3: Ski Iowa Loop, follows the Heritage Trail along a river that cuts through creases in the bluffs to reach the Mississippi.

Ride 2: The Winneshiek County Ramble, takes you to the western edge of the Driftless Area. There are plenty of hills, but you have a respite on a rail-trail along a ridgeline, then end with a white-knuckle descent into the town of Decorah.

If you thought Iowa was basically flat, these first three rides will change your mind!

"The majestic bluffs that overlook the river, along through this region," Mark Twain wrote, "charm one with the grace and variety of their forms, and the soft beauty of their adornment." This ride gives you a close look at those Mississippi River bluffs, from bottom to top and down again, plus some sweet—and flat—miles along the river.

0.0 mi. From T.J. Hunter's Pub and Grill (where a solid breakfast with coffee and a tip costs about six dollars), coast down Main Street and turn right onto Front Street, which is also the Great River Road.

Lansing was settled in 1848, but wasn't incorporated until 1864. By that time, it was already a port of call for river traffic. Grain and merchandise were shipped from here, and milled logs were sent downriver. You'll see little evidence of that early industry, however, as you coast through town. The Main Street businesses, many still housed in 19th-century storefronts, are geared more towards tourism and river recreation than shipping. Excursion, sport fishing, and houseboats have replaced the barges and riverboats at the waterfront.

0.9 miles. After passing the Sports Complex, turn right towards Waukon on County Road X42 and head up the slight grade. Bluffs rise from the edge of the road on your right; Village Creek meanders through the narrow valley on your left. Heading in a southerly direction, the road crosses the creek and runs through the hamlet of Village Creek. The bluffs close in on both sides, and the ride gets steeper: the next three miles will put you in your lowest gear.

7.5 miles. You reach the top of the bluff as you pass Thompson Corner at the intersection with County Road A52 (Elon Drive). Stay on County Road X42 and enjoy the view across hilltop farmlands and wooded valleys. Now you have five miles of fun rollers and one steep (but short) climb.

13.1 miles. As the road starts to curve east, you pass Saint Joseph's Cemetery and collect your reward for the climbing you've done so far: a beautiful two-mile descent to Harpers Ferry on the Mississippi River.

15.2 miles. Cross Cold Creek and turn left at the stop sign onto the Great River Road (County Road X52), which you left back in Lansing. If you go straight east at this intersection, you'll find Harpers Ferry's business district. The census credited a mere 310 souls to this town, but that number is augmented dramatically by boaters, anglers, and tourists in the summer. The town boasts several restaurants and a convenience store along with marinas and services for the summer folks.

Heading north on the Great River Road, the first three miles are lovely, with a paved shoulder to keep you comfortably out of the path of the occasional car. The bluffs rise precipitously from the flat plain on your left.

18.0 miles. The paved shoulder ends as the road climbs into the bluffs. Gear down for a steep, mile-and-a-half push between forested slopes, then shift back onto your big chain ring for a screaming-fast descent. Glance left as you speed downhill to see the Wexford Church, reputed to be the oldest church west of the Mississippi. The descent ends a short distance past the church; you go back to your granny gear for the climb up the next bluff.

Lafayette Ridge Drive marks the crest of that climb. Now you have more than two miles of downhill to get back to the river's edge.

26.3 miles. It's comfortably flat as you cruise beside a wide, island-encumbered stretch of the river known as Columbus Lake. Ski-boats and fishermen share the wide water against a backdrop of wooded islands and the Wisconsin shore. On your left, the bluffs jut up, capped by limestone cliffs. Ahead, you can see Lansing and the Blackhawk Bridge over the Mississippi.

29.1 miles. Turn left onto Main Street (State Highway 9) in Lansing, and pedal up the hill to your starting point.

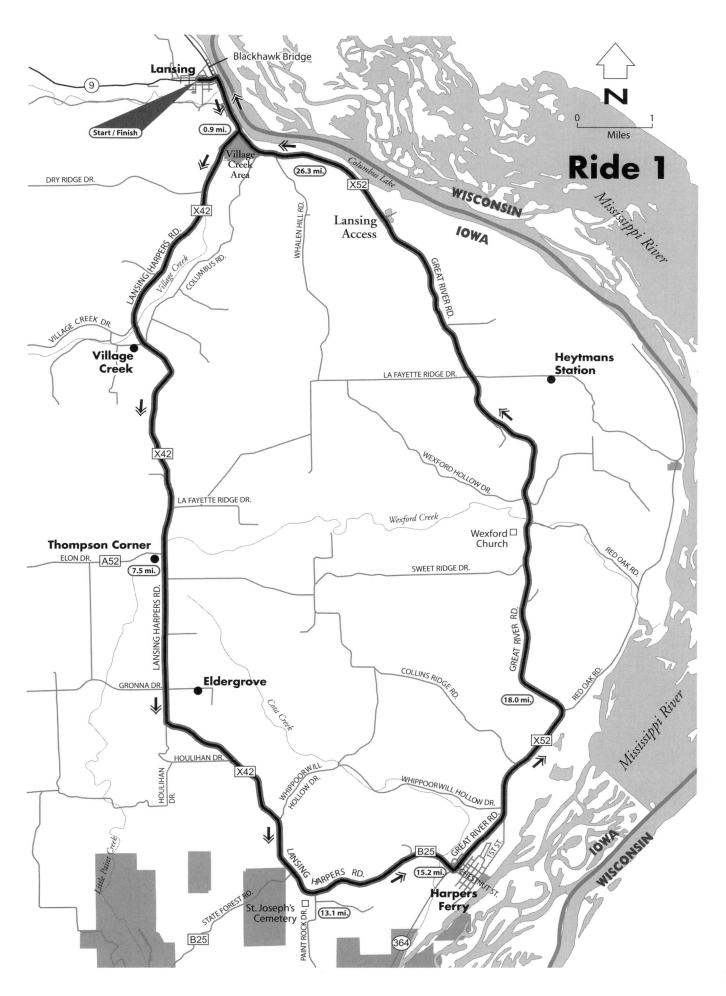

Blackhawk Bridge

Lansing

(9)

Start / Finish

0.9 mi.

DRY RIDGE DR.

Village
Creek
Area

X42

LANSING HARPERS RD.

Village Creek

COLUMBUS RD.

VILLAGE CREEK DR.

Village
Creek

X42

LA FAYETTE RIDGE DR.

Thompson Corner

ELON DR. A52

7.5 mi.

LANSING HARPERS RD.

GRONNA DR. Eldergrove

Coon Creek

HOULIHAN DR.

HOULIHAN DR.

X42

Little Paint Creek

WHIPPOORWILL HOLLOW DR.

LANSING HARPERS RD.

STATE FOREST RD.

St. Joseph's
Cemetery

PAINT ROCK DR. 13.1 mi.

B25

26.3 mi.

X52

Columbus Lake

WHALEN HILL RD.

Lansing
Access

WISCONSIN

IOWA

GREAT RIVER RD.

LA FAYETTE RIDGE DR.

Heytmans
Station

WEXFORD HOLLOW DR.

Wexford Creek

Wexford
Church

SWEET RIDGE DR.

RED OAK RD.

COLLINS RIDGE RD.

GREAT RIVER RD.

18.0 mi.

RED OAK RD.

X52

WHIPPOORWILL HOLLOW DR.

GREAT RIVER RD.

B25

15.2 mi.

1ST ST.

CHESTNUT ST.

Harpers
Ferry

364

Mississippi River

IOWA

WISCONSIN

N

0   1
Miles

Ride 1

3

RIDE 2
Winneshiek County Ramble

LOCATION: State and county roads and the Prairie Farmer Trail between Decorah and Calmar
DISTANCE: 33.5-mile loop
SURFACE: Paved roads and crushed-limestone trail
TERRAIN: Lots of hills on the roads; flat rail-trail
DIFFICULTY: Strenuous
SERVICES:
  Restrooms: At start/finish, businesses and restaurants in Ridgeway and Calmar
  Water: Same, and at Prairie Farmer Trail head in Ridgeway
  Food: Restaurants and convenience stores in Decorah, Ridgeway, and Calmar
  Camping: Pulpit Rock Campground at Decorah City Park, Decorah; Pine Creek Cabins and Campgrounds, Decorah
  Lodging: Motels and a bed and breakfast in Decorah, bed and breakfast in Calmar
  Bike Shop: Decorah Bicycles, College Street, Decorah
STARTING POINT: Pulpit Rock Campground at Decorah City Park on Pulpit Rock Road, on the west side of Decorah

Your legs work hard for the first ten miles of this ride, but then you have about twice that distance on an easy, mostly shaded rail-trail and a gentle, ridge-top road. The final few miles have more short climbs before you reach—and *descend*—the steepest, longest hill of the ride.

0.0 miles. Kick off from the Pulpit Rock Campground of Decorah City Park and turn left onto Pulpit Rock Road, which crosses U.S. Highway 52 and becomes Madison Road, then starts on a 1.4-mile climb out of the Upper Iowa River valley.

Madison Road heads due west, with few curves and no flats: you're either grinding up or speeding down hills. Each crest rewards you with a panoramic view across hilltop farms and wooded valleys.

6.0 miles. On your right is the Madison Lutheran Church, built in 1906. Just beyond it is perhaps the prettiest view of this stretch as you look across the hollows carved by Tenmile Creek. The hills are steep, but comfortably rounded by age. The row crops are planted across the slopes, broken by erosion-control strips of grass that make interesting patterns on the hillsides.

8.9 miles. You speed downhill to a T intersection; brake hard for the stop sign at this blind corner. Turn left onto County Road W14, and head south towards Ridgeway atop a low ridge ahead.

10.1 miles. Cross State Highway 9 and enter Ridgeway, "Where Big Things Come in Small Packages." The "big things" aren't readily apparent, but the "small package" contains just 295 people. Off-route to your right on Railroad Street, the Chatterbox Café/T&J's Lounge is a good place for a break.

Three blocks up from State Highway 9, turn left at the stop sign onto County Street (a sign directs you to Spillville). Then, a quarter mile on, follow the Recreational Trail sign and turn sharply left, almost reversing your course, to reach the Prairie Farmer Trail head. There's a shelter here with a picnic

table, some playground equipment, and a water hydrant. Head south on the trail.

The Prairie Farmer Trail was developed in 1992 on an Old Milwaukee Road right-of-way. The surface is crushed limestone, fine for road tires, though after wet weather it can be clingy-soft. The grades are insignificant—you probably won't shift gears between here and Calmar. Long stretches of the trail are lined with trees, which give welcome shade and protection from winds.

13.6 miles. Here's a trailside rest area overlooking corn and soybean fields that cover the hills as far as you can see. It's a very pleasant ride, far from roads and traffic noise. All you hear as you cruise south on the trail are birdsongs, wind-rustled leaves, and the soft crunch of your tires.

19.4 miles. Pass another trailside bench, then emerge from the woods to cross 175th Street and curve through the outlying residences of Calmar, "The Crossroads of Northeast Iowa." Pass beneath the water tower and reach trail's end at the old train depot, now the Town Clerk's office.

20.7 miles. At the former depot, turn right onto U.S. Highway 52 (Maryville Street). Across the highway is the Train Station Restaurant, serving a good lunch at a very reasonable price, and decorated with a wonderful collection of historical town photos, train schedules, and advertisements. Follow U.S. Highway 52 as it turns east to take you out of town.

22.9 miles. Turn left onto Middle Calmar Road (County Road W38). You immediately cross some very rough railroad tracks; take them cautiously. The next six miles as you head north towards Calmar are great cruising. The road holds to a winding and scenic ridgeline, with gentle dips and rises, then makes a curving descent into the Trout Creek valley. When you pass Middle Ossian Road, start gearing down for your last two climbs of this ride. They're steep but short, separated by a flat stretch that lets you catch your breath.

30.8 miles. You're going downhill, still picking up speed as you enter the Decorah city limits. Get on your brakes *now*—the descent gets steeper and there's a busy intersection after you pass beneath the highway bridge.

31.5 miles. Turn right at the stop sign onto Short Street, then go left onto South Mill Street and pedal through a residential district, past some very nice old homes.

32.2 miles. Turn left onto West Water Street. The Norwegian-American Museum is across the street, a tribute to the Norwegian immigrants who settled Decorah in the mid-1800s. Ride up West Water Street one block and bear right onto College Drive.

Things get a little confusing here: there's a sign prohibiting bicycles on the sidewalks, then, as you turn onto College Drive, another sign prohibits bicycles on the road. Fortunately, there's no indication that either prohibition is enforced.

Pass Decorah Bicycles and an ice cream shop (are you *sure* you want to pass the ice cream shop?) on College, then cross the Upper Iowa River.

32.4 miles. Just across the bridge, turn left onto Fifth Avenue, following the sign to Pulpit Rock Campground. In about a half mile, you cross a one-lane bridge over the river, then take the first left onto Pulpit Rock Road and follow it back to your starting point.

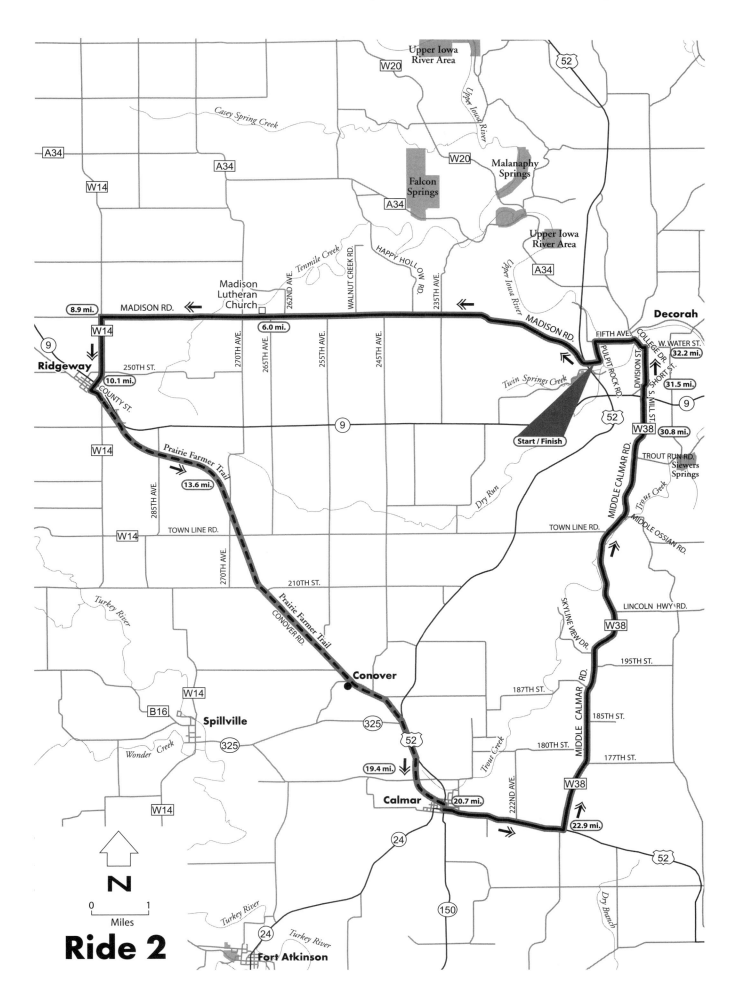

Upper Iowa
River Area

W20

52

Casey Spring Creek

A34

A34

W14

Falcon
Springs

W20

Malanaphy
Springs

A34

Upper Iowa
River Area

Tenmile Creek

262ND AVE.

HAPPY HOLLOW RD.

235TH AVE.

Upper Iowa River

Madison
Lutheran
Church

8.9 mi.

MADISON RD.

MADISON RD.

Decorah

W14

9

Ridgeway

270TH AVE.

265TH AVE.

255TH AVE.

245TH AVE.

WALNUT CREEK RD.

6.0 mi.

250TH ST.

10.1 mi.

COUNTY ST.

9

FIFTH AVE.

W. WATER ST.

32.2 mi.

PULPIT ROCK RD.

DIVISION ST.

COLLEGE DR.

S. SHORT ST.

9

Twin Springs Creek

52

31.5 mi.

W38

30.8 mi.

W14

Prairie Farmer Trail

13.6 mi.

285TH AVE.

Dry Run

S. MILL ST.

TROUT RUN RD.
Siewers
Springs

MIDDLE CALMAR RD.

Trout Creek

TOWN LINE RD.

TOWN LINE RD.

270TH AVE.

W14

MIDDLE OSSIAN RD.

210TH ST.

Turkey River

Prairie Farmer Trail

CONOVER RD.

SKYLINE VIEW DR.

LINCOLN HWY RD.

W38

195TH ST.

187TH ST.

185TH ST.

W14

Conover

B16

Spillville

325

325

Wonder Creek

Turkey River

24

W14

325

52

19.4 mi.

Calmar

20.7 mi.

Trout Creek

180TH ST.

222ND AVE.

177TH ST.

MIDDLE CALMAR RD.

W38

22.9 mi.

52

24

150

N

0   1
Miles

Ride 2

Turkey River

Turkey River

Fort Atkinson

Dry Branch

Start / Finish

RIDE 3
Ski Iowa Loop

LOCATION: County roads and the Heritage Trail between Sageville and Graf
DISTANCE: 23.2-mile loop
SURFACE: Paved roads and crushed-limestone trail
TERRAIN: A flat rail-trail heading out, then serious hills for the return trip
DIFFICULTY: Strenuous
SERVICES:
Restrooms: At start/finish, tavern in Durango, pit toilet at mile 6.7, trailhead in Graf
Water: At start/finish, tavern in Durango, vending machine in Graf
Food: Tavern in Durango
Camping: None nearby
Lodging: Motels, hotels, and bed and breakfasts in Dubuque
Bike Shop: Several in Dubuque
STARTING POINT: Heritage Trail head on Rupp Hollow Road (County Road D12), off U.S. Highway 52 in Sageville, north of Dubuque

Lead Led the Way

Lead lured the first European settlers to Iowa. As early as 1634, French-Canadian Jean Nicolet reported that Indians from the Sauk, Mesquakie, and Ho-Chunk tribes were mining and smelting ore from deposits near present-day Dubuque to trade for European goods.

European exploitation of the lead deposits began in earnest in 1788, when Julien Dubuque won permission from the Mesquakies to mine their lead. Establishing himself on the site of the city that bears his name, he applied to Spain, which claimed everything west of the Mississippi, for a grant of land. He called the tract "The Mines of Spain" and finally won his grant in 1796.

For 22 years, Dubuque clung to his tract through Spanish, French, and American claims. He mined the lead, engaged in fur trading, and grew rich. When he died in 1810, his settlement included cultivated fields, a wharf, blacksmith shop and forge, mill, smelting furnace, and several hundred Indian and French residents.

Upon Dubuque's death, his Indian friends buried him in a wooden tomb on a bluff above the river. Creditors and land speculators from Saint Louis rushed to claim the mines, but the Mesquakies burned all the standing buildings and stood firm against further encroachment by the whites.

Non-Indian settlement in Iowa became legal in 1834 under the terms of the Black Hawk Purchase. Dubuque's Mines of Spain were put quickly back into production. A large portion of the lead shot fired during the Civil War came from these mines, which operated until 1914.

In 1897, a Gothic Revival monument was placed on the hilltop above Dubuque's long-decayed tomb, where it still stands. The Mines of Spain is now a State Recreation Area.

From the Sundown Mountain Ski Area, you look across farms nestled in the hollows between the hills.

This ride takes you past both the bottom and top of one of Iowa's few Alpine ski areas. Obviously, it entails some hill-climbing . . . but there's an out. The first 11 miles are on the Heritage Trail with almost unnoticeable grades. To avoid the hills, you can simply turn around in Graf and return on the trail instead of taking the roads.

0.0 miles. Out of the Heritage Trail's parking lot in Sageville, cross Rupp Hollow Road (County Road D12) and follow the trail northwest into the forest. Bluffs rise steeply on your left; on your right is a sleepy-looking pond and small clearings surrounded by woods. The trail follows the Little Maquoketa River through a crease in the bluffs. It's completely shaded and the river is mostly hidden in the forest. You may hear traffic noise in this stretch—the trail is right below U.S. Highway 52.

3.7 miles. Cross Burtons Furnace Road in Durango. Durango has all of 11 households, but it also has a trailside tavern that serves cold beer and warm burgers. Cross a small stream with a big name —the Middle Fork Little Maquoketa River—as you leave Durango. The trail's rise is imperceptible and the surface is good even for skinny road tires. Breaks in the forest canopy permit trailside wildflowers: Canadian thistles, lobelia, daisies, and black-eyed Susans color the way. Other than birds singing and varmints rustling the leaves, it's wonderfully quiet.

7.4 miles. Pass limestone cliffs rising on your right, while the river meanders through a clearing on your left.

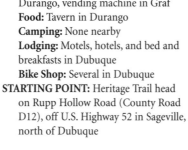

You're in the heart of the bluffs now, the steep slopes clothed in oak, ash, maple, black walnut, and hickory.

8.2 miles. On your left through the screen of trees are the ski lifts of Sundown Mountain Ski Area. The name is a bit pretentious—with a 475-foot vertical drop, this is hardly a mountain, and the area faces the rising, not the setting sun. Less than a mile beyond Sundown's trails, you cross Asbury Road.

11.5 miles. Enter Graf, a settlement with about twice the population of Durango. At the trailhead park are a shelter, picnic tables, and restrooms. Bottled water is available from a machine across the road.

This is the turnaround point. Climb the embankment out of the trailhead and turn right on Graf Road for a scenic—and hilly—trip back to the starting point or, if you prefer an easy ride, retrace your route on the Heritage Trail.

13.4 miles. After a short, shallow climb from Graf, go right at the stop sign onto Asbury Road (County Road D17), heading east towards the ski area.

14.4 miles. Cross the Heritage Trail, then a bridge over the river. Gear down for a steep two-mile climb that takes you past Sundown Mountain's ski lodge. The view from the top is spectacular, though partially blocked by new housing.

17.2 miles. Asbury Road turns right, Lewis Road comes in from the left, and you continue straight, up a sharp, short climb on Lore Mound Road. For the next mile, the road is curvy, narrow, and downhill. At the stop sign, turn right onto Derby Grange Road.

19.2 miles. Glide downhill to the stop sign and bear right, then take the left turn to continue on Derby Grange Road. *Watch for this turn*—it's easy to sail off mistakenly on Hales Mill Road. If you cross a creek, you missed the turn.

Enjoy a pretty ride through this little hollow, then cross two steel bridges over Cloie Branch and make another three-quarter-mile climb to pass the Derby Grange Golf Course and Dubuque Little League fields.

21.3 miles. At the stop sign, go left on the paved shoulder of Kennedy Road. Kennedy soon turns right—you bear left on Rupp Hollow Road (County Road D12). From here, it's all downhill—literally—for the mile and a half back to the Heritage Trail's parking lot.

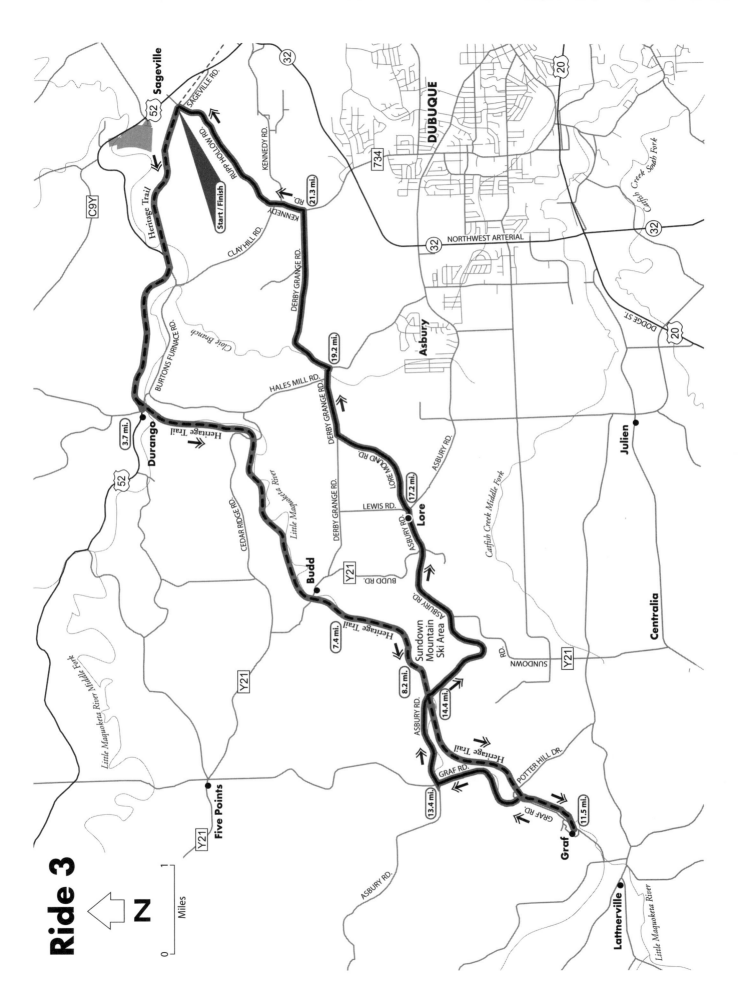

Ride 3

N

0 1 Miles

Sageville

DUBUQUE

Sageville Rd.

Heritage Trail

Rupp Hollow Rd.

Start / Finish

Kennedy Rd.

21.3 mi.

Kennedy Rd.

Clay Hill Rd.

Burtons Furnace Rd.

Clair Branch

Derby Grange Rd.

Hales Mill Rd.

19.2 mi.

Asbury

Derby Grange Rd.

3.7 mi.

Durango

Heritage Trail

Cedar Ridge Rd.

Little Maquoketa River

Loremound Rd.

Asbury Rd.

17.2 mi.

Lewis Rd.

Lore

Julien

Derby Grange Rd.

Asbury Rd.

Budd

Y21

Budd Rd.

Heritage Trail

7.4 mi.

8.2 mi.

Asbury Rd.

Sundown Mountain Ski Area

Sundown Rd.

Centralia

Y21

14.4 mi.

Heritage Trail

Potter Hill Dr.

Graf Rd.

13.4 mi.

Graf Rd.

11.5 mi.

Graf

Little Maquoketa River Middle Fork

Y21

Five Points

Y21

Asbury Rd.

Lattnerville

Little Maquoketa River

Northwest Arterial

Catfish Creek South Fork

Catfish Creek Middle Fork

Dodge St.

734

52

32

20

C9Y

RIDE 4
Smell the Chocolate Ride

LOCATION: Jefferson City Trail and Waverly Rail Trail between Denver and Waverly
DISTANCE: 20.6 miles out and back
SURFACE: Paved trails and city streets
TERRAIN: Very flat, with one gradual slope
DIFFICULTY: Easy
SERVICES:
    Restrooms: At start/finish, portable toilets at mile 2.9 and mile 7.0, convenience store in Waverly
    Water: At start/finish, convenience store in Waverly
    Food: Restaurants, taverns, and convenience stores in Denver and Waverly
    Camping: Brandt Park, Denver
    Lodging: Motels in Waverly
    Bike Shop: Bike Tech, Main Street, Cedar Falls
STARTING POINT: Forrest Avenue Park on the west side of State Street at the northern end of Denver

The Cedar River Valley

West of the Driftless Area, Iowa settles onto the Iowan Surface, a mostly flat land with occasional long, low hills and shallow, meandering rivers flowing northwest to southeast. The last of the glaciers didn't reach this area, but their melt water created miles-wide valleys. The Cedar River Valley is one of these.

The Cedar was once known as the Red Cedar River, from the trees that grew along it. Those trees are long gone. From headwaters just north of the Iowa/Minnesota border, the river collects water from many tributaries and joins the Iowa River south of Iowa City.

The Cedar River Valley is simply great for bicycling. The land rolls nicely—your granny gear won't get much, if any, use, but you'll use all of your rear gear cluster as well as your middle and outer gear rings. There are hundreds of miles of paved, low-traffic county roads, most in excellent condition. Towns are well spaced for rest stops, and large enough to support the restaurants, taverns, and convenience stores that are essential to the feeding and watering of bicycle tourists.

The icing on this cake is the trail development. Over the past several decades, Cedar Valley communities have aggressively developed abandoned rail lines and other routes into multi-use trails. A number of the trails follow the Cedar River and its tributaries, winding through riverside woodlands that provide cool temperatures and shade for those hot summer days, as well as lots of opportunities to spot wildlife.

Trail development in the Cedar Valley is ongoing—every year, old trails are extended and improved and new ones are built. Bicycling is going to get better and better in the Cedar River Valley!

With only one gentle hill and a couple of embankments to climb, this out-and-back ride is great for a family outing with young children or an easy afternoon's cruise.

0.0 miles. From the Forrest Avenue Park on the north end of Denver, turn left (north) onto the bike lane along State Street. This is the Jefferson City Trail, named in commemoration of Denver's original moniker.

0.8 miles. At the intersection with Larrabee Avenue, the bike lane turns into a 10-foot-wide paved trail parallel to U.S. Highway 63. Pedal up the shallow rise with a cattail-filled ditch on your right and farmland across the highway on your left.

1.9 miles. The trail descends to turn left underneath the highway and becomes the Waverly Rail Trail, heading west. There's a small rest area here with benches in the shade of the highway bridge.

The last train on this right-of-way was a traveling restaurant, the Star Clipper Dinner Train, which served multi-course gourmet meals as it made a slow journey from Waverly to here and back. The train was moved to Michigan in 1997 and the City of Waverly bought the right-of-way two years later for the trail. The trail gets considerably more use than the dinner train did.

2.9 miles. Cross Killdeer Avenue, where there's a small trailhead with a portable toilet. About a half mile farther along is a high trestle, from which you have an expansive view of corn and soybean fields spreading across long, gentle slopes. The riding is easy, the shade is cool, and birds are singing all around you.

7.0 miles. Continuing west on the trail, you pass another trailside portable toilet, then gear down for a sharp rise over Garden Street. The downhill on the other side is steep enough to let you coast awhile. The next mile takes you through a green tunnel of overhanging branches.

8.4 miles. On your left is the Cedar River, and just ahead is a bridge over a stream flowing into it. There are benches and a small viewing platform where you can watch the river pass by. As you enter the city of Waverly, the trail becomes a divided bikeway with lampposts down the median strip and a couple of picnic tables on your right.

8.9 miles. Pass a Kwik Star convenience store, which has restrooms for trail users, and cross First Avenue SE, then Bremer Avenue, Waverly's main thoroughfare. The old train depot is here, another reminder that you're on a railroad right-of-way.

9.1 miles. Cross the intersection of First Avenue NE and Third Street NE (nobody will ever accuse Waverly of being overly creative in naming its streets), then turn right onto Second Avenue NE. Make an immediate left onto Cedar Lane Road.

Follow Cedar Lane Road around a wide, scenic bend in the Cedar River, bearing left at each intersection. You'll pass the Waverly Water Ski Club's docks and ski jump, and by now your nose should be tingling.

10.3 miles. Pass Pelikan Park and turn left onto Horton Road. You'll quickly cross the Cedar River, and now your nose is on full alert: There's chocolate in the air!

11.1 miles. The source of your nose's delight is on the left, the Nestle Chocolate plant, which produced the makings for the World's Largest Latte. The cup it was poured into is on display in the parking lot. Just beyond the plant's entrance, cross Sixth Avenue NW and turn left onto the Waverly Rail Trail again. It's still a superslab of bike trails as it passes the Nestle parking lot.

The trail crosses the Cedar River on a spectacular, 23-foot-wide bridge. When the Star Clipper sold its ribbon of right-of-way to Waverly, this bridge was the jeweled clasp at its end. Unfortunately, the company sold the steel in the bridge to a salvage company. The City successfully blocked that move, but it was dicey for a time.

11.5 miles. Cross Second Avenue NE, where you turned off the trail earlier, then cross Bremer Avenue again and follow the trail back to Denver.

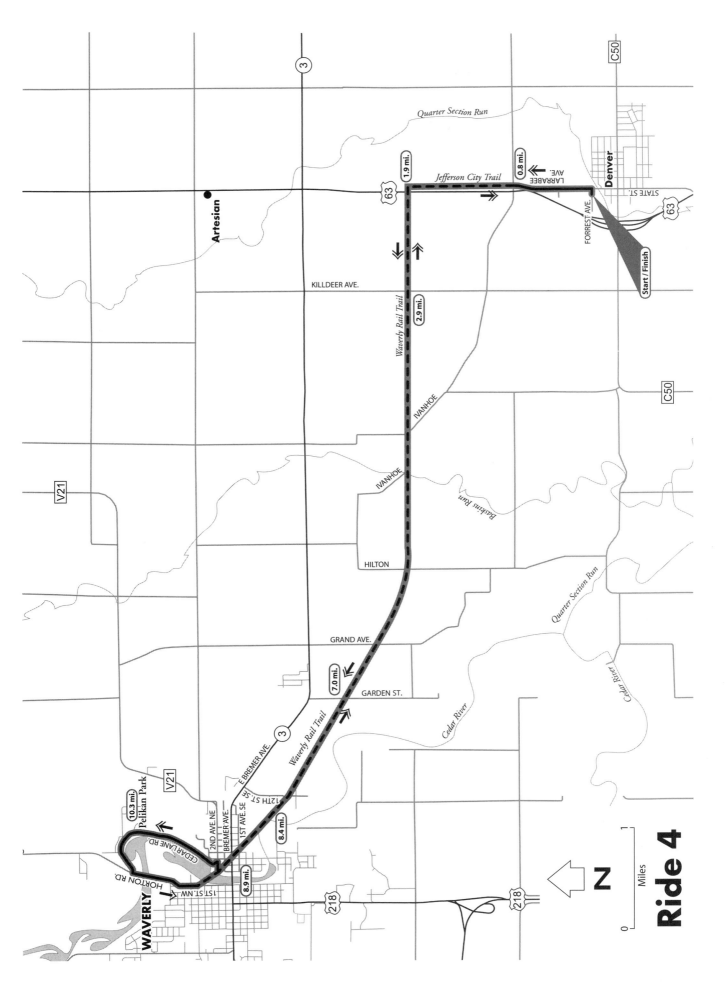

Ride 4

N

Miles

0 ——— 1

WAVERLY

Denver

Artesian

Start / Finish

Quarter Section Run

Jefferson City Trail

Waverly Rail Trail

0.8 mi.

1.9 mi.

2.9 mi.

7.0 mi.

8.4 mi.

8.9 mi.

10.3 mi.

Pelikan Park

LARRABEE AVE.

FORREST AVE.

STATE ST.

KILLDEER AVE.

IVANHOE

IVANHOE

HILTON

GRAND AVE.

GARDEN ST.

E. BREMER AVE.

12TH ST. SE

1ST AVE. SE

BREMER AVE.

2ND AVE. NE

CEDAR LANE RD.

HORTON RD.

1ST ST. NW

Bashins Run

Cedar River

Quarter Section Run

Quarter Section Run

Cedar River

3

63

63

C50

C50

V21

V21

218

218

RIDE 5
Finding the Lost County Seat

LOCATION: Butler County Nature Trail, Rolling Prairie Trail, county and state roads between Shell Rock and Allison
DISTANCE: 30.0-mile loop
SURFACE: Paved trail, crushed-limestone trail, paved roads
TERRAIN: Flat on trails, gently rolling hills on roads
DIFFICULTY: Easy to moderate
SERVICES:
  Restrooms: Convenience store in Shell Rock, businesses in Clarksville, Wilder County Park and in Allison
  Water: Same
  Food: Restaurants and convenience stores in Shell Rock, Clarksville, and Allison
  Camping: Shell Rock Park (tents), Shell Rock; Heery Woods State Park, Clarksville; Wilder County Park, Allison
  Lodging: Motels in Waverly
  Bike Shop: None nearby
STARTING POINT: Butler County Nature Trail head on County Road T63, about .4 miles north of State Highway 3 in Shell Rock

Variety rules on this ride: you start on a shaded, crushed-limestone trail, switch to an asphalt-paved trail across open country, then go onto the county roads to discover the ghost of a town that used to be.

0.0 miles. Swing your leg over your bike and head north on the Butler County Nature Trail, off County Road T63 in Shell Rock. This trail was developed in 1989, and nature has been encroaching on it ever since. The crushed-limestone surface is smooth enough for your road tires, but keep an eye out for potholes and rough spots.

Through the trees on your right, you'll glimpse an oxbow lake, left behind when the Shell Rock River, a tributary of the Cedar, changed its course many years ago. Though the trail roughly parallels the Shell Rock's course, you won't actually see the river from this trail.

0.4 miles. Cross Glen Hall Road and pedal through the stacks of bricks and pavers in the Shell Rock Brick Works yard, then follow the trail back into the woods. Through the trailside trees, you have flickering views across the land's swells. Birds twitter in the overhead canopy and squirrels and rabbits scamper across the trail. The trail is cool, shaded and protected from winds, and almost perfectly level.

4.8 miles. Cross a trestle over Beaver Creek. Look for deer tracks in the mud flats next to the stream, and turtles sunning themselves on half-sunken branches. The trail crosses more open space now, and prairie flowers are everywhere.

5.5 miles. The trail ends abruptly at the Schmadeke family's driveway. Turn right on the driveway to reach County Road C33, where you turn left, heading west.

6.6 miles. County Road C33 brings you to the shaded streets of Clarksville. Turn left onto the ultrawide Main Street. (Momma Mia's Pizza here offers a delicious alternative to franchise pizza places.) Pedal four blocks down Main and turn right on Jefferson Street.

7.7 miles. Cross two extremely rough sets of railroad tracks carefully, then turn left into the gravel parking lot of the Rolling Prairie Trail head. Go through the parking lot, up the gravel path, and turn right onto the asphalt trail.

8.4 miles. Crossing a high trestle, you get your first look at the Shell Rock River. The trail is sunny and smooth, a strip of sleek asphalt arrowing west across farmland. Redwing blackbirds trill as you invade their territory and goldfinches are solidified sunbeams flitting across the trail. On both sides, a sea of crops stretches to the horizon, interrupted only by island-like farmsteads.

13.9 miles. Shortly after you cross the hardtop Newell Avenue, the asphalt ends and you continue on a well-packed gravel trail. (Plans are in the works to extend the paved trail west another 20 miles to Coulter, but it'll take a few years.) The trail turns left and narrows, then enters Wilder County Park and you're back on asphalt. Cruise through the park and campground to the parking lot and the park road out to State Highway 3, where you turn right.

15.1 miles. Turn left onto State Highway 14. There's a convenience store at this corner. (To reach the business district of Allison, turn right here, then zigzag through the residential streets to Main Street. There's a restaurant and a tavern in town.) State Highway 14 takes you between corn and soybean fields over undulating land. The slopes are gentle and the view goes on forever across the fields.

18.1 miles. Turn left onto Butler Center Road (County Road C45), heading east. The two-lane county road has a nice, smooth surface and hardly any traffic.

18.5 miles. You'll notice a couple of street signs stuck in the fence line at the edge of the cornfield, where there are no streets. When you reach Madison Road, coming in from your right, you're in what remains of Butler Center.

Butler Center, platted in 1856, quickly grew large enough to become the seat of Butler County. In 1880, however, the Dubuque & Dakota Railroad built its line through Allison, four miles away. The next year, the county seat was moved to Allison, and Butler Center's citizens soon followed, taking most of the buildings with them. The town gradually reverted to prairie, then became the farmland you see now. An historical marker on a boulder about 20 yards up Madison Road, signs marking long-gone streets, and a single farmhouse are all that remain of Butler Center.

From Butler Center, County Road C45 makes a beeline east across the low hills. It's a road that lets your mind wander as you pass widely spaced farmyards and homes and watch hawks lazing on the breezes.

28.2 miles. County Road C45 merges with County Road T63; bear left to follow County Road T63 into Shell Rock. The road becomes Cherry Street through the center of town and across the Shell Rock River. Shell Rock's a pleasant-looking town, but the streets are empty save for a pickup or two parked in front of the local restaurant or tavern. At Grove Street, you'll see a Bike Route sign pointing to the right: ignore it and continue straight.

29.6 miles. Turn left at the stop sign onto North Public Road. There's a Kwik Star convenience store here. A block up the road, cross State Highway 3, continuing straight on North Public Road (County Road T63) to your starting point at the Butler County Nature Trail.

Ride 5

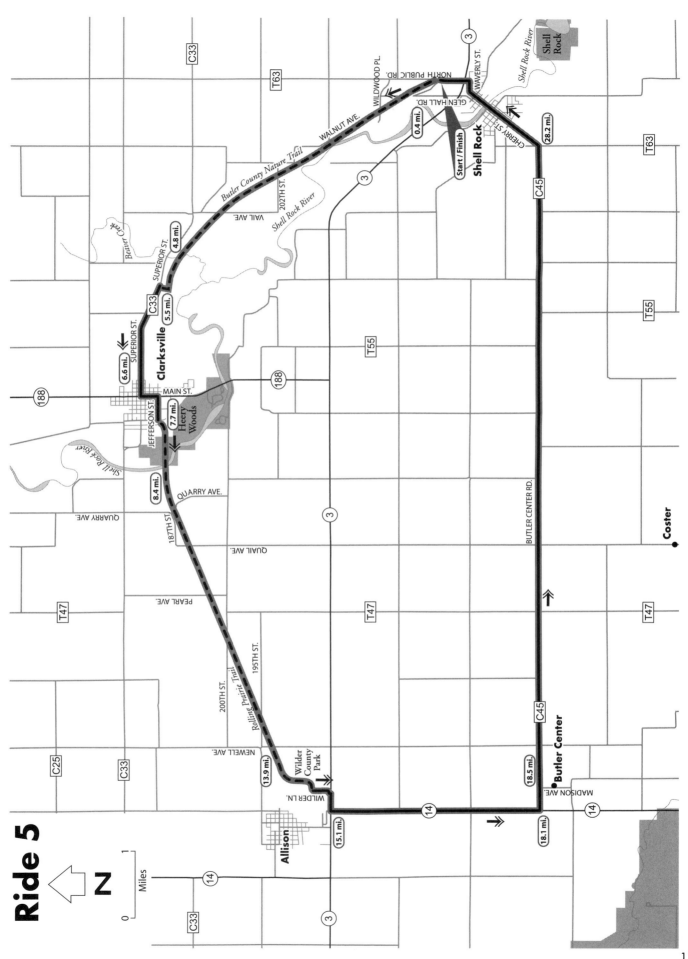

N

Miles
0 1

Shell Rock

Shell Rock River

Shell Rock

Shell Rock River

WAVERLY ST.

NORTH PUBLIC RD.

GLEN HALL RD.

WILDWOOD PL.

Start / Finish

0.4 mi.

28.2 mi.

CHERRY ST.

Walnut Ave.

Butler County Nature Trail

202ND ST.

VAIL AVE.

Shell Rock River

4.8 mi.

SUPERIOR ST.

Beaver Creek

C33

5.5 mi.

SUPERIOR ST.

Clarksville

6.6 mi.

MAIN ST.

JEFFERSON ST.

7.7 mi.

Heery Woods

Shell Rock River

8.4 mi.

QUARRY AVE.

QUARRY AVE.

187TH ST.

QUAIL AVE.

PEARL AVE.

200TH ST.

195TH ST.

Rolling Prairie Trail

NEWELL AVE.

13.9 mi.

Wilder County Park

WILDER LN.

Allison

15.1 mi.

14

18.1 mi.

14

Butler Center

18.5 mi.

MADISON AVE.

BUTLER CENTER RD.

C45

C45

Coster

T63

T55

T47

T63

C33

T63

T55

T47

C25

C33

C33

188

188

3

3

3

3

14

T47

T55

14

11

RIDE 6
Say "Hi" to Chuck Ride

LOCATION: County roads between Cedar Falls and
New Hartford
DISTANCE: 33.2-mile loop
SURFACE: Paved roads
TERRAIN: Low rolling hills and flats
DIFFICULTY: Moderate
SERVICES:
> **Restrooms:** Businesses in Cedar Falls and New Hartford
> **Water:** Same
> **Food:** Restaurants and convenience stores in Cedar Falls
> and New Hartford
> **Camping:** Washington Union Access (primitive only),
> Black Hawk County Park and Antique Acres Camp-
> ground, Cedar Falls; George Wyth State Park, Waterloo
> **Lodging:** Motels, hotel and bed and breakfasts in Cedar
> Falls and Waterloo
> **Bike Shop:** Bike Tech, Main Street, and Europa Cycle &
> Ski, University Avenue, Cedar Falls

STARTING POINT: Cup of Joe on the corner of First Street
(State Highway 57) and Main Street in downtown
Cedar Falls

Low-traffic county roads through wide-open farmland,
some fun rollers, a scenic wetland area and river valley, and a
relaxed cruise over the flats make this a great sampler of bicycling in the northern Cedar River Valley.

0.0 miles. From the Cup of Joe espresso bar, head south
on Main Street through Cedar Falls' prosperous-looking downtown. There's a restaurant, art gallery, nightclub, or upscale
retail store at every hand, plus a beautifully restored historic
hotel and theater. At Sixth Street, Main Street goes from two
lanes to four; the speed limit is 35 mph, the traffic is light, and
the outside lane's wide enough to share.

1.5 miles. Turn right onto Seerley Boulevard, which
turns into a divided street with a center strip of trees and
flower gardens as it climbs the gradual slope to the University
of Northern Iowa's campus. Turn right onto College Street,
then go left onto 23rd Street at the traffic light. The redbrick,
Georgian-style UNI dorms are on your left.

2.4 miles. Just past Campus Street, bear right at the parking lot entrance and follow the side path down to the underpass
beneath Hudson Road. You emerge at the UNI Wellness Center;
turn right, then bear left at the V and follow the side path
around the Wellness Center, then south past the UNI Dome.

3.1 miles. Turn right to head west on the paved shoulder on 27th Street. You pass UNI's Native Roadside Vegetation
Center, which is responsible for much of the prairie plantings
along Iowa's highways. Once you cross Union Road, 27th
becomes County Road D17 and runs straight as a chalk line
across low hills clothed in corn and soybeans. The paved
shoulder ends at the Black Hawk/Grundy County line, but
traffic is so light you won't miss it.

11.5 miles. Check out the tree growing out of the top of
an old, ceramic silo next to the farmhouse on your right—Ma
Nature *does* persist, doesn't she? At the T intersection, turn
right to head north on County Road T55 (U Avenue). The
next two miles give you some good rollers—grab some speed
on the downs and you'll easily make it over the ups.

13.5 miles. County Road T55 turns right, but you continue straight north to the stop sign, then continue straight on
State Highway 57. You have a short climb, then a mile-long
downhill before State Highway 57 curves left; keep going
straight at the curve, onto New Hartford's Main Street. Cross a
double set of railroad tracks, follow the curve to the right and
pedal into Senator Charles "Chuck" Grassley's hometown.

Chuck Grassley has been Iowa's senator since 1980. He's
the only active farmer in the United States Senate—he comes
home to this community of 652 souls regularly to make sure
his crops are still growing. Grassley, the Chairman of the Senate Finance Committee, has a reputation for pinching each
nickel in his own pocket until Jefferson winces, though the
size of the federal deficit suggests a looser grip on public
funds. Wave a symbolic "hello" to Chuck.

On the right, just before you reach the stop sign, is
Ingalls Little House Cafe, which offers a great breakfast and
lunch at prices that can entice even Senator Grassley.

15.9 miles. Turn left onto Broadway Avenue (County
Road T55). You pass a Kwik Star convenience store, then cross
Beaver Creek and climb a short but steep hill out of New
Hartford.

16.6 miles. At the hilltop cemetery, turn right onto
Beaver Valley Road (County Road C67). You can coast for
about a half mile and try to find a smooth path over the
expansion cracks (they seem to be least offensive right in the
center of the lane). The road starts a gradual rise that turns
into a couple of short, steep climbs. At the top, you head down
over a fast roller, then have a long run-out to the Black Hawk
County line, where County Road C67 takes on a layer of
smooth asphalt.

23.3 miles. At the stop sign, turn left onto Union Road
North (County Road D75). On your left is the Beaver Valley
Wetlands: look for herons, egrets, Canada geese, and a variety of
ducks.

24.8 miles. Turn right onto Cedar-Wapsi Road West
(County Road C57). You can go for speed down this hill—the
railroad tracks up ahead are very smooth—and coast all the
way to the Cedar River. This area is known as Turkey Foot
Heights, where the Shell Rock and West Fork Rivers join the
Cedar River. It was so named because of the river confluence's
resemblance to the footprint of a wild turkey. As you cross
the bridge, look to your left to see the junction of the Shell Rock
and Cedar Rivers. Daniel Boone's son, Nathan, is reputed to
have camped near here for three days while exploring this area.

27.5 miles. At the stop sign, turn right onto Waverly
Road (County Road V14). From here south to Cedar Falls, the
road is basically flat—settle into a comfortable gear and
cruise. You'll pass Antique Acres, with old tractors and farm
machinery scattered about. There's a show of antique equipment here every August that draws collectors from all over the
country. As you cruise into the North Cedar district, watch for
Biemann's Chuck Wagon Restaurant on your left. They serve
what's arguably the best cheeseburger and beer fries in town.

32.8 miles. Cross a rough railroad track, then go
through the traffic light at First Street (IA 57) and pedal one
block to turn left on Second Street. Two blocks down, turn left
onto Main Street to get back to Cup of Joe.

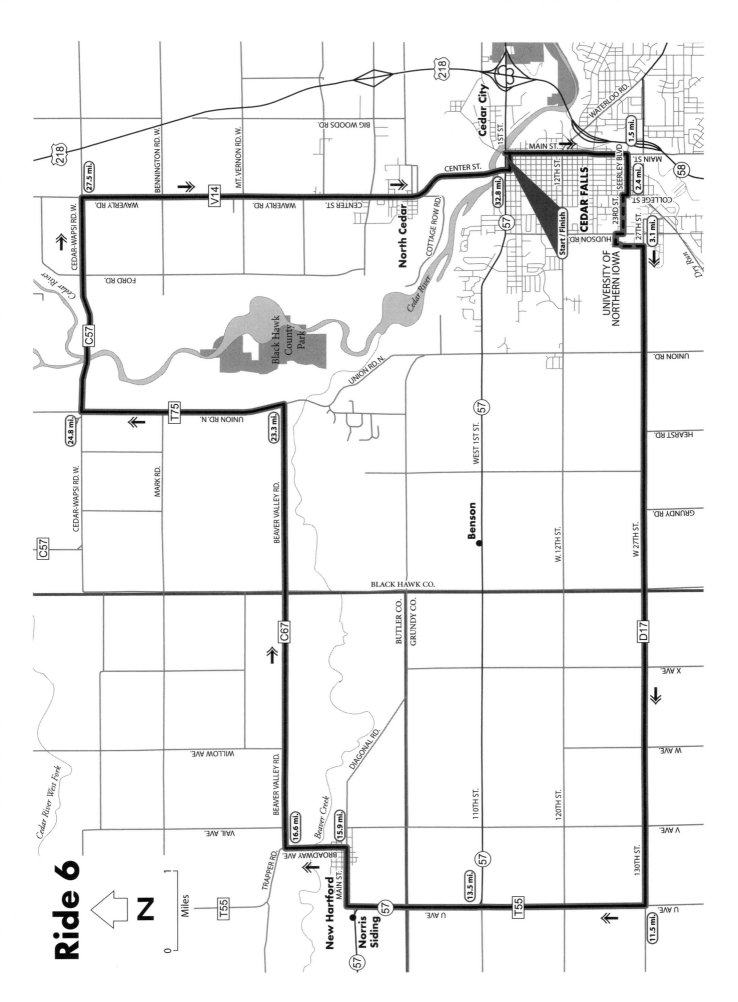

Ride 6

N

Miles
0   1

Cedar City

218

218

27.5 mi.

BENNINGTON RD. W.

MT. VERNON RD. W.

BIG WOODS RD.

CEDAR-WAPSI RD. W.

WAVERLY RD.

FORD RD.

V14

WAVERLY RD.

CENTER ST.

CENTER ST.

North Cedar

COTTAGE ROW RD.

Cedar River

Black Hawk County Park

Cedar River

1ST ST.

MAIN ST.

12TH ST.

CEDAR FALLS

32.8 mi.

57

Start / Finish

23RD ST.

SEERLEY BLVD

27TH ST.

MAIN ST.

WATERLOO RD.

1.5 mi.

58

2.4 mi.

COLLEGE ST.

3.1 mi.

UNIVERSITY OF NORTHERN IOWA

HUDSON RD.

Dry Run

C57

Cedar River

24.8 mi.

T75

UNION RD. N.

23.3 mi.

UNION RD. N.

UNION RD.

HEARST RD.

GRUNDY RD.

W 27TH ST.

WEST 1ST ST.

57

Benson

W. 12TH ST.

W. 27TH ST.

CEDAR-WAPSI RD. W.

C57

MARK RD.

BEAVER VALLEY RD.

BLACK HAWK CO.

BUTLER CO.

GRUNDY CO.

C67

D17

X AVE.

W AVE.

Cedar River West Fork

WILLOW AVE.

DIAGONAL RD.

110TH ST.

120TH ST.

V AVE.

16.6 mi.

Beaver Creek

15.9 mi.

VAIL AVE.

BEAVER VALLEY RD.

BROADWAY AVE.

MAIN ST.

New Hartford

TRAPPER RD.

T55

Norris Siding

57

57

U AVE.

57

13.5 mi.

T55

130TH ST.

U AVE.

11.5 mi.

Cedar River West Fork

13

RIDE 7
Tour de Parks

LOCATION: Cedar Trails System in Cedar Falls and
    Waterloo
DISTANCE: 16.9-mile loop
SURFACE: Paved trails and streets
TERRAIN: Basically flat, with two very short hills
DIFFICULTY: Child's play
SERVICES:
  Restrooms: At start/finish, Island Park, Black Hawk
  County Park, George Wyth State Park, Pfeiffer Park
  Water: Same
  Food: Restaurants in Cedar Falls
  Camping: Black Hawk County Park, Cedar Falls; George
  Wyth State Park, Waterloo
  Lodging: Motels, hotels, and bed and
    breakfasts in Cedar Falls and Waterloo
  Bike Shop: Bike Tech, Main Street, and
    Europa Cycle & Ski, University Avenue,
    Cedar Falls
STARTING POINT: Peter Melendy Park,
  on the northeast corner of First Street
  (State Highway 57) and Main Street in
  downtown Cedar Falls

The Cedar Trails System

With nearly 70 miles of interconnected, paved trails, the Waterloo-Cedar Falls metropolitan area is the mecca of Iowa bicycling.

The development of the 52-mile Cedar Valley Nature Trail from Waterloo to Cedar Rapids in the late 1970s generated tremendous public interest in recreational trails. In the early 1980s, the Cedar Falls Rotary Club took the lead in creating the first two miles of the metro trail system, from downtown Cedar Falls to George Wyth State Park. Spurred by forward-looking citizens, the five cities that make up the metro area developed a plan for a trail network to link parks, schools, shopping, residential areas, and industrial parks.

Trail planners took full advantage of the scenic Cedar River and its tributaries. Trails now run through the floodplain forests on both sides of the Cedar, and along Dry Run and Black Hawk Creeks. Borrow pits for highway construction have been turned into small lakes surrounded by parklands, with trails along their shores. Prairie plantings provide ever-changing fields of flowers.

The planners decided early on that connections between trails were vital, and created trail loops instead of lines. You can ride anything from a four-mile circle around a lake to a 40-mile loop around the cities, all on paved trails. The Cedar Trails System links Cedar Falls, Waterloo, Evansdale, and Hudson; connects seamlessly to the Cedar Valley Nature Trail; and is a part of the American Discovery Trail, a coast-to-coast trail in the making.

The system grows every year as new trails are opened. At present, the long-range plan envisions over 90 miles of interconnected trails in the metro area, plus trails that will extend north all the way to the Minnesota border.

The *Gateway to the Trails* sculpture in Peter Melendy Park is an appropriate starting point for what may be the best trail ride in Iowa. You'll wind through forests and prairies, into or past a dozen parks, along the Cedar River, and around Big Woods Lake. Spring, summer, or fall, it's drop-dead gorgeous.

0.0 miles. From Peter Melendy Park, cross Main Street and head west on the side path—the Cedar Valley Lakes Trail—along First Street (State Highway 57). Pass a "history row" of a restored single-room schoolhouse and early gas station, and the Ice House Museum, then turn right to cross the Cedar River. You'll loop through Tourist Park and under the bridge you just crossed, then glide through Island Park.

Coming out of the Island Park, there's a great series of curves to swoop through. Bear right when you reach the Y and slip under another bridge, then wind along next to a placid backwater until you come out onto Cottage Row Road. Across the road, summer homes, raised twelve feet above the ground to escape floods, line the river.

The trail turns away from the road to jog around a small horse pasture and farm fields bordered by woods. Watch for wild turkeys—a flock of about 30 birds lives here.

As you enter Black Hawk County Park, the floodplain forest is dotted with bluebells and other wildflowers.

Between the park's campgrounds, there's a trailhead with a restroom, water, picnic tables, and a shelter. The trail leaves the park as a side path heading east along Lone Tree Road.

4.4 miles. The side path goes straight east, but for a prettier ride, turn right onto Hiawatha Road and cruise through a nice area of modest homes. Turn right onto Pine Street, then left onto Longview Avenue. Longview turns left a half mile after you cross Center Street and becomes Central Avenue. At the stop sign, go right onto Lake Street for a pleasant stretch past wetlands and open country.

6.3 miles. At the stop sign, cross Big Woods Road and bear right onto the Big Woods Lake Trail. It circles the lake, curving through a fragrant stand of pines and the Rotary Prairie Restoration, where prairie flowers and grasses delight your eyes. Leaving Big Woods Park, you have a gorgeous, winding mile between a pair of small lakes before coming back into downtown Cedar Falls.

8.3 miles. Be careful on the railroad tracks here—they can catch a wheel. Before the bridge, turn right to curve under the road and into Gateway Park. (Going straight over the bridge takes you back to Peter Melendy Park.) You're back on the Cedar Valley Lakes Trail, riding beside the river, through the park and into the riparian forest.

9.6 miles. Bear left at the Y in the trail and enter George Wyth State Park. You'll catch glimpses of Alice Wyth Lake through the trees on your left.

10.8 miles. Bear right at the Y and pass Fisher Lake, which is on your left. There's an overlook deck where you can pause to admire the lake's water lilies. Continuing on the trail, you wind through woods and wetlands, enjoying the cool shade and keeping an eye out for deer.

12.4 miles. The trail widens to road width: turn left onto the trail up and over the river on the highway bridge. On the far side, turn right onto the South Riverside Trail, a converted rail bed through the Hartman Nature Reserve. The shaded, straight trail converges with the river after about two miles, and a densely wooded bluff rises on your left.

15.4 miles. Push up a short, steep climb into Pfeiffer Park and bear left at the top. (Krieg's Crossing bike bridge is on your right, leading to the Cedar Valley Lakes Trail.) Cruise through the park, then coast downhill beneath the Highway 58 bridges.

Bear left at the Y at the bottom of the hill, then turn right onto the side path along Waterloo Road. Across Dry Run Creek, turn right again onto the side path along Utility Parkway. Follow that trail as it leaves the road, crosses some railroad tracks, and skirts the Washington Park Golf Course.

16.6 miles. Cross Fourth Street and climb the levee again. Bear left at the top, drop into the parking lot, and go straight on Second Street. At the traffic light, turn right on Main Street and ride down the block to your starting point.

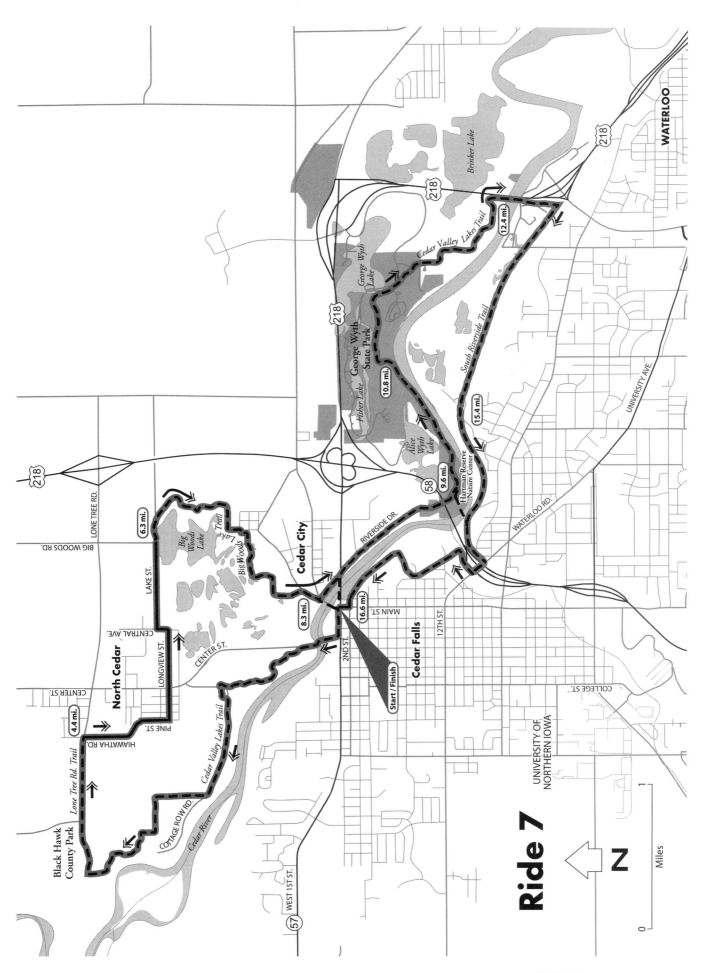

Ride 7

Black Hawk County Park

North Cedar

Cedar City

Cedar Falls

Waterloo

George Wyth State Park

Hartman Reserve Nature Center

University of Northern Iowa

Start / Finish

Big Woods Lake

Big Woods Lake Trail

Fisher Lake

Alice Wyth Lake

George Wyth Lake

Brinker Lake

Cedar Valley Lakes Trail

Cedar Valley Lakes Trail

Lone Tree Rd. Trail

South Riverside Trail

Cedar River

4.4 mi.
6.3 mi.
8.3 mi.
9.6 mi.
10.8 mi.
12.4 mi.
15.4 mi.
16.6 mi.

BIG WOODS RD.
LONE TREE RD.
LAKE ST.
CENTRAL AVE.
LONGVIEW ST.
CENTER ST.
PINE ST.
HIAWATHA RD.
CENTER ST.
COTTAGE ROW RD.
2ND ST.
MAIN ST.
WEST 1ST ST.
12TH ST.
COLLEGE ST.
RIVERSIDE DR.
WATERLOO RD.
UNIVERSITY AVE.

218
218
218
218
58
57

N

Miles
0   1

RIDE 8
Over the Burned Bridge

LOCATION: Cedar Valley Nature Trail and county roads between La Porte City and Brandon
DISTANCE: 22.1-mile loop
SURFACE: Paved and crushed-limestone trail, paved roads
TERRAIN: Flat trail, gentle hills on the roads
DIFFICULTY: Easy
SERVICES:
Restrooms: Businesses and trailheads in La Porte City and Brandon
Water: Same
Food: Restaurants and stores in La Porte City and Brandon
Camping: McFarlane County Park, La Porte City
Lodging: Bed and breakfast in La Porte City; motels, hotels, and bed and breakfast in Waterloo
Bike Shop: None nearby
STARTING POINT: Cedar Valley Nature Trail head off Eighth Street (Commercial Street) in LaPorte City

The Battle for the Trail

When people proposed turning the Illinois Central Railroad's abandoned Cedar Valley Road from Waterloo to Cedar Rapids into a recreational trail, opposition from the adjacent landowners was immediate and widespread. Nowhere in the 52-mile stretch was that opposition stronger than in La Porte City.

The landowners raised claims of ownership, nearly all of which were found to be groundless. They protested that the trail would bring Vandals, Visigoths, and other bicycling Barbarians across their land. At one public meeting to discuss the proposed trail, a local farmer warned that livestock would be stolen by trail users. A tiny, middle-aged woman shot back, "For the life of me, I can't figure how I'm going to get one of your heifers draped across my handlebars."

Frustrated by the courts and a juggernaut of trail support, some opponents resorted to sabotage. Trees were felled across the nascent trail, dead livestock were dumped in the right-of-way, and nail-studded boards were buried just beneath the trail's surface. The ultimate sabotage, however, was the burning of the old railroad bridge over Spring Creek.

The arsonist, however, had gone too far. Iowans are fair-minded folk, and even trail opponents were offended by the destruction. The sabotage ended, the opposition receded, and the trail went through.

Thirty years later, the Cedar Valley Nature Trail brings a stream of bicyclists through La Porte City and provides a first-class recreational facility for the town. Now, La Porte City decorates its downtown with banners showing bicyclists on a trail and celebrates an annual Trails Day. The town slogan is "All Trails Lead to La Porte City."

This ride takes you on the sweetest section of the 52-mile Cedar Valley Nature Trail, a leafy tunnel filled with the music of birds. You can ride the trail as an out and back, or make a loop on county roads through some of Iowa's richest farmland.

0.0 miles. Head east on the trail from the Cedar Valley Nature Trail head in La Porte City. You quickly pedal through La Porte City's backyards, past the grain bins and elevator, then leave town on the tree-lined path. The trail seems utterly flat—its steepest grade is only 2 percent.

1.0 miles. Pass the La Porte City Country Club's golf course and cruise into an open area. There are several crossings between pastures along here—watch out for the grated cattle guards buried in the trail.

2.2 miles. At King Road, there's a trailhead with water, a small shelter, and a picnic table. To the left on the road is McFarlane County Park, with restrooms at its campground. Cross King Road on the trail, which changes from asphalt to a crushed-limestone surface as it plunges back into the woods. It's smooth enough for road tires, but keep an eye out for occasional rough spots.

You break into the open after about a half mile of woods to cross the Cedar River on a long trestle, then slip back into the sun-dappled shade. The woods are deep and cool, with only the songs of birds and buzz of insects to disturb their stillness.

4.0 miles. Cross the Spring Creek Bridge. The original bridge, left over from the railroad, was burned by trail opponents when the conversion of this abandoned rail line was just getting started. Fortunately, the trail developers had insured all the bridges on the right-of-way just weeks before the arson, so the bridge was quickly rebuilt.

5.0 miles. On your right, the Cedar River sweeps by below a pair of benches set at the bluff's edge. A little farther along is an historical marker commemorating a pioneer homestead; there, the trail and the river diverge again.

6.1 miles. As you enter Buzzard's Glory Quarry, you pass crumbling structures that once loaded cement into railroad cars. The quarry, long out of use, is now only a calm pond surrounded by limestone cliffs. A shelter and picnic tables are here, along with information displays about the quarry operation and the Purdy family, which once owned this land.

Beyond the quarry, the trees thin out as you pedal between rising embankments. The trail slices through a 12,000-year-old dune formed by winds piling up the floodplain sands.

10.2 miles. You've emerged from the woods and crossed a gravel road to pass a grain elevator and bins. Ahead is the Brandon trailhead, with restrooms, a shelter, and picnic tables. Bear left onto Branard Street just before you reach the trailhead.

Two blocks up Branard Street, turn left, heading west on Main Street (County Road V71). There's not much to Brandon's business district: Across from you is a small grocery; a block to the right is a restaurant with good home cooking.

At the yield sign, bear right to follow County Road V71, then take the first left onto Brandon Road (County Road D48). This takes you westward, around gentle curves and over low hills with long views across the fields.

14.7 miles. Stay on County Road D48 as it turns left; Clark Road (County Road V65) continues straight. A sign points to La Porte City. The countryside is green and beautiful, and as you top a rise, you have a magnificent 360-degree view across the rolling land. Woods mark the Cedar River's course; ahead and to your left you can see the La Porte City grain elevator.

19.6 miles. Bear left at the V in the road and cross the Cedar River, then another long bridge over a branch of Wolf Creek. County Road D48 is now County Road L, and as you enter La Porte City's limits, it becomes Eighth Street and takes you back to your starting point.

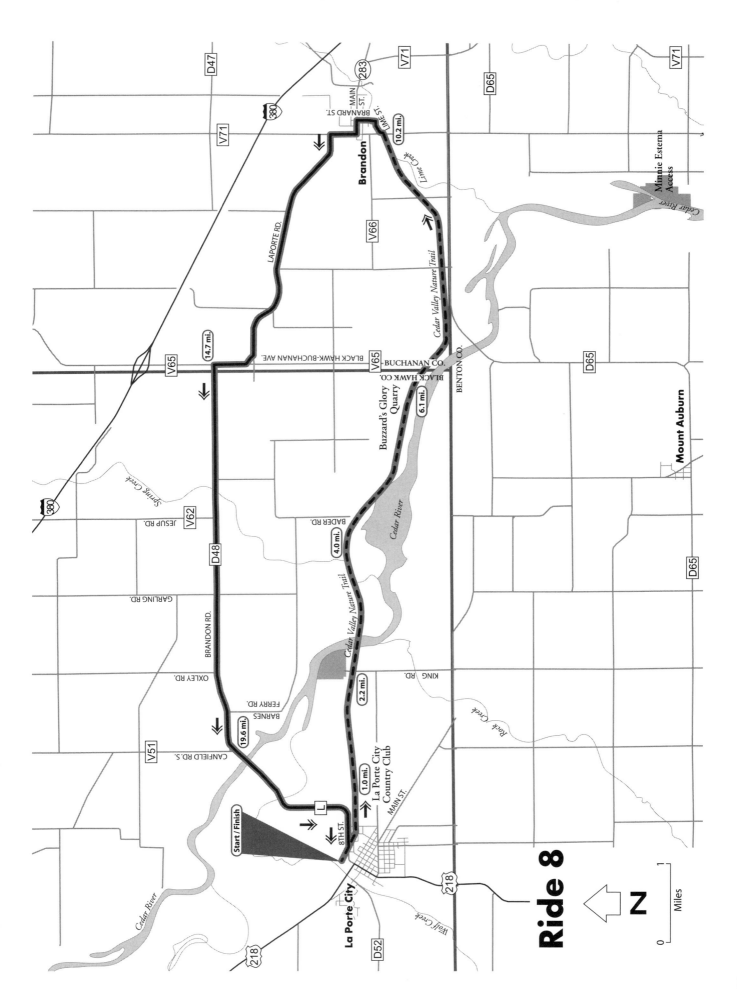

Ride 8

N

Miles
0   1

17

RIDE 9
Cycling Past the Caves

Keep an eye out for miniature horses as you travel County Road E17 west of Andrew.

LOCATION: County, state, and federal roads looping north of Maquoketa
DISTANCE: 27.5-mile loop
SURFACE: Paved roads
TERRAIN: Rolling hills; one steep climb and descent
DIFFICULTY: Moderate
SERVICES:
> **Restrooms:** Businesses in Maquoketa, convenience store in Andrew, Maquoketa Caves Nature Center (open on summer weekends only)
> **Water:** Same
> **Food:** Restaurants, grocery, convenience stores in Maquoketa; convenience store in Andrew
> **Camping:** Maquoketa Caves State Park, Maquoketa
> **Lodging:** Hotel, motels, and bed and breakfasts in Maquoketa
> **Bike Shop:** Magellan Bike & Ski Repair, Dearborn Street, Maquoketa

STARTING POINT: Intersection of Main and Platte (State Highway 64) Streets in Maquoketa

The Maquoketa Caves

A side trip into Maquoketa Caves State Park is well worth the effort—and it does take some effort, since there's a steep hill involved.

Of the dozen-plus caves, the largest is Dancehall Cave, which has walkways and a lighting system (the lights are dim; bring your flashlight). You have to stoop to enter, but you'll have plenty of headroom once you get inside the 1,100-foot-long cavern.

The other caves are of varying accessibility—they were all formed long before the Americans with Disabilities Act was passed, and it's hard to retrofit a cave. But you don't have to go underground to appreciate rock formations like the natural bridge above Raccoon Creek or the 17-ton Balanced Rock.

Artifacts found in 13 sites within the park indicate that Native Americans used the caves for hundreds, perhaps thousands of years before deer-hunting white settlers discovered them in 1834. The caves became a popular site for picnics and weekend outings during the late 19th and early 20th centuries; Dance Hall Cave got its name from the soirees held there. Unfortunately, many of the cave's milk-white stalactites and stalagmites were "collected" by early souvenir hunters.

The first section of land for this state park was acquired in 1921. During the 1930s, the Civilian Conservation Corps and Works Progress Administration developed facilities in the park, including the stone lodge, the Dancehall Cave walkway system, the hiking trail linking the caves, and several picnic shelters. A recent renovation project has restored these structures and brought the park facilities up to modern standards.

This ride takes you out of Maquoketa, over rolling country divided by the Maquoketa River's many tributaries, then back along a ridgeline to town. The views of hills and wooded valleys are breathtaking.

0.0 miles. From the intersection of Main and West Platte streets (Platte Street is also State Highway 64) in Maquoketa, pedal north on Main Street. Go through the traffic light at Quarry Street, then turn right a few blocks later onto Pershing Road.

1.7 miles. At State Highway 62, turn left, heading north again, and coast down to cross the Maquoketa River. The next three miles are a gradual climb up from the river past croplands dotted here and there by single-family homes. The roadside ditches are filled with wildflowers: Queen Anne's lace, coneflowers, black-eyed Susans, and Canadian thistles. Traffic is fast and moderately heavy on State Highway 62, but the sightlines are very long and the motorists are courteous.

At the top of the climb, you're rewarded with a lovely view to your right, looking down a hollow to a small pond and woods beyond. To the left, look out across cornfields with erosion-control grass strips in geometric patterns on the hillsides.

7.8 miles. After a mile or so along the ridgeline, you have a short climb to enter Andrew, home of Iowa's first governor. This town was a player in the mid-1800s struggle to determine the Jackson county seat. Over a 30-year period, the county held semi-regular votes on the matter, with Andrew, Bellevue, Fulton, and Centreville all in contention. Unassuming Maquoketa, however, eventually won out when it became a railroad hub; the railroad brought enough population for the city to win the final vote by 179 votes—a virtual landslide. Even then, however, Andrew held onto the county jail. There's not much left in Andrew nowadays, at least along State Highway 62.

8.2 miles. Turn left (west) onto County Road E17 (150th Street). As you top the short rise, you're confronted with a beautiful view of downhill rollers between rich farm fields. County Road E17 is a smooth, concrete two-lane with hardly any traffic, so you can crank up some speed for a roller coaster ride down to Cedar Creek. On the far side of the creek, you hit an uphill too steep for your momentum to carry.

12.5 miles. Still heading west, cross the four-lane U.S. Highway 61. There are three sets of nearly invisible rumble strips in the concrete surface before the stop sign. They're mild enough to cross without jarring your teeth out, but it's more comfortable to pass them on the right.

The start of the mile-long climb from U.S. Highway 61 is steep enough for your granny gear, but about a third of the way up you hit a flat stretch. After that, the climb is much easier.

15.2 miles. After another fun run over rolling hills, you descend to cross the North Fork of the Maquoketa River, then have a steep, mile-long climb back up to the ridge. This section of road has a paved shoulder.

18.0 miles. Welcome to the former town of Iron Hill, now home to little more than the Rural Recycling Center. At the T, go left onto Caves Road (County Road Y31.) For the next eight miles, you wind along a ridge with extensive, beautiful views on both sides. As you pass the road to Maquoketa State Park, note the Maquoketa Caves Nature Center. It's worth a visit if you're there on a weekend. From there, you pedal easily over gentle rises and falls along the tops of the hills. Traffic is light, the road's smooth, and the view never quits.

26.3 miles. Turn right onto U.S. Highway 61. There's a narrow shoulder punctuated by rumble strips that's useable, though not really comfortable. Fortunately, you only need to travel about a quarter mile before taking the exit to West Platte Street.

At the traffic light at the end of the exit ramp, go left on West Platte Street (State Highway 64). There's a side path along this road, but it only goes for a couple of blocks before ending abruptly—you're better off staying on the road, which takes you back into Maquoketa and to your starting point.

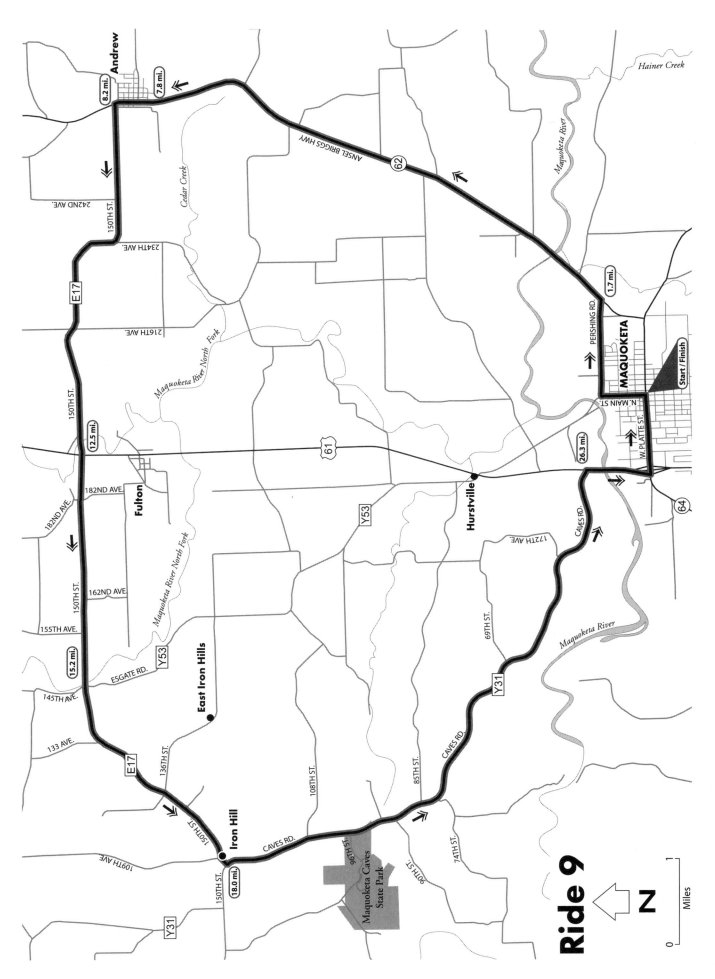

Ride 9

N

0 ——— 1
Miles

RIDE 10
Street to Stream Ride

Kick off this ride from the sculpture in Cedar Rapids' Greene Park.

LOCATION: Cedar Rapids streets and the Sac & Fox Trail
DISTANCE: 15.7-mile loop
SURFACE: Paved streets; crushed-limestone trail
TERRAIN: Short hills on streets; flat trail
DIFFICULTY: Easy
SERVICES:
  Restrooms: Businesses in Cedar Rapids, Bertram Road Trailhead, Indian Creek Nature Center
  Water: Same
  Food: Restaurants in Cedar Rapids
  Camping: Morgan Creek Park, Cedar Rapids; Pleasant Creek State Recreation Area, Palo
  Lodging: Motels, hotels, and bed and breakfasts in Cedar Rapids
  Bike Shop: Several in Cedar Rapids
STARTING POINT: Greene Park on Third Avenue SE between Fifth and Seventh streets SE

Czech Village

During the late 19th and early 20th centuries, thousands of Czech and Slovak immigrants came to Cedar Rapids and the surrounding communities. Czech Village is a restored shopping district in what was the center of the Czech community. Before the Second World War, Czech was the preferred language in this district, but nowadays you're not likely to hear much but English. The village is on the south side of the Cedar River, less than half a mile off the Street to Stream Ride route.

You enter the village via the Lion Bridge, which is decorated with antique-style lights and adorned with eight concrete lion heads, a traditional symbol of the Czech people. Czech Village is not large—just a couple of blocks—and it's not touristy. The closest thing to a tourist trap is Czech Cottage, a gift shop with lots of imports from the Czech and Slovak Republics.

Zindricks Czech Restaurant features real Czech recipes—this is not Americanized food. The koláčes from the Sykora Bakery will make your mouth think it died and went to heaven.

Over on 16th Street SW is the National Czech and Slovak Museum and Library. Founded in 1974 as the Czech Fine Arts Foundation, the museum has been housed in several places; it finally settled here in 1993. Presidents Bill Clinton of the U.S., Václav Havel of the Czech Republic, and Michael Kováč of the Slovak Republic were present for its dedication on October 21, 1995.

From the heart of downtown Cedar Rapids, this ride takes you on bike-friendly streets with nice, wide lanes, then onto the Sac & Fox Trail along Indian Creek, where you leave the urban environment without leaving the city.

0.0 miles. Head northeast on Third Avenue SE from the sculpture in Greene Park. This is a one-way street, and the right-hand lane is extra wide, perfect for shared bicycle/car use. You're quickly out of the downtown commercial district and into a pleasant-looking residential neighborhood.

1.7 miles. At the traffic light on 19th Street NE, bear right onto Linden Drive, another street with wide lanes. It takes you past the Brucemore Historical Site's back entrance. Built in 1886, Brucemore is a 21-room, red brick, Queen Anne-style mansion that was occupied in succession by three of Cedar Rapids' most prominent families. It's worth a little side jaunt to check it out.

Just past the Brucemore entrance, go left at the stop sign to head north onto Forest Drive. This is definitely a high-rent area: the homes are large, lovely, and expensive looking.

2.8 miles. At the four-way stop, turn right onto 27th Street Drive, then bear right at the yield sign onto Country Club Parkway SE. Heading south now, you pass a golf course on your left and have a couple of ups and downs on this residential street. Turn left at the stop sign onto Cottage Grove Avenue and rocket down a steep hill to cross Indian Creek.

4.4 miles. There's a rather imposing hill ahead, but you dodge right onto Sunland Drive, another residential street. At the T intersection, go left onto Cottage Grove Parkway SE.

When Cottage Grove Parkway Ts into East Post Road, ride across the grass on your right to get onto the Sac & Fox Trail.

At the entrance, the trail is a bit rutted by erosion, but it smooths out quickly. Your road tires will have no problems on this surface. The trail quickly plunges into lush woods and weaves southwards along Indian Creek. It's shady, cool, and lovely—a great ride on a hot day.

7.1 miles. Emerge from the woods to the Rosedale Road trailhead. Bear right to cross the road, then continue on the trail with Indian Creek on your right. The trail winds through woods, crossing and re-crossing the creek. You're on the outskirts of Cedar Rapids now, and the woods are home to deer, wild turkeys, and other wildlife—keep your eyes peeled.

8.6 miles. On your right is the Bertram Road trailhead with a portable toilet and water fountain. Now you're entering the Cedar Greenbelt area. There's a hiking trail leading off to your right that makes about a half-mile loop before rejoining this trail.

9.1 miles. A bridge crosses the stream on your left to go up to the Indian Creek Nature Center, where there are restrooms and water, and you continue winding south and west through the gorgeous Greenbelt woods. The trail veers right and comes to the Cedar River for a moment, then turns from the river to travel along a power line easement.

10.5 miles. At the fork in the trail, go left to cross the bridge over a runoff waterway, then go left again at the T intersection and continue along the river to trail's end at the Cole Street trailhead. Ride through the parking lot and climb the embankment, cross two sets of railroad tracks, and continue on the road.

12.5 miles. At the stop sign, angle left onto Otis Road SE, a two-lane blacktop with no center or fog lines. Pass the Kazimour Orchards, then bear left, staying on Otis, when Memorial Drive intersects from the right.

15.0 miles. Now you're back in urban surroundings. At the stop sign, cross 12th Avenue and angle right onto Sixth Street SE. At Fourth Avenue SE (downtown Cedar Rapids is not a city of startling road names), turn left and pedal one block to Fifth Street SE, where you turn right. Another block and you're back at Greene Park.

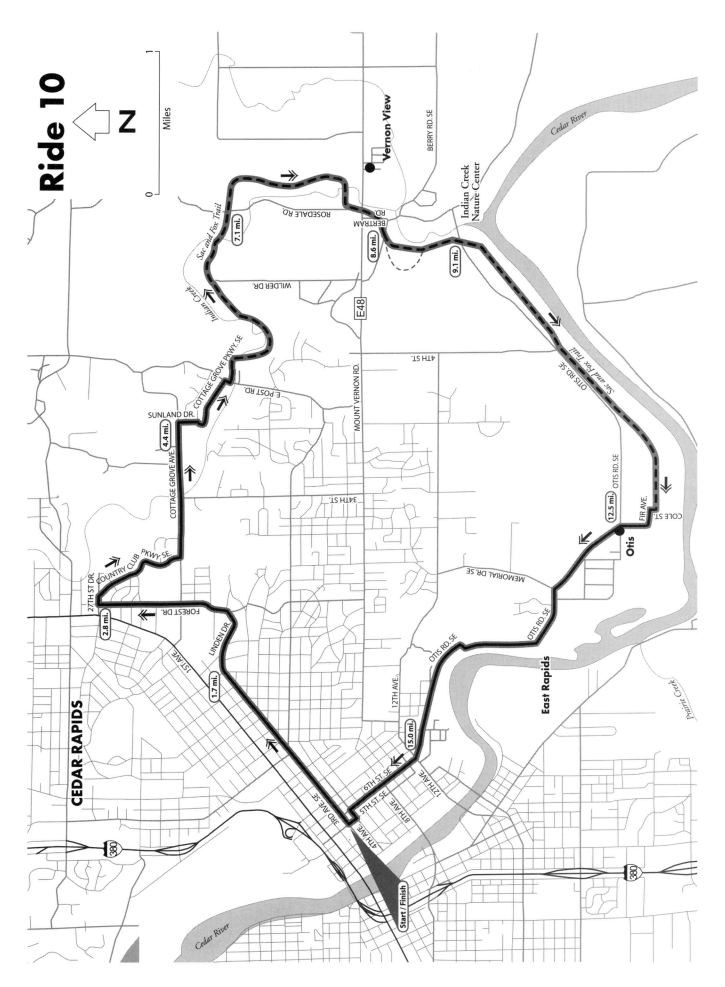

Ride 10

N

Miles
0   1

CEDAR RAPIDS

Cedar River

27TH ST DR.

COUNTRY CLUB PKWY SE.

2.8 mi.

SUNLAND DR.

COTTAGE GROVE AVE.

COTTAGE GROVE PKWY. SE.

4.4 mi.

E. POST RD.

Sac and Fox Trail

7.1 mi.

Indian Creek

WILDER DR.

ROSEDALE RD.

BERTRAM RD.

8.6 mi.

Vernon View

BERRY RD. SE

Cedar River

Indian Creek Nature Center

9.1 mi.

E48

MOUNT VERNON RD.

4TH ST.

34TH ST.

OTIS RD. SE

Sac and Fox Trail

12.5 mi.

OTIS RD. SE

FIR AVE.

COLE ST.

Otis

MEMORIAL DR. SE.

OTIS RD. SE

OTIS RD. SE

East Rapids

Prairie Creek

15.0 mi.

12TH AVE.

12TH AVE

8TH AVE

5TH AVE

6TH ST. SE

5TH ST. SE

3RD AVE. SE

4TH AVE

1ST AVE.

LINDEN DR.

FOREST DR.

1.7 mi.

Start / Finish

380

380

FIR AVE.

RIDE 11
Sugar Bottom Sojourn

The Devonian Fossil Gorge

Below the Coralville Dam, there's a window into time: an exposed portion of the primeval seafloor. Hundreds of millions of years ago, in the Devonian Period, Iowa was located near the Earth's equator and covered by warm, shallow seas similar to today's Caribbean Sea. That sea was populated by animals, and their fossilized remains are now on wonderful display in the Devonian Fossil Gorge.

The Coralville Dam on the Iowa River was completed in 1958 as part of a comprehensive flood control system for the Mississippi River. In the summer of 1993, a record flood swept down into Coralville Lake. As the lake rose to record levels, the water blasted out of the dam's emergency spillway in an overflow that lasted 28 days, releasing as much as 17,000 cubic feet per second. The deluge obliterated the road and campground below the spillway and scoured away 17 feet of soil, creating a shallow gorge and exposing the limestone bedrock.

When the waters finally receded, they revealed a treasure trove of perfectly preserved fossils from the Devonian Period. The Army Corps of Engineers, cooperating with area scientists and local residents, developed a plaza, walkways, and viewing areas in the newly cut gorge, paid for with over $400,000 in donated money and services.

In the Fossil Gorge, you'll see prominent ledges composed entirely of densely packed fossils—a life-layer known as a biostrome. You can walk the smooth, gently undulating rock surface of the Iowa River's original bed, see ancient corals, crinoids (prehistoric animals related to today's star fish), clam-like brachiopods, and bryozoans (moss animals). There are even sections of arthodires, huge armored fish that once swam here. It's a not-to-be-missed opportunity to read a chapter of Iowa's geological history from the depths of time.

LOCATION: Local, county, and state roads around Coralville Lake
DISTANCE: 18.6-mile loop
SURFACE: Paved town, county, and state roads
TERRAIN: Lots of short, steep hills and curves
DIFFICULTY: Moderate
SERVICES:
    Restrooms: Businesses in North Liberty and at start/finish, recreation areas and visitor center around Coralville Lake
    Water: Same
    Food: Restaurants, taverns, and convenience stores in North Liberty, convenience store at 3.5 miles
    Camping: Army Corps of Engineers campgrounds around Coralville Lake; Lake Macbride State Park, Solon
    Lodging: Motels, hotels, and bed and breakfasts in Cedar Rapids and Iowa City
    Bike Shop: Several in Cedar Rapids and Iowa City
STARTING POINT: Beaver Kreek Centre on North Dubuque Road (County Road W66) on the south side of North Liberty

The U.S. Army Corp of Engineers is dam big (or big on dams—take your pick). This ride takes you across their Coralville Dam and around the lake it created by plugging up the Iowa River. The ride starts on flats, but then offers up hills that'll tax your thighs.

0.0 miles. Beaver Kreek Centre is a badly spelled shopping center on the southern edge of North Liberty. From its parking lot, turn right (southeast) onto North Dubuque Street (County Road W66). Located between Cedar Rapids and Iowa City, North Liberty's becoming a bedroom community to both. As you curve between farm fields mixed with housing developments, you can muse on names like "Stoney Point" and "Spring Valley," which have no basis in the actual terrain. Spring Valley, for instance, is high and dry.

2.9 miles. Turn left onto West Overlook Drive. There's a paved shoulder that makes a nice bike lane, but it ends as you enter the Army Corps of Engineers' domain. The Corps manages the dam and land around Coralville Lake. Woods line the road, which dips and rises on easy grades. Curves keep the scenery fresh.

3.9 miles. Bear right at the stop sign, then go right at the next stop sign, getting onto Prairie du Chien Road. You have a steep, short descent and curve around the Coralville Dam's

The Coralville Dam was completed in 1958, controlling runoff from 3,084 square miles of watershed.

spillway, then pay for the downhill with a short, sharp climb onto the dam to cross the Iowa River. Coralville Lake is on your left; the diminished Iowa River flows out below you on the right. Looking down gives a better perspective on the magnitude of the dam; looking across the lake shows one benefit of its construction.

On what is essentially a park road, you rise gradually past the Visitor Center on your left, then a disc golf course on your right. You have curves ahead, along with sharp descents and climbs.

6.3 miles. Go left at the stop sign to head east on Newport Road (County Road F8W), another winding blacktop. The hills are short but steep, and awkwardly spaced: you'll use most of your gears over the next mile and a half before you get to a flatter stretch along the ridgeline. Varied farmland surrounds you: cornfields, pasture, and woods, with occasional houses and farm buildings. At the tops of the climbs, look across the hills and valleys; in the valleys, you're hemmed in by crops and trees.

9.1 miles. Turn left onto Sugar Bottom Road (County Road F70) for a quarter-mile downhill to cross Turkey Creek, then shift down for a mile-and-a-half climb back up. Admittedly, it's a bad reward-to-work ratio, but the road ahead is marvelously curvy, with long flats and a couple of short, steep drops. You go through a little hamlet of houses, Broganville; in late July and August, there's a farm stand here with sweet corn. The kids manning the stand are saving up to buy a saddle horse.

14.8 miles. At the stop, turn left onto Mehaffey Bridge Road (County Road F28) for a screaming-fast descent past the Sugar Bottom Recreation Area and across a narrow neck in Coralville Lake. Motor traffic has been light to none since you left North Liberty, but it picks up on Mehaffey Bridge Road. This is a popular bicycling route, however, so motorists are accustomed to—and courteous of—bicyclists.

17.8 miles. At the four-way stop sign at Penn Avenue in North Liberty, go straight, then turn left onto Dubuque Road at the next stop. That takes you back to your starting point at Beaver Kreek Centre.

Ride 11

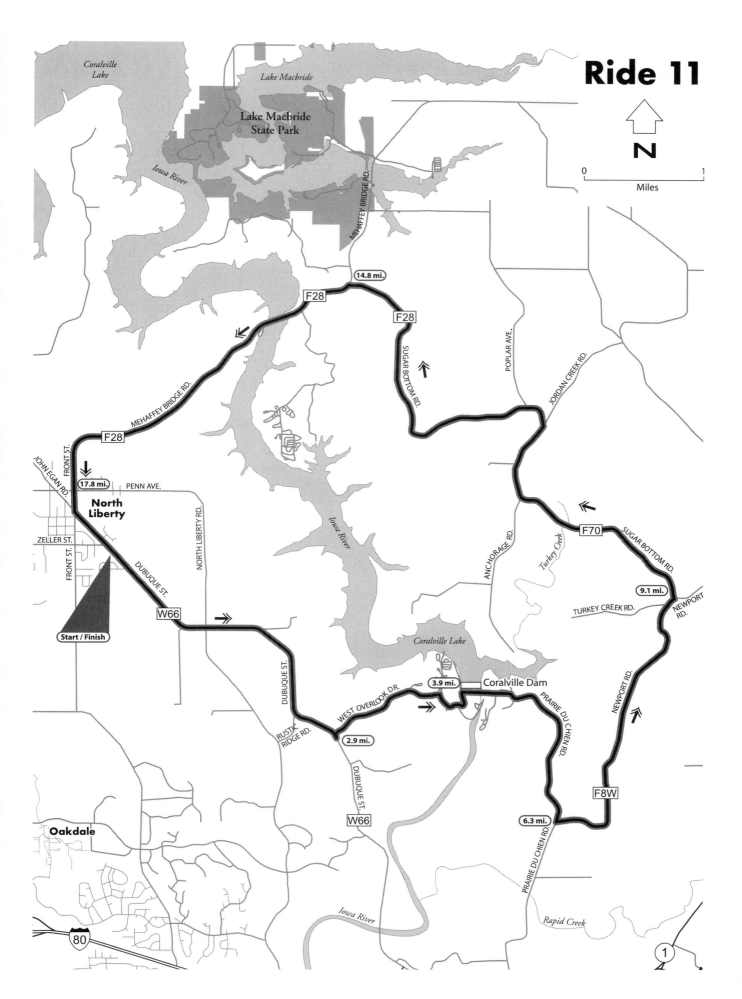

Coralville
Lake

Lake Macbride

Lake Macbride
State Park

Iowa River

MEHAFFEY BRIDGE RD.

N

0 — 1
Miles

14.8 mi.

F28

F28

SUGAR BOTTOM RD.

POPLAR AVE.

JORDAN CREEK RD.

MEHAFFEY BRIDGE RD.

F28

JOHN EGAN RD.

FRONT ST.

17.8 mi.

PENN AVE.

**North
Liberty**

ZELLER ST.

FRONT ST.

NORTH LIBERTY RD.

NORTH LIBERTY RD.

DUBUQUE ST.

W66

Iowa River

ANCHORAGE RD.

Turkey Creek

F70

SUGAR BOTTOM RD.

9.1 mi.

NEWPORT RD.

TURKEY CREEK RD.

NEWPORT RD.

Start / Finish

DUBUQUE ST.

RUSTIC RIDGE RD.

Coralville Lake

WEST OVERLOOK DR.

3.9 mi.

Coralville Dam

PRAIRIE DU CHIEN RD.

2.9 mi.

DUBUQUE ST.

W66

F8W

6.3 mi.

PRAIRIE DU CHIEN RD.

Oakdale

80

Iowa River

Rapid Creek

1

23

RIDE 12

Around the Amanas

LOCATION: Kolonieweg Trail, county, state, and federal roads between Amana and Marengo
DISTANCE: 27.1-mile loop
SURFACE: Paved trail and paved county, state, and federal roads
TERRAIN: Gentle swells through a river valley, with a couple of shallow climbs and descents
DIFFICULTY: Easy
SERVICES:
  Restrooms: Businesses in Amana, Middle Amana, Marengo, South Amana, and Homestead
  Water: Same
  Food: Restaurants in Amana, Middle Amana, Marengo, and Homestead
  Camping: Amana Colonies RV Park, Amana
  Lodging: Motels, hotels, and bed and breakfasts in Amana
  Bike Shop: None nearby
STARTING POINT: The Kolonieweg Trail heads off 48th Avenue, south of the Colony Inn and shopping area in Amana

The Mill Race

It took the Inspirationists of the Amana Colonies four years, from 1865 to 1869, to construct the seven-mile-long Mill Race from the Iowa River near West Amana, through Middle Amana and Amana into Price Creek, which flows back into the river. The Mill Race provided water power for two textile mills and one flour mill.

Three boats were built as transport for a small steam shovel that helped dig the canal, and were later used to dredge the canal, combating the continuous silting problem. To let the dredge boat pass, eight wooden bridges over the canal had to be removed, then reassembled after the boats went by. The bridges could be taken down and put back together in just a few hours by a team of carpenters aided by horses.

The dredge boat had a four-man crew who lived on board and worked through spring, summer, and fall. The communal kitchen house in whichever village the boat was nearest provided meals to the crew; women brought food baskets down to the Mill Race three times a day. According to folklore, the canal is deepest near Middle Amana because the meals there were the best of the colonies, and the boat crews were wont to linger in that area.

In the 1920s, the Amana Society replaced the mills' shaft drives with electrical generators, which kept the Mill Race waters moving steadily enough to prevent siltation. The last dredge boat was permanently dry-docked in 1921.

The flood of 1993 wreaked havoc with the Mill Race, weakening its walls so much that it could no longer provide as much water as the generators needed to operate. The Amana Colonies Historic Sites Foundation and the Amana Society are working to repair and restore the waterway.

The Amana Colonies, seven small villages along the Iowa River, were settled in 1855 by a religious society of German immigrants, the "Community of True Inspiration," or Inspirationists. Their beautifully preserved red brick and sandstone buildings now house a variety of stores, restaurants, inns, and other attractions.

0.0 miles. The Kolonieweg Trailhead is next to the former train depot in Amana, which now houses part of the Old Creamery Theater. Head west on the paved trail beside the Mill Race, which once powered the mills in Amana and Middle Amana. During the Amanas' communal period, 1855-1932, a stroll along the levee beside the Mill Race between the two towns was considered a fine Sunday afternoon outing. Now the path provides a pleasant start to your ride.

0.7 miles. After crossing U.S. Highway 151 (State Highway 6), bear right at the Y in the trail and ride around the east side of Lily Lake. The lake was the holding tank, controlling the water's flow to downstream mills. Now it serves as home to Canada geese and habitat for tens of thousands of yellow lotus water lilies, which bloom through July and August.

1.3 miles. A spur veers left to the parking lot at the picnic area on Lily Lake, but you cross State Highway 220 and turn left (west) with the trail (the right-hand fork leads to the Amana Colonies Visitor Center).

Cross a small stream lined with poplars. There are over 11,000 trees along this watercourse, planted in 1991-92 by Dr. Lewis Licht of the University of Iowa. From data collected here, Dr. Licht proved that a dense planting of poplars along streams can greatly improve the quality of water by filtering agricultural runoff and controlling erosion.

2.3 miles. The trail crosses back over State Highway 220 and circles the west end of Lily Lake, but you get on the road to continue west. Pass the Maytag Plant, where Amana appliances are produced, and pump up a short hill into Middle Amana. The village is off to your right.

Still heading west, you pass a beautiful stand of pampas grass as you cruise the flats of the river valley. A sharp curve in the road before you reach the turnoff for High Amana is known as Geist Ecke, or Ghost Corner, supposedly haunted by white, filmy apparitions.

5.6 miles. At the 3-way intersection where the road to West Amana cuts off and State Highway 220 turns left, continue straight onto County Road F15. Now you're beyond the boundaries of the original 26,000 acres bought by the Inspirationists.

The two-lane county road flows easily over the slight swells of the river valley. Grass-covered hills rise from the road on the right; on the left you look across vibrantly green farm fields to the tree-lined course of the Iowa River.

11.4 miles. Turn left to go south on M Avenue (County Road V66), where a brick sign welcomes you to Marengo: "Our Town—Make it Yours!" Crossing the river, you ride through a modest residential neighborhood; the business district is several blocks west. The road changes its name to Eastern Avenue.

13.8 miles. At the convenience store, turn left onto U.S. Highway 6. The road rolls gently as you pedal east down the valley. You pass Macht Nicht, the home of the Iowa Rocker, which a sign says is the "Rockingest Rocker," whatever that may mean.

19.0 miles. There's an antiques and quilt shop here at the intersection with State Highway 220 in South Amana. The quilts are gorgeous and probably worth their prices. Stay on U.S. Highway 6, cruising a flat three miles before the junction with U.S. Highway 151, where you start a gradual climb. Coast down the far side, then climb a somewhat steeper hill to Homestead.

23.5 miles. Homestead is a small collection of buildings that the Inspirationists bought so they'd have a depot on a railroad line. There's a good downhill to the Iowa River: here you'll hit your top speed of the ride. Cross both the river and the Mill Race.

26.6 miles. Turn right onto the Kolonieweg Trail and cruise back to the starting point.

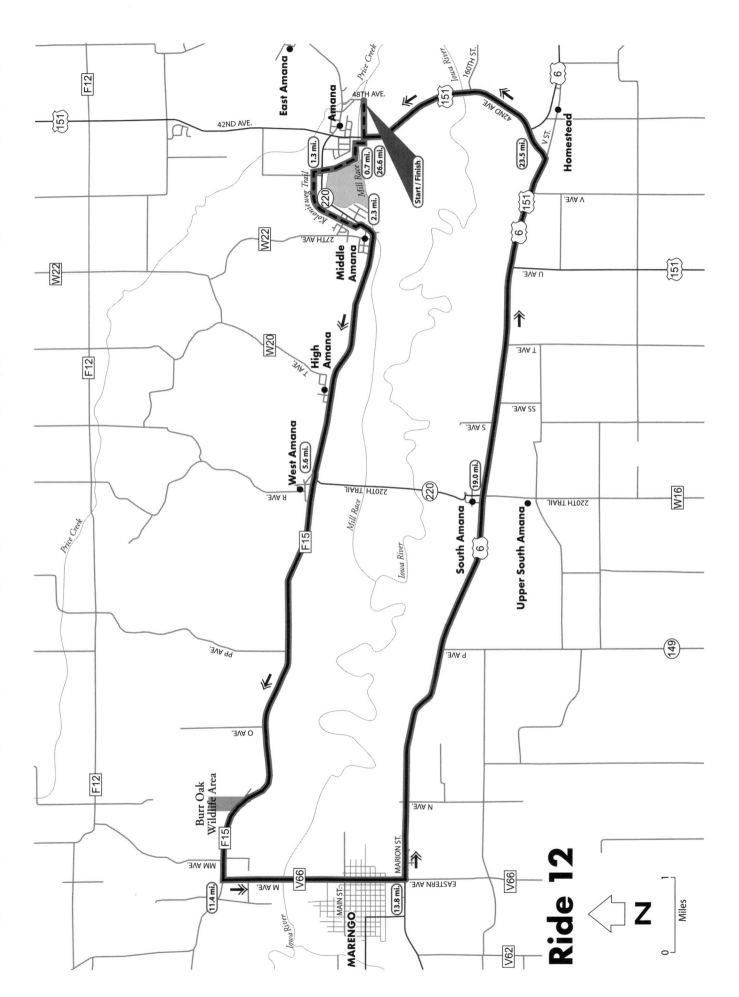

Ride 12

N

Miles
0   1

RIDE 13
Buffalo Bill's River Ride

LOCATION: Road loop from Le Claire to Princeton and back

DISTANCE: 20.6-mile loop

SURFACE: Paved county and state roads

TERRAIN: Mostly flat along the river, then a long climb followed by easy rolls and a great descent

DIFFICULTY: Moderate

SERVICES:

Restrooms: At start in Le Claire, businesses in Princeton, convenience store/tavern at Argo

Water: Same

Food: Same

Camping: Interstate RV Park, Davenport

Lodging: Motels and bed and breakfasts in Le Claire, bed and breakfast in Princeton

Bike Shop: Jerry and Sparky's Bicycle Shop, Locust Street; On Two Wheels, Eastern Avenue, Davenport

STARTING POINT: RiverWay Park in Le Claire, on the river side of U.S. Highway 67/Cody Road (also the Great River Road)

Along the Mississippi

It's the Father of Waters, the longest river in the U.S., one of history's greatest liquid highways. From Lake Itasca in northern Minnesota to the Gulf of Mexico below New Orleans, the Mississippi River has carried the produce and natural resources of the country's center to markets all over the world.

River commerce built towns all along the Iowa shore. Once they were centers of industry, boat-building, and shipping, but as dams tamed the river and railroads took over more and more of the freight, the river towns' importance diminished and their populations shrank. Some all but disappeared, others held their own, and the exceptional ones managed to thrive.

These next three rides are a sampler of river towns. On Ride 13: Buffalo Bill's River Ride, you'll visit Le Claire, once home to dozens of river pilots, and Princeton, a once-thriving town cut to half its size by the decline in river shipping. Ride 14: The Mississippi River Trail Ride takes you through Davenport, a city that has prospered along with its fellow Quad Cities—Bettendorf, Iowa; Moline and Rock Island, Illinois. The Quad Cities owe a large part of their prosperity to the railroads' decision to build the first bridge across the Mississippi there, an advantage that was increased in the 20th century when Interstate 80 followed the railroads' example.

On Ride 15: Riding the River Road, you'll cruise through Buffalo, Montpelier, and Fairport, small towns that have never aspired to any sort of prominence. This stretch of riverbank sports fishing camps, summer homes, and campgrounds: for these towns, the river means recreation and tourism.

All three of these rides feature flat terrain and long stretches with river views—great country for bicycling!

Your ride starts in William "Buffalo Bill" Cody's hometown, cruises up the Mississippi River to Princeton, then climbs out of the valley and spins over rolling farmland before heading back to the river and Le Claire. The last five miles tilt downhill.

Before you start pedaling, you might enjoy the Buffalo Bill Museum in RiverWay Park, with its eclectic assortment of Buffalo Bill memorabilia, riverboat artifacts and photographs, arrowheads, spear points, and fossils. Museum admission includes access to the Lone Star, a steam-powered towboat that set the record of 99 years in continuous service, from 1869 to 1968.

0.0 miles. Pedal up Wisconsin Avenue from Le Claire's RiverWay Park and cross the railroad tracks and Front Street. Turn right onto Cody Road (U.S. Highway 67), as the Great River Road is called in this town, and ride north through Le Claire's historic district.

The town was founded in 1829 by Antoine Le Claire, a fur trader and frontiersman. During the mid-19th century, it was home port to more riverboat captains and pilots than any other town on the Mississippi. Just below town, the river turns west through what was once the Upper Rock Island Rapids, an extremely dangerous, rock-bound gorge. Wing dams and revetments built in the late 1800s drowned those rapids and the ancient gorge.

3.4 miles. In 1804, the golf course on your left was the site of a pitched battle between the Sac and Fox tribes (now the Mesquakies) and the Sioux. Legend has it that nearly a thousand Indians were killed. Your ride, however, is quite peaceful and easy as you travel north, with frequent views of the Mississippi on your right. The riverbank is dotted with summer homes and fishing camps, which become more numerous as you enter Princeton.

5.3 miles. Turn right on Chestnut Street and cross the railroad tracks. There are large crossing lights here to mark the turn. Take the tracks cautiously—they're very rough.

Turn left onto River Drive and glide through Princeton, which was incorporated in 1857, combining three settlements into a town of nearly a thousand souls. The decline of river traffic that came with the railroads halved that population by 1900. The Inter-Urban Railroad from Clinton to Davenport finally reached Princeton in 1904 and revived the town somewhat; still, Princeton today holds fewer people than in 1860.

5.7 miles. Turn left on Lost Grove Road (County Road F45). Cross the Great River Road and head west, out of the valley. It's a much easier and shorter climb here than it was up north in the bluffs, but it's still a climb. You reach the top in just under a mile.

Much of the river towns' population moved to the farmland above the river, working the land instead of the water. The land is rich and the farms look prosperous as you spin easily up shallow grades and coast pleasantly on the down slopes.

10.7 miles. At the stop sign, turn left to head south on County Road Z30/F45. This is a part of the Cody Trail, a scenic auto route, but don't worry about hordes of motoring sightseers. Traffic is light to nonexistent. The road goes south as truly as a bullet from Buffalo Bill's rifle. There's a long, gradual grade up to County Road F45's turn to Eldridge; you continue straight on County Road Z30 between the cornfields rustling in the breeze.

14.5 miles. The Argo General Store, which triples as a restaurant and tavern, is all that's left of the former town of Argo. At the four-way stop, turn left (east) onto Territorial Road (County Road F51). From here on, the road goes down. The grade is slight at first, then much steeper after you pass the Cody School. Speeding down, you pass an 1886 one-room schoolhouse and a little wayside chapel. Both buildings are in a state of neglect, and neither appears to be open to the public.

19.4 miles. Territorial Road ends at a T intersection and you turn right onto Cody Road to return to Le Claire. This side of the road has an intermittent paved shoulder to ride into town. Turn left at Wisconsin Street to get back to RiverWay Park.

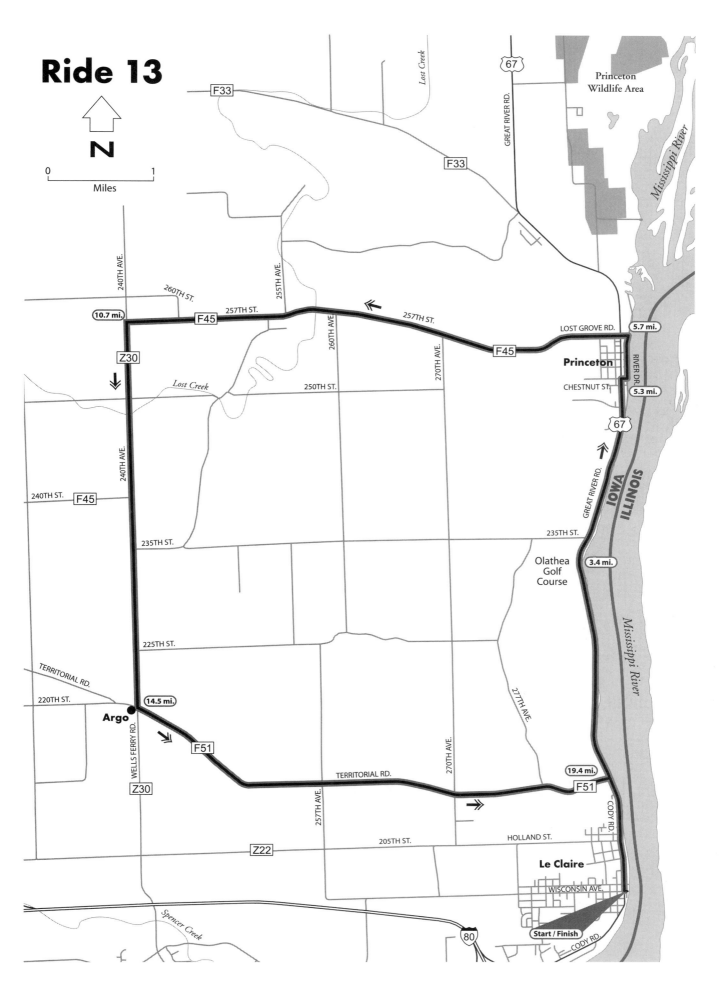

Ride 13

N

0   1
Miles

Lost Creek

Princeton
Wildlife Area

67

GREAT RIVER RD.

Mississippi River

F33

F33

240TH AVE.

260TH ST.

257TH ST.

255TH AVE.

10.7 mi.

F45

257TH ST.

257TH ST.

F45

LOST GROVE RD.

5.7 mi.

Z30

260TH AVE.

270TH AVE.

Princeton

RIVER DR.

Lost Creek

250TH ST.

CHESTNUT ST.

5.3 mi.

240TH AVE.

67

240TH ST.

F45

GREAT RIVER RD.

IOWA

ILLINOIS

235TH ST.

235TH ST.

Olathea
Golf
Course

3.4 mi.

Mississippi River

225TH ST.

TERRITORIAL RD.

277TH AVE.

220TH ST.

14.5 mi.

Argo

WELLS FERRY RD.

F51

270TH AVE.

19.4 mi.

TERRITORIAL RD.

F51

Z30

257TH AVE.

205TH ST.

HOLLAND ST.

CODY RD.

Z22

Le Claire

WISCONSIN AVE.

Spencer Creek

80

Start / Finish

CODY RD.

RIDE 14
Mississippi River Trail Ride

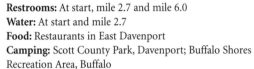

LOCATION: Mississippi River Trail in Davenport
DISTANCE: 11.3 miles out and back
SURFACE: Paved trail
TERRAIN: A flat trail along the river
DIFFICULTY: Child's play
SERVICES:

> **Restrooms:** At start, mile 2.7 and mile 6.0
> **Water:** At start and mile 2.7
> **Food:** Restaurants in East Davenport
> **Camping:** Scott County Park, Davenport; Buffalo Shores Recreation Area, Buffalo
> **Lodging:** Hotels, motels, and bed and breakfasts in the Quad Cities
> **Bike Shop:** Jerry and Sparky's Bicycle Shop, Locust Street; On Two Wheels, Eastern Avenue, Davenport

STARTING POINT: Channel Cat Water Taxi parking lot at Lindsay Park in East Davenport

The Davenport Murder

Born in 1783 in England, George Davenport landed in New York City in 1804, joined the U.S. Army, and ended up on the American frontier. After his discharge, he joined a company running supplies to a fort that was being built on an island in the Mississippi River, between what would become the Quad Cities. George soon set out on his own and, within a decade, established several trading posts along the river. The Indians with whom he traded liked and respected him and their furs soon made him wealthy enough to build his own mansion on the island.

When the Black Hawk Purchase opened the Iowa side of the river to white settlement in 1834, George, Antoine Le Claire, and several others established a town opposite the army's fort. They named it Davenport, apparently at Le Claire's suggestion (Antoine's namesake town is just a few miles upriver).

On July 4, 1845, while his family attended the Independence Day celebration in Stephenson, Illinois (later to become Rock Island), robbers broke into Davenport's mansion and found him there. One account says they shot George, another says he was beaten and left for dead when the booty from his safe turned out to be less than expected. Whichever happened, George clung to life long enough to describe his assailants.

A gang operating out of Nauvoo, Illinois, were the prime suspects. Edward Bonney, a private detective, infiltrated the gang and apprehended the murderers. Eight men were charged in the crime. One escaped and disappeared. Four were found guilty of murder and hanged. Two others received prison sentences, and charges were dropped against the last.

George Davenport was buried on the grounds of his mansion in a ceremony performed by his friends, the Fox Indians. Later, a minister performed a second funeral for the white mourners.

Davenport's riverfront is adorned with parklands threaded by a beautiful multi-use trail. You'll see the Mississippi River at work and play, and catch glimpses of the natural Mississippi through waterfowl and riverbank critters.

0.0 miles. From the eastern end of the Water Taxi parking lot, jump onto the Mississippi River Trail. Go left at the trail's fork, then left again at the T intersection to head downriver. (If you go to the right at this intersection, you'll reach trail's end at the Bettendorf city limits.) Cross Mound Street carefully. Mound Street leads up to the East Davenport Historic District, an attractive, rather upscale neighborhood of restaurants, taverns, coffee shops, and stores. Many of the commercial buildings built by early settlers are still standing.

The trail widens to road-width as it passes behind the Iowa American Water Company waterworks, then narrows again as it curves to the river's edge.

0.5 miles. Pass a lovely gazebo and *Watching the Ferry*, a sculpture of two boys looking out over the river. This bend was once known as Stubbs' Eddy (the outside of a river's curve is an "eddy"), named after a soldier who retired from the U.S. Army at Arsenal Island in 1834. Legend has it that Stubbs lived in a cave near here with a collection of animals, including a pet pig.

1.5 miles. Pass beneath Government Bridge, the successor to the first bridge across the Mississippi. Built to carry the railroad in 1856, that bridge was replaced in 1873; the second bridge was supplanted in 1894-95 by the present structure. There's a bike/pedestrian walkway over the bridge, connecting with trails on Arsenal Island and, on the far side, the Illinois Mississippi River Trail in Rock Island and Moline.

Continue downriver on Iowa's trail to pass Lock and Dam 15. Before this dam was built, the Upper Rapids, an 18-mile stretch of whitewater, made navigation a terror. Now this wide, rock-free expanse of river is known as Lake Davenport, a popular boating area.

Watch yourself crossing the entrance and exit to the Rhythm City Casino, just past Lock and Dam 15. Drivers entering and leaving the casino are thinking wins and losses, not paying attention to bicyclists.

2.3 miles. Pass under the Centennial Bridge and come into Centennial Park. Here you can bear left to ride along the floodwall or go right to stay on the main trail. (The floodwall path ends at a boat ramp; cross the ramp and the parking lot to rejoin the main trail.)

3.2 miles. Slip under the Crescent Railroad Bridge. On your right, the city has pulled back a bit, separated from the trail and river by waving grasses and wildflowers. Approaching Credit Island, you're likely to see egrets and herons in the pond on your right.

4.3 miles. The trail ends at the Credit Island Park Road. Bear right at the fork and go slowly so you can enjoy a delightful sculptural rendition of Seurat's painting, *A Sunday Afternoon on the Island of La Grande Jatte*. In the background is a wetland pond with more wading birds. During the winter months, the trees around this pond are dotted with dozens of bald eagles.

Just past the artwork, partially concealed in a grove of oaks on the left, is a cold war-era U.S. Army M103 heavy tank. The irony of juxtaposition is food for thought as you ride.

Credit Island was a popular amusement park a century ago; now it's home to a municipal golf course, large expanses of grass, and huge oak trees—as pleasant a venue as you're ever likely to find for biking. Keep bearing to your left as you circle the island.

6.7 miles. Pass the clubhouse and tennis courts and exit Credit Island Park, then hop back onto the trail and head back upriver. From this direction, you have a postcard-quality view of the Mississippi River bridges and Davenport skyline.

11.2 miles. After a pleasant ride back along the trail, you return to the pavilion at Lindsay Park. Turn right to get to the Water Taxi parking lot.

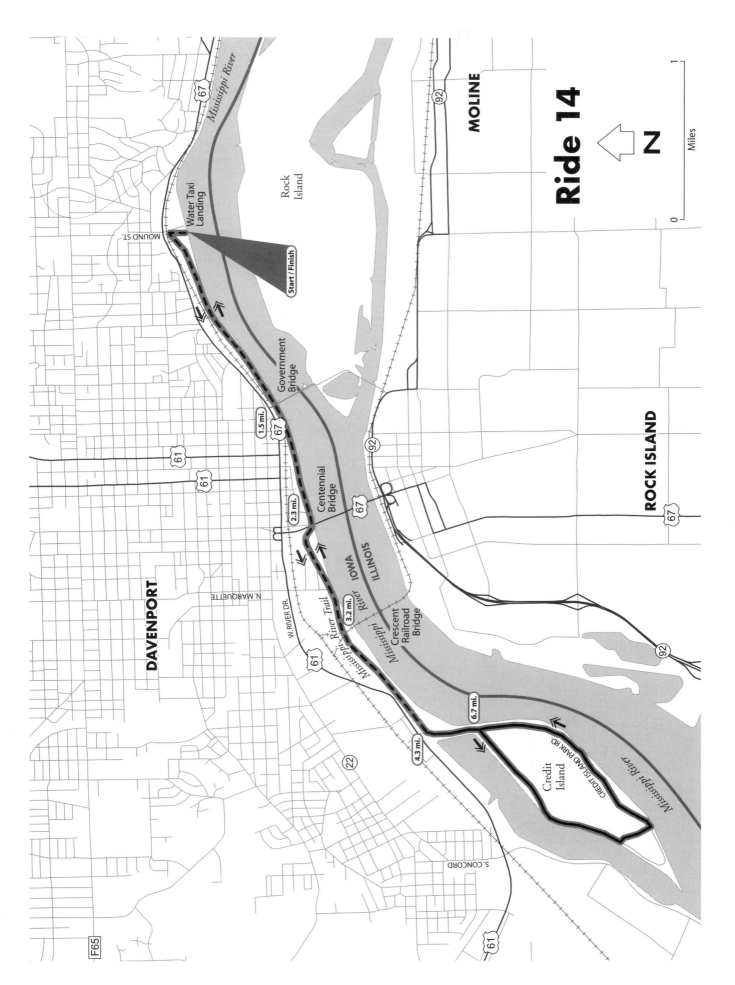

DAVENPORT

Mississippi River

MOUND ST.

Water Taxi
Landing

Start / Finish

Government
Bridge

Rock
Island

MOLINE

Ride 14

N

0   1
Miles

1.5 mi.

67

61

61

Centennial
Bridge

2.3 mi.

67

92

N. MARQUETTE

W. RIVER DR.

Mississippi River Trail

61

IOWA

ILLINOIS

3.2 mi.

Mississippi River

Crescent
Railroad
Bridge

67

92

ROCK ISLAND

67

6.7 mi.

22

4.3 mi.

Credit
Island

CREDIT ISLAND PARK RD.

Mississippi River

92

S. CONCORD

61

F65

29

RIDE 15
Riding the River Road

LOCATION: Great River Road between Muscatine and Buffalo

DISTANCE: 16.6 miles one way

SURFACE: Paved trail, paved roads

TERRAIN: Mostly flats along the river, with a couple of low hills

DIFFICULTY: Easy

SERVICES:

Restrooms: Weed Park, Muscatine; frequent riverside campgrounds and recreation areas; businesses in Buffalo

Water: Same

Food: Restaurants and convenience stores in Muscatine and Buffalo

Camping: Fairport State Park, Fairport; Wildcat Den State Park, Montpelier; Clark's Ferry Recreation Area, Montpelior; Buffalo Shores Recreation Area, Buffalo

Lodging: Motels in Muscatine, bed and breakfast in Montpelior

Bike Shop: Harpers Schwinn Cyclery, Grandview Avenue, Muscatine; McNeill AJH Hardware, First Street, Montpelior

STARTING POINT: The children's fishing pond at Weed Park on the east end of Muscatine

You've ridden other portions of the Great River Road, but this stretch may be the best of them all. The river is wide and steady here, and across its broad expanse are wooded islands and the bluffs of Illinois. In the shallows, you'll see wading birds and waterfowl; on the water, long tows of barges toil, filled with grain and gravel, corn and cement. There are only two hills on this ride, both with easy grades and great river vistas from their crests.

0.0 miles. From the wooden fishing deck at the children's fishing pond in Muscatine's Weed Park, a paved trail leads east and ducks into the woods, following the pond's drainage down to State Highway 22, the Great River Road. Turn left onto the highway to head east up the river valley.

Muscatine is a city of many names: Casey's Woodpile in 1833, Newburg in 1836, and Bloomington after 1839. But Bloomington got confused with too many others—Indiana and Kentucky also had towns of that name—and was sometimes mistaken for Burlington as well. After ten years of misdelivered mail, the town's name was changed to refer to the Mascoutin Indian tribe. The fourth name was a keeper: No other city in the U.S. or, it's thought, in the whole world, is named Muscatine.

Muscatine was an important lumber center in the mid-1800s, but in the 1890s, buttons began to take over. Made from freshwater clamshells, the buttons manufactured here were stronger than those made from animal horns, and more closely resembled the "pearl" buttons made from imported marine shells. By the beginning of the 20th century, Muscatine was the world's largest pearl button manufacturer, with more than half its workforce employed at the task.

The Great River Road you're traveling is two lanes of smooth pavement. Traffic is moderate for the first mile or so, then becomes lighter once you pass the Hohn factory. On your right, a double set of railroad tracks parallels the road; beyond it are trees lining the river's banks. Watch for the display of yellow water lilies spreading beautifully from the summer cottages into the shallows along the river.

4.2 miles. Climb the ride's first low hill on a gentle grade. At the top is a long, beautiful view of Mississippi River islands and the bluffs of the Illinois side.

6.4 miles. Cruise through the hamlet of Fairport, a cluster of homes anchored upriver by a marina and the Chart House and Lounge. There's a gradual climb out of Fairport before you pass the Fairport Fish Hatchery. Check out the giant fisherman carved out of a tree trunk at the fish hatchery entrance. He's poised in mid-cast, with his line extended behind him, tangled in the branches of a tree.

8.2 miles. Pass the Shady Creek Recreation Area on your right. Corn and soybean fields are on your left, and the roadside ditches are filled with wildflowers. As you pass Wildcat Den Avenue, note the stands of pampas grass, their white and silver fronds glinting in the sun.

At about ten and a half miles, you encounter a gradual, half-mile climb to get over a railroad spur coming down the hill on your left and going over to the coal-burning Fair Station Power Plant on the river. The view from the top of this hill is excellent, and then you have a nice, long downhill.

12.0 miles. Enter the town limits of Montpelier, another cluster of homes, summer cottages, and fishing camps on the riverbank. There are restrooms and a water fountain at Clark's Ferry Recreation Area. There are no businesses along the road through Montpelier except Varner's Caboose Bed and Breakfast, where the guest rooms are housed in an old railroad caboose. You quickly leave Montpelier and get back to pastures and crops on your left; the river is obscured behind the trees on your right.

You catch a glimpse of riverside industry as you pass the Cargill salt and grains plant, its conveyors stretching out to the river, and the PCS phosphate plant. Beyond the industrial sites, crops take up as much of the riverside flatland as possible and stretch up the hill on your left.

15.6 miles. Pass the Buffalo Shores Recreation Area and cruise into the town of Buffalo, the first settlement in Scott County. It was homesteaded in 1833 by Benjamin Clark, who came across from Andalusia, Illinois. Three years later, he platted the town with his friends, Captain E. A. Mix and Dr. E. Pillsbury, and named the site for Pillsbury's hometown of Buffalo, New York. At one time, Buffalo had a local coal mining industry, and later a shell button factory. Neither of these industries is at all in evidence now: Buffalo is an easygoing riverfront town with just a few businesses on the Great River Road.

16.6 miles. Your ride ends at Clark's Landing, a restaurant and pub in the center of the village.

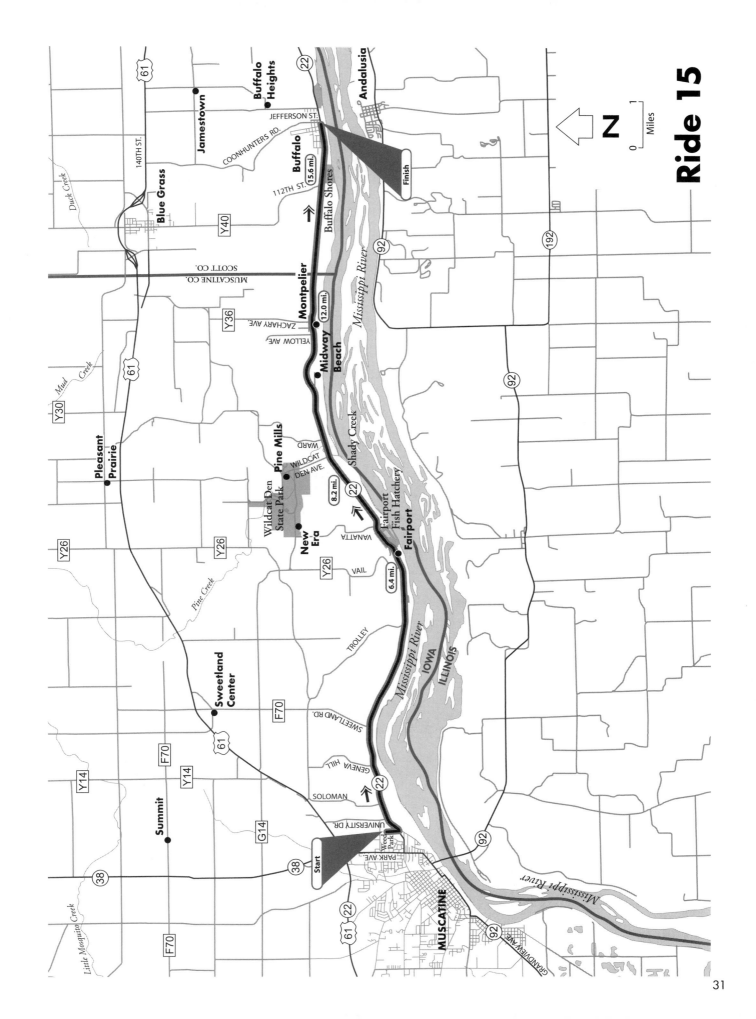

Ride 15

N

0 —— 1
Miles

RIDE 16
George Never Slept Here

A lovely stand of pampas grass surrounds a linden tree south of Washington.

LOCATION: State and county roads between Washington and Wayland
DISTANCE: 26.1-mile loop
SURFACE: Paved roads
TERRAIN: Rolling hills; some short, steep climbs and descents
DIFFICULTY: Moderate
SERVICES:
    Restrooms: City Park and businesses in Washington, businesses in Wayland
    Water: Same
    Food: Restaurants and convenience stores in Washington, tavern and convenience store in Wayland
    Camping: Marr Park, Ainsworth
    Lodging: Hotel, motels, and bed and breakfasts in Washington
    Bike Shop: Rider Sales, Third Street, Washington
STARTING POINT: City Park in the center of Washington, at the corner of Washington and Iowa streets

George Washington never visited Washington, Iowa, and certainly never slept here. He's here in spirit, however: his bust adorns a time capsule that was placed in City Park on July 4th, 1976, and is due to be opened in about seventy years.

Washington calls itself "The City of Flowers and Trees" and claims the title of "The Cleanest City in Iowa." It's an attractive town with a prosperous-looking business district centered around the square of the City Park. Winga's Café is your basic small-town, home-cooking, good-food café, and there's an espresso bar next door that's totally unpretentious. The residential areas are nicely kept, including some turn-of-the-century homes.

And yes, there are plenty of trees and flowers.

0.0 miles. Start at City Park, at the corner of Washington and Iowa streets, and head east on Washington. After one block, it becomes State Highway 92 with a 25 mph speed limit that increases to 30 mph as you cruise through a nice residential area.

1.2 miles. Turn right to go south on Airport Road (County Road W61). Almost immediately, you're away from town and into farmland. Even the airport produces crops—the runways and taxi-ways are carved through a cornfield. The smooth county road is beeline-straight and easy over swells in the land, bordered by corn and bean fields that extend to the horizons. Traffic is nearly nonexistent.

3.7 miles. Get a little break from farmland by going right on East Trio Lane. It loops down a small slope and passes a little lake surrounded by nice homes, then comes back up to Airport Road. Turn right on 275th Street, pass the end of the lake, and push up a gradual slope.

4.8 miles. At the stop sign, go left, south again, on Wayland Road (County Road W55). (If you turn right, you'll return to Washington.) Coast down a long slope and cross the West Fork of Crooked Creek—a waterway you'll see several times on this ride—then make a long, gradual climb from the creek's hollow. The roadside ditches are filled with prairie flowers and there's a gorgeous stretch of pampas grass after

you get out of the hollow.

The slopes are gentle until you descend another long hill and cross Crooked Creek again, then make a climb that'll get you into your lowest gears.

9.7 miles. Cross 320th Street (County Road G62) and continue south on County Road W55 as the road flows across the land's gentle swells. There's a steep descent to cross Willow Creek, then a steep climb out of that hollow.

12.6 miles. Cross State Highway 78 and continue straight into the town of Wayland. At the four-way stop, turn right onto Main Street to idle through the small business district resting in the shadow of the water tower. There are a tavern and a small grocery store here if you're in need of food or drink.

Main Street curves to the right, becomes Lincoln Street, and intersects State Highway 78 on the western edge of town. Turn left, heading west. After a pleasant stretch of road with long views across pasturelands dotted with prairie flowers, you have a half-mile descent to cross Crooked Creek again, then rise gently to the hamlet of Coppock.

16.0 miles. Turn right onto County Road W47 and start a gradual climb through the cluster of houses and mobile homes that is Coppock. Livestock comprises an interested segment of Coppock's population: As you climb the hill, you'll be watched by horses, then a cluster of goats, and finally a pair of llamas who seem to enjoy the sunlight glinting off bicycle spokes.

From the crest of the climb out of Coppock, you have a nice ridge to ride, with long views of jumbled hills and hollows, farmland and forest. The land rises and falls in long, gentle swells, like an ocean bay on a calm day. There's a drop to cross the West Fork of Crooked Creek and a short, steep climb out of that hollow, but little else to get you out of your big chain ring.

23.7 miles. At the stop sign, go left on County Road W55. There's a lovely view to the left of horses grazing in a shallow valley, the hayfield behind them dotted with round hay bales. Traffic picks up a bit, but the sight lines are good and drivers give you plenty of room.

25.6 miles. There's a blinking red light and four-way stop at the intersection with Van Buren Street in Washington. County Road W55 turned into Iowa Avenue as you entered the outskirts of town; your lane is very wide, with plenty of room to share with motor vehicles as you cruise through the residential area and back to your starting point.

Ride 16

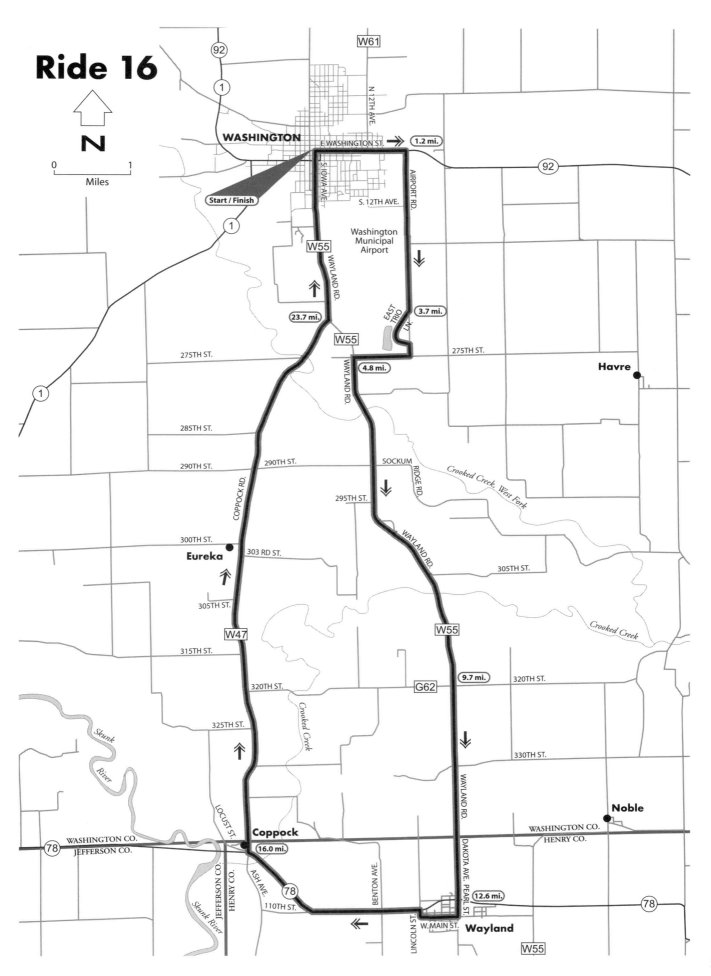

N

0   1
Miles

92

1

W61

WASHINGTON

N 12TH AVE.

E. WASHINGTON ST. → 1.2 mi.

92

Start / Finish

1

S. IOWA AVE.

S. 12TH AVE.

AIRPORT RD.

Washington
Municipal
Airport

W55

↑ 23.7 mi.

WAYLAND RD.

EAST
TRIO
LN.

↓

3.7 mi.

W55

275TH ST.

Havre

WAYLAND RD.

4.8 mi.

275TH ST.

285TH ST.

290TH ST.

290TH ST.

SOCKUM

Crooked Creek, West Fork

COPPOCK RD.

295TH ST.

↓

RIDGE RD.

300TH ST.

Eureka

303 RD ST.

WAYLAND RD.

305TH ST.

Crooked Creek

↑

305TH ST.

W47

315TH ST.

W55

9.7 mi.

320TH ST.

G62

320TH ST.

320TH ST.

Crooked Creek

Skunk River

325TH ST.

↑

330TH ST.

WAYLAND RD.

Noble

LOCUST ST.

Coppock

16.0 mi.

WASHINGTON CO.
JEFFERSON CO.

78

WASHINGTON CO.
HENRY CO.

HENRY CO.

Skunk River

ASH AVE.

78

110TH ST.

BENTON AVE.

DAKOTA AVE.

PEARL ST.

12.6 mi.

78

←

LINCOLN ST.

W. MAIN ST.

Wayland

W55

RIDE 17
The Foolish Fort Ride

LOCATION: City, county, and state roads between Fort Madison and Denmark
DISTANCE: 19.6-mile loop
SURFACE: Paved city, county, and state roads
TERRAIN: Rolling hills, very steep climb at the start and a fast descent at the end
DIFFICULTY: Moderate
SERVICES:
  Restrooms: Businesses in Fort Madison
  Water: Same
  Food: Restaurants, convenience stores, grocery in Fort Madison
  Camping: Duck Haven Campground, Fort Madison
  Lodging: Hotel, motels, and bed and breakfasts in Fort Madison
  Bike Shop: None nearby
STARTING POINT: Old Settlers' Park on the corner of Fourth Street and Avenue E in Fort Madison

The Fort that Failed

Fort Madison, the first U.S. Army installation west of the Mississippi, was built in 1808 as a "factory"—a government-run trading post. It was a mistake from start to finish.

The cession of the Indian land upon which the fort was built happened when William Henry Harrison, governor of the Indiana Territory, got a bunch of "chiefs" of the Sac and Fox tribes drunk and bribed them into selling tribal land. The sale stipulated a 25-year delay before the U.S. would actually take possession of the land; Fort Madison was a sort of surety on the eventual transfer.

The sober Indians denied the right of the drunken ones to sell out, and weren't at all happy about the fort. Their displeasure, however, wasn't strong enough to overcome the advantage of having a trading post, or the annuities paid to those who'd signed the treaty. Besides, the fort was so stupidly situated that the Indians probably knew they could take it out whenever they wanted.

Fort Madison stood on the flats beside the river, and it wasn't long before the soldiers realized anyone inside was a sitting duck for snipers on the hill behind it. To protect against this, they put a blockhouse on top of the hill, connected to the fort by a long, palisaded walkway. That solved one problem, but there was no solution to the nearby ravine, which provided ideal cover to gather forces out of sight of the fort's defenders and launch an attack.

When the War of 1812 broke out, the British encouraged the Indians to do just that. Warriors killed one soldier and forced the rest inside the fort's walls, where they were trapped until the Indians tired of the siege and drifted off to their fall hunt. The Indians returned in spring to take potshots at anyone foolish enough to show his head above the palisades, quickly convincing the fort's commander that his position was untenable. In the dead of night, he snuck his forces into boats, set the fort on fire, and headed down the Mississippi River.

So ended the brief, feckless career of Fort Madison. It wasn't until 1833, after the Black Hawk Treaty ended the east's Indian wars, that the area was again settled and a new Fort Madison—this time without the fort—began to grow.

Architectural gems from the 19th century line the first half mile of this ride; then it's up from the Mississippi River and the town, into undulating countryside. The ride ends with a six percent grade back down to Fort Madison's historic district.

0.0 miles. From Old Settlers' Park, the first public park in Fort Madison, head west on Avenue C, a wide, shaded street lined with handsome, Victorian-era homes. At Central Park, turn right onto Ninth Street and gear down for a steep half mile up. Catch your breath when you turn left on Avenue C, then angle right onto Old Denmark Road to tackle another three-tenths of a mile of very steep road.

That's the hardest climb of this ride. The next time you see a hill this steep, you'll be heading *down* it.

2.0 miles. Turn right at the stop sign and go north on County Road X32/J42. You soon pass Rodeo Park on your left. Since 1947, this has been the site of the Fort Madison Tri-State Rodeo, one of the top PRCA rodeo events of the year. The road is gentle along here, laid out across low swells as you pass the municipal airport and the Spring Lake Golf Course.

Keep an eye out for the Quarry Creek Elk & Bison Company. There are a bunch of bison roaming around, chewing grass and wondering what ever happened to the millions of their species that used to roam this country.

5.6 miles. Cross County Road J48 (108th Street) and pedal down and up long,

Fort Madison's historic district is filled with beautiful, 19th century homes.

gentle grades, with forever views across the farmlands. The land seems flat as you look over it, but your legs tell you it isn't.

8.7 miles. You reach a T intersection at State Highway 16. If you're looking for a rest break, the town of Denmark is about a quarter mile to your left, with a convenience store and tavern. To continue on the loop, go right, heading east. Traffic is light and the riding's easy, with long flats between the shallow rolls of the land. The roadside ditches are splashed with wildflowers.

11.4 miles. Turn right to head south on County Road X38. Ignore the sign that says it's nine miles to Fort Madison: you're closer than that. The hills are a little steeper, but there's nothing that calls for your granny gear. Though you've been pedaling past corn and soybean fields, pastures and hayfields, there have always been roadside homes and farms in sight. Not all of the houses are occupied. You'll see a couple of brick farmhouses, built in the 19th century, deserted in the 20th, and deteriorating in the 21st. They're indications of Iowa's rural depopulation, which is particularly apparent in the state's southern counties.

17.8 miles. On your right is a grassy, park-like field with benches set out around a baseball diamond. Its connection to the Iowa State Penitentiary is evidenced by the razor wire topping the chain-link fence around it.

18.4 miles. Turn right onto U.S. Highway 61. This is a four-lane highway with a 45-mph speed limit; traffic can be heavy during commute hours. Ahead is a nice view across the Mississippi River to Illinois, and in a half mile you'll see a sign warning trucks of the six percent grade. Enjoy the downhill!

On your left as you rocket down into Fort Madison, you'll notice the stone walls of Iowa's first prison, the Iowa State Penitentiary, built over 160 years ago. It's a grim-looking place.

19.4 miles. Squeeze your brakes hard to slow down for the right turn onto Avenue E, which takes you back to Old Settlers' Park.

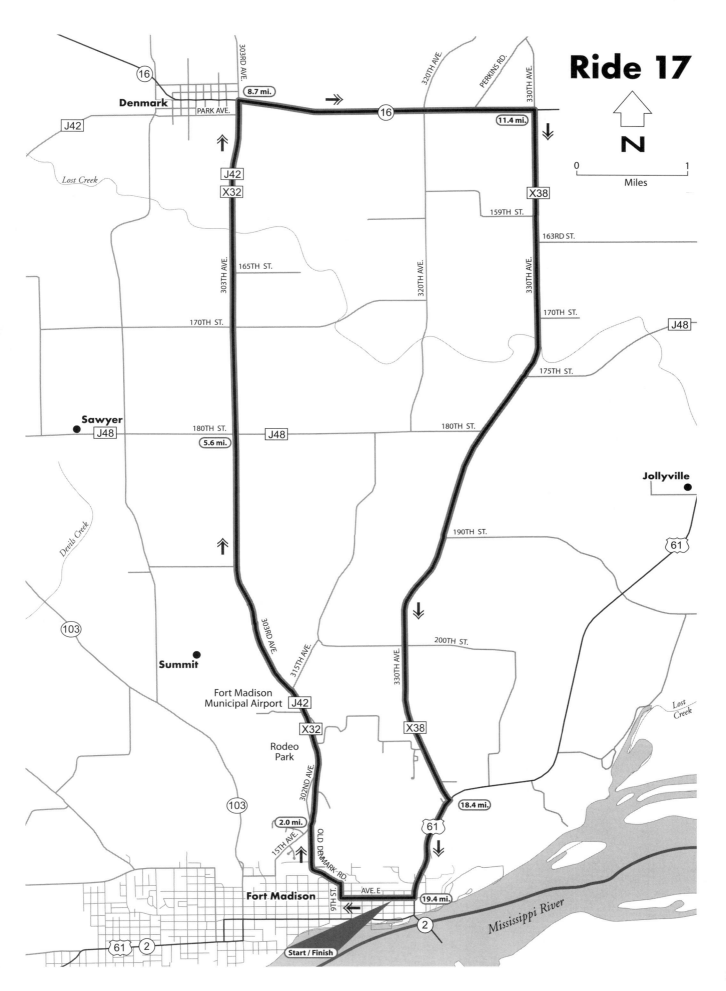

Ride 17

N

0 —— 1
Miles

Denmark

Sawyer

Jollyville

Summit

Fort Madison
Municipal Airport

Rodeo
Park

Fort Madison

Mississippi River

Start / Finish

Lost Creek

Devils Creek

Lost Creek

Perkins Rd.

303rd Ave.

320th Ave.

330th Ave.

315th Ave.

302nd Ave.

330th Ave.

15th Ave.

Old Denmark Rd.

9th St.

Ave. E

Park Ave.

165th St.

170th St.

180th St.

159th St.

163rd St.

170th St.

175th St.

180th St.

190th St.

200th St.

J42

X32

J48

X38

J48

16

16

61

103

103

61

2

61

2

8.7 mi.

11.4 mi.

5.6 mi.

18.4 mi.

2.0 mi.

19.4 mi.

RIDE 18

The Villages of Van Buren County

Downtown Bonaparte is listed on the National Register of Historic Places.

LOCATION: County and state roads between Bentonsport and Farmington
DISTANCE: 27.2 mile loop
SURFACE: Paved roads and one gravel street in Bentonsport
TERRAIN: One short, steep climb; low rolling hills and riverside flats
DIFFICULTY: Moderate
SERVICES:
  Restrooms: City Park in Bentonsport, National Historic Riverfront Park in Bonaparte, and businesses in Farmington
  Water: City Park in Bentonsport, businesses in Bonaparte and Farmington
  Food: General store in Bentonsport, restaurants and taverns in Bonaparte and Farmington
  Camping: Lacey-Keosauqua State Park, Keosauqua; Bentonsport River Side Park (no hookups); Shimek State Forest, Farmington
  Lodging: Hotel in Keosauqua, bed and breakfasts in Bentonsport
  Bike Shop: None nearby
STARTING POINT: The Vernon Bridge, at the foot of Sanford Street in Bentonsport

Mormon Music

Following the murder of their founder, Joseph Smith, in 1844, the adherents of the Church of Jesus Christ of the Latter Day Saints abandoned their community in Nauvoo, Illinois, and began a years-long migration to Utah's Great Salt Lake. In February of 1846, the first group of Mormons, led by Brigham Young, crossed the Mississippi River into Montrose, Iowa, and began blazing the trail west.

Iowa was sparsely settled and what few roads existed were rudimentary at best. The pioneers slogged through the mud of thawing ground and melt-swollen waterways. They entered what is now Van Buren County at Farmington, traveled along the northeast side of the Des Moines River, and camped for a day of rest and repairs at Reed's Creek. Traveling with this group was the Pitt Brass Band, musicians who were a source of inspiration and cheer to the struggling pioneers. A contingent from Farmington visited the encampment at Reed's Creek and invited the band to put on a concert. They played first at the hotel, then at the schoolhouse, where the concert continued until nearly dark. They were rewarded with supper and five dollars.

After a day's rest, the Mormons crossed the river at a ford in Bonaparte, just downstream of the present Highway 2 bridge, and camped a few miles farther on at Richardson's Point. The Pitt Brass Band was again invited to perform in nearby Keosauqua, but this time Brigham Young struck a better bargain. After a brief preliminary show, the band put on a concert at the courthouse and netted $25.00 above their expenses. Returning the next night, they again packed the house and profited another $20.00.

The jingle of coins gave the band an extra treble note as they continued their journey, and helped pay for the Mormons' migration.

In the early 19th century, the Des Moines River was the main travel and shipping corridor through Van Buren County, giving rise to towns along its banks. This ride takes you through three of those river towns, two of which have been designated as National Historic Districts.

0.0 miles. Clip into your pedals at the Vernon Bridge in Bentonsport, a town that takes its history seriously—indeed, it seems still to be living it in many ways. It's hard to imagine this village of about 40 residents as a thriving port of call for riverboats, with a population of nearly a thousand people. Now the main street is more National Historic District than commercial center. Most of the well-preserved buildings sport fading signs that give their histories. There are no paved roads in town; Bentonsport didn't even get electricity until 1956.

Ride two blocks north on Sanford Street's gravel surface and turn right at the T intersection to head east on County Road J40. You have a steep half-mile climb from the village, then a couple of gentle rolls before you get a long, gradual descent back into the river valley.

4.0 miles. County Road J40 curves to parallel the Des Moines River and brings you into the Bonaparte National Historic District. Bonaparte, settled in 1837, was originally known as Meek's Mills. At its peak, the town had a population of over a thousand, but in 1903 a flood destroyed the wing dam that had provided power for mills. The Meek Mill was soon sold to pay debts and a fire ravaged the downtown. Bonaparte never recovered from these disasters, and by 1986 it was on the verge of extinction. It was rescued by local citizens who brought the commercial district back to life, renovated historic structures to attract tourism, and developed new businesses. You'll see the fruits of those labors as you cruise through town.

Cross Main Street and go left on Washington Street, which becomes County Road J40 again on the town's outskirts. You have a pleasant ride north through the Lindsay Wilderness Area, with forest on both sides, as you climb out of the valley in a series of easy steps. At the top of the climb, you're rewarded with a great view across hills and hollows.

6.4 miles. Turn right with County Road J40, heading east. The land rolls gently, with short flat stretches between and on top of the hills, and the roadside ditches are ablaze with wildflowers. The road surface is good and there's hardly a car in sight.

9.9 miles. Go right on County Road W46 (100th Avenue), which straddles the line between Van Buren and Lee Counties. It runs south in a flat beeline for the first mile or so, then develops some nice rolls, with longer downs than ups, as you go through Shimek State Forest. You have a comfortable downhill into the river valley again.

16.4 miles. County Road W46 has become Olive Street as you've coasted into Farmington. It merges with State Highway 2 at the four-way stop; continue straight on State Highway 2. Most of Farmington's business district is off route to your left. This is the oldest village in Van Buren County, yet it seems the least interested in its history.

Pass the Bridge Café and Supper Club as you head west across the river. (If it's lunchtime, this is a good spot for home cooking and low prices.) You have a narrow paved shoulder for the gradual climb up from the river. This section of highway is part of the Mormon Pioneer Trail, one of the network of routes the Church of Jesus Christ of the Latter Day Saints followed on their trek from Nauvoo, Illinois, to Salt Lake City, Utah.

21.3 miles. State Highway 2 curves left, but you keep going straight on County Road W40. There's a very short rise and then it's downhill for a mile to cross the river again and come back into Bonaparte. Turn left as soon as you cross the bridge and follow County Road J40 back to Bentonsport.

27.1 miles. Unfortunately, you can't enjoy the run-out from the steepest descent of the ride: turn left onto Sanford Street and coast the last two blocks to your starting point.

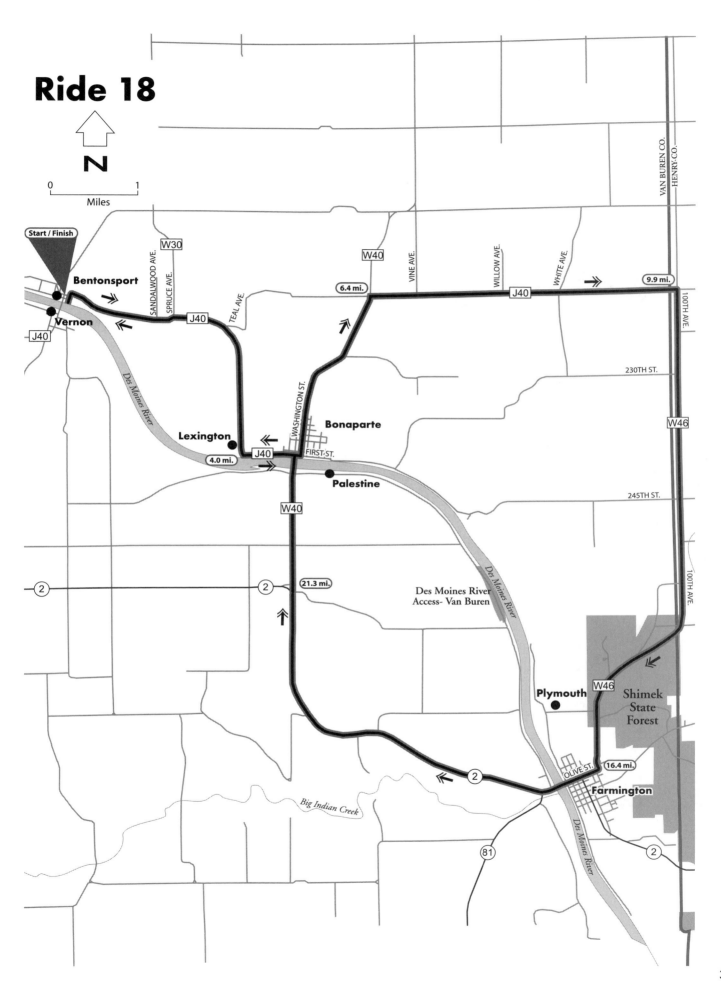

Ride 18

N

0   1
Miles

Start / Finish

Bentonsport

W30

SANDALWOOD AVE.

SPRUCE AVE.

J40

Vernon

J40

TEAL AVE.

W40

6.4 mi.

VINE AVE.

WILLOW AVE.

WHITE AVE.

9.9 mi.

J40

100TH AVE.

230TH ST.

W46

WASHINGTON ST.

Bonaparte

Lexington

J40

FIRST ST.

4.0 mi.

Palestine

245TH ST.

W40

Des Moines River

2

2

21.3 mi.

Des Moines River
Access- Van Buren

VAN BUREN CO.

HENRY CO.

Plymouth

W46

Shimek
State
Forest

100TH AVE.

2

OLIVE ST.

16.4 mi.

Farmington

Big Indian Creek

81

2

CENTRAL IOWA

RIDE 19
Rice Lake Roundabout

LOCATION: County and state roads between Joice and Lake Mills
DISTANCE: 14.9-mile loop
SURFACE: Paved roads
TERRAIN: Low, gentle swells of land
DIFFICULTY: Easy
SERVICES:
Restrooms: At businesses in Joice, off-route in Lake Mills, Rice Lake State Park
Water: Same
Food: Restaurants and taverns in Joice and Lake Mills, Rice Lake Golf Course clubhouse
Camping: Pilot Knob State Park, Forest City
Lodging: Motels in Lake Mills
Bike Shop: None nearby
STARTING POINT: Community Park, at the corner of Main and Lindon streets in Joice

The Des Moines Lobe

Fifty thousand years ago an ice sheet formed in the Hudson's Bay region in Canada and inexorably spread south over land already littered by previous glaciers. This Ice Age, the Wisconsinan Event, would carve the final shapes on the landscape we know today.

The ice spread southward for 20,000 years, retreated, then advanced again. It reached as far south as today's Des Moines, stayed for three millennia, then began its slow, final retreat. The glacier left behind a hummocky moraine country, a land of gentle swells punctuated by glacial deposits of soil and rocks, and "prairie potholes" formed when buried ice melted to leave small, shallow lakes and interconnected wetlands. Rivers formed to carry the melt water, carving steep, deep valleys through the accumulated glacial deposits and the occasional boulder.

Start in a tiny, somnambulant town, cruise through rich farmlands, pass the former hometown of Iowa's longest-serving governor, and spin around a lovely lake. This is the landscape most people think of as Iowan, and it's great for easy cycling.

0.0 miles. Joice is so out of the way that not even a state highway intrudes on its peace and quiet. In the block-long business district, Nellie's Café and Frank's Place indicate a community in which everyone is on a first-name basis.

From Community Park, head west on Main Street through two blocks of an attractive residential area, then turn right at the stop sign to go north on Western Street (County Road S14).

0.7 miles. Be careful crossing the railroad tracks here; the angle is bad and you might catch a wheel. The road turns to the left, parallel to the tracks, and becomes County Road S10. Off to your right are some of the turbines of the Top of Iowa Wind Farm. Eighty-nine turbines, mounted on 235-foot-high towers in rows across nearly 5,500 acres of farmland generate enough power to supply about 24,000 homes.

County Road S10 glides north smoothly across the low, gentle swells of land, and you're likely the only vehicle traveling on it. To your left, grasslands lead to the screen of trees around Lower Rice Lake.

1.5 miles. Cross 425th Street, a gravel road, and County Road S10 becomes Bluebill Place. You pass through a wetlands area and the land opens up into corn and soybean fields stretching out to far horizons, broken only by tree-dotted watercourses and fence lines.

3.6 miles. It's hard to believe that this intersection with 448th Avenue was once a hamlet called Bristol. There's nothing here now but a small farmhouse with a beautiful garden. Glide down a slight slope through more wetlands and grasslands of a Wildlife Management Area.

4.4 miles. At the stop sign, turn left onto Worth County Road 105. The water tower and grain elevator of Lake Mills are ahead of you in the west, on a road as straight as a taut string. Farmland stretches out on both sides, broken by small hummocks crowned with trees.

6.6 miles. North Third Avenue splits off, going straight towards the elevator as you curve left with County Road 105. On your right is the Norwegian Monument Prairie Planting, established in 1995 and now replete with tall grasses and prairie flowers. Across the prairie planting is a monument to Norwegian immigrants who came into this area in the middle of the 19th century, spreading westward from settlements in Wisconsin and Minnesota. A sculpture, *The Promise of America*, depicts an immigrant family arriving in the New World.

Terry Branstad, governor of Iowa from 1983 until 1999, was born near here and practiced law in Lake Mills before getting into politics. He was the youngest governor in Iowa history when he was first elected, and held onto the office longer than anyone had ever put up with it before.

7.4 miles. County Road 105 became Main Street as you came into Lake Mills. At Winnebago Street (County Road R74), turn left to continue the loop. For a food or restroom break, go straight on Main Street into the business district, where there are convenience stores, restaurants, and taverns.

There's a side path trail running along the west side of the road for about a half mile to the elementary school. Traffic on this road is so light that the trail is superfluous. Pass a horse farm on your left as you travel south, leaving Lake Mills behind and cruising a stretch of hayfields, grasslands, and wetlands.

10.2 miles. Turn left to go east on County Road A34 (425th Street). Pass a golf course on your left, then the entrance to Rice Lake State Park and the Rice Lake Golf and Country Club. On the horizon ahead are the wind farm's turbines.

The road curves and enters a forested section, which opens on the right to a pretty view of Lower Rice Lake. Cross the waterway connecting the lake's two sections and enjoy a postcard-quality vista of the main part of the lake on your left.

13.3 miles. Cross the railroad tracks and turn right onto Bluebill Lane (County Road S10), heading south to Joice.

14.8 miles. At the stop sign, turn left onto Main Street to return to the starting point.

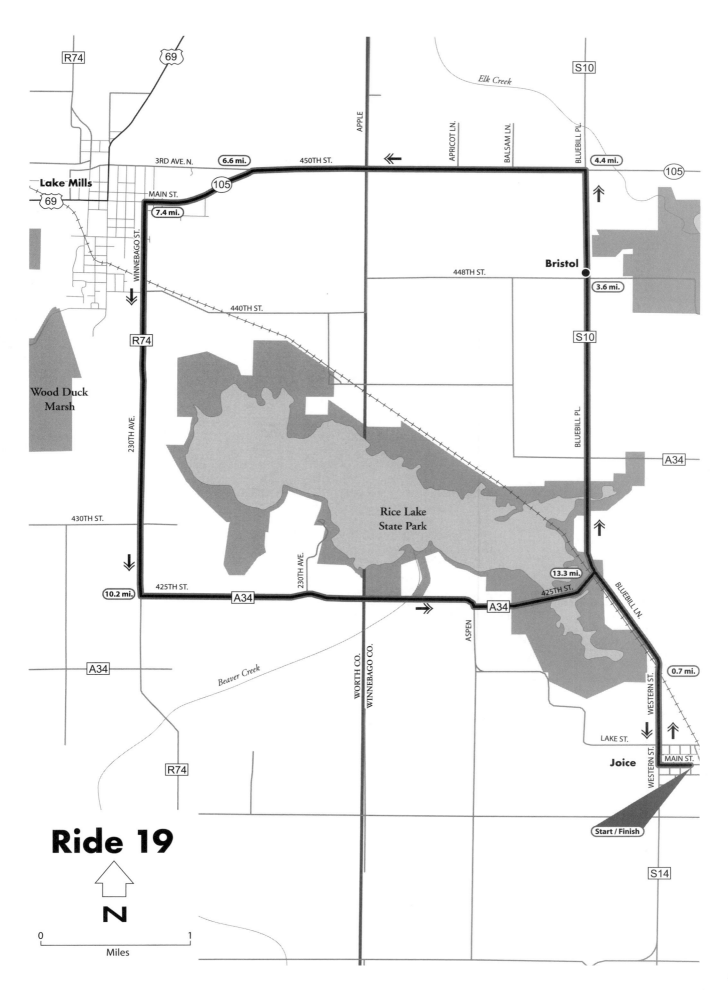

R74

69

R74

69

Lake Mills

3RD AVE. N.   6.6 mi.   450TH ST.

105

MAIN ST.

7.4 mi.

WINNEBAGO ST.

440TH ST.

R74

Wood Duck
Marsh

230TH AVE.

430TH ST.

425TH ST.

10.2 mi.   A34

A34

R74

APPLE

Elk Creek

APRICOT LN.

BALSAM LN.

BLUEBILL PL.

S10

4.4 mi.

105

Bristol

448TH ST.

3.6 mi.

S10

A34

Rice Lake
State Park

230TH AVE.

13.3 mi.

425TH ST.

BLUEBILL LN.

A34

ASPEN

Beaver Creek

WORTH CO.
WINNEBAGO CO.

0.7 mi.

WESTERN ST.

LAKE ST.

WESTERN ST.

Joice   MAIN ST.

Start / Finish

S14

Ride 19

↑

N

0   1

Miles

41

RIDE 20
Who Named This Lake?

LOCATION: County and city roads around Clear Lake
DISTANCE: 14.4-mile loop
SURFACE: Paved roads
TERRAIN: Gentle swells, lots of flats
DIFFICULTY: Easy
SERVICES:
    Restrooms: At start/finish, Clear Lake State Park, businesses in Ventura, McIntosh Woods State Park
    Water: Same
    Food: Restaurants, taverns and convenience stores in Clear Lake and Ventura
    Camping: Clear Lake State Park, Clear Lake; McIntosh Woods State Park, Ventura
    Lodging: Motels and bed and breakfasts in Clear Lake
    Bike Shop: Lakeside Cyclery, Clear Lake
STARTING POINT: Public boat access at the southwest corner of City Square Park in Clear Lake

Enjoy the beach at Clear Lake State Park, but don't expect clear water.

The Day the Music Died

Everyone with ears in the baby boom generation has heard Buddy Holly's "Peggy Sue," Ritchie Valens's "Donna," and the Big Bopper's "Chantilly Lace." The deaths of these three musicians was a tragedy to countless teenagers and an irreplaceable loss to rock and roll.

Holly, along with Ritchie Valens and J. P. "The Big Bopper" Richardson, played a concert at the Surf Ballroom in Clear Lake on February 2, 1959. They boarded a chartered Beechcraft Bonanza at the nearby Mason City airport in the wee hours of February 3rd, bound for their next gig in Fargo, North Dakota. The band members were traveling by bus—the three headliners had decided to take a plane so they'd arrive in Fargo with time to get some laundry done before their show.

The plane took off from the runway towards the south, circled once to get onto its heading, and disappeared into the light snow falling from the night sky.

Minutes later, the plane inexplicably fell from that sky and crashed into a field of crop stubble about six miles north of Clear Lake. Buddy Holly, Ritchie Valens, and the Big Bopper were killed, along with the airplane's pilot.

It was the Day the Music Died.

They're gone but not forgotten. Ken Paquette, a rock and roll fan from Wisconsin, created a memorial to the three performers at the site of the crash. A stainless steel guitar and a set of three stainless steel records now mark the spot. The guitar bears the performers' names; the records represent "Peggy Sue," "Donna," and "Chantilly Lace."

And on the first weekend of February each year, the Surf Ballroom pays tribute to the performers with a dance that features their music.

You start this ride in Clear Lake, a town that comes particularly alive in the summer. Regrettably, that name promises something the lake doesn't deliver: clear water. Like almost all of Iowa's lakes and rivers, Clear Lake is clouded with silt and nutrient runoff, much of it from homeowners' overzealous lawn care.

0.0 miles. From the lake's public access boat ramp on the southwest corner of City Square Park, pedal away from the lake on Main Street and make an immediate right onto South Shore Drive to pass the water tower. You leave the main business district, pass summer rental cottages and condominiums crowded along the lakeshore. Across 12th Street, a bike lane appears along the road.

1.4 miles. Bear right on Lakeview Drive. You've seen precious little of the lake so far, thanks to the wall-to-wall summer homes. To check out some attractive and interesting cottages, make a little jog at 25th Avenue to stay on Lakeview. Turn left at 26th Avenue to rejoin South Shore Drive and its bike lane.

There are gentle rolls to this road as you pass Clear Lake State Park, following South Shore Drive south, then east. At about three miles out, you have your first good view of the lake stretching out on your right; on your left is a wetland and open fields. This doesn't last long; lakeside homes soon line the road again.

5.0 miles. South Shore Drive turns left, heading away from the lake, and becomes Dogwood Avenue once you pass the Girls Scouts' Camp Tanglefoot. At the T intersection, turn right onto County Road B35 (235th Street) to go west. The paved shoulder/bike lane ends here, but you won't miss it—there's hardly any traffic on County Road B35. The road is almost flat, with a good smooth surface that your bike glides over with little effort. In the distance, you can see the turbines of the Cerro Gordo County Wind Farm; the 55 turbines here were erected in 1999. On your right, you have a nice long view over cornfields to the tree-surrounded lake.

7.4 miles. County Road B35 Ts into County Road S14 (Balsam Avenue) and you turn right, heading north. Farmland gives way to a pond and wetlands, the Ventura Marsh State Game Management Area. Pedal across a broad causeway over the Clear Lake narrows and enjoy fine lake views on both sides. There are summer homes along the shore of the big lake, with shallow-draft party barges at their docks.

8.8 miles. Pedal up a gradual rise into the small town of Ventura. There's the Steak House Café and Lounge, but if you'd rather have a milkshake than a beer, the tiny Viking Drive Inn is your choice. A very decent burger with fries at the Viking is about half the price of the same at the Steak House.

Turn right onto Lake Street and ride through a couple of residential blocks before you come out parallel with the lakeshore again. Lake Street is utterly flat and runs right next to the lake for a couple of miles, passing McIntosh Woods State Park. It becomes North Shore Drive as you re-enter the town of Clear Lake.

Your view of the lake is unobstructed for another mile—the road's too close to the shoreline to permit houses on that side—so you can look across boat docks and out to the wide reaches of the lake. There are "Share the Road" signs posted and the moderate motor traffic is very courteous. Bicycles are welcome around here!

13.9 miles. You've been riding through crowded commercial establishments, condos, and lakefront homes for a while when you pass the Surf Ballroom on your left. A block beyond the Surf, turn right onto Fourth Street, a one-way street. Go down a block to the lake, then take a left onto North Lakeview Drive at the water's edge. Follow it for a quarter mile and you're back at the starting point.

Ride 20

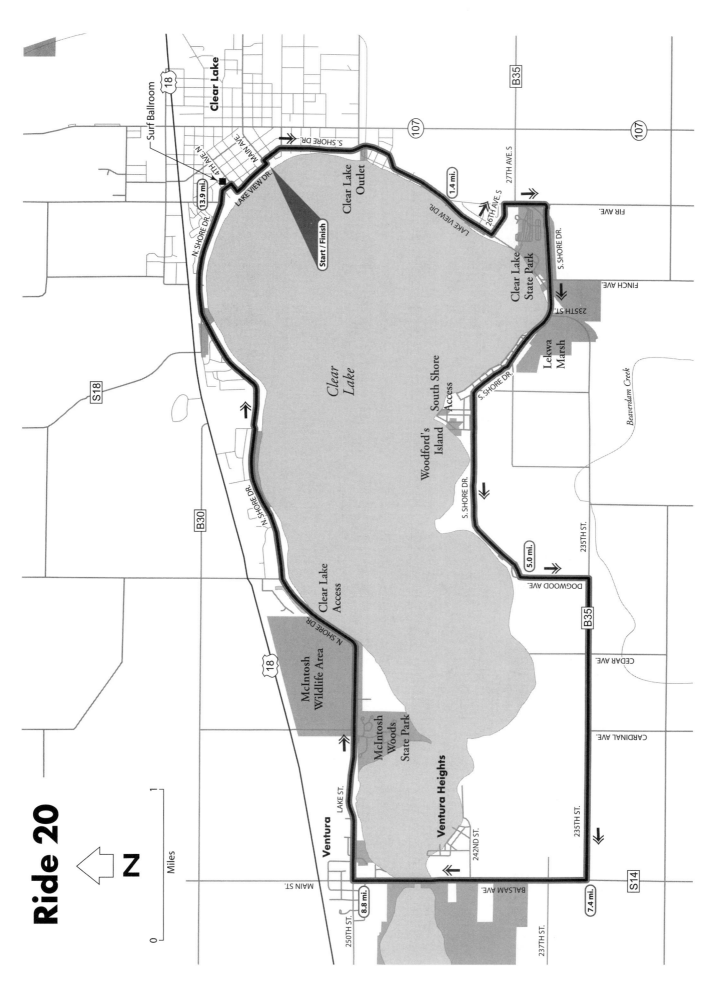

N

Miles
0   1

RIDE 21
Bikin' to Burt

LOCATION: City, county, and state roads between Algona and Burt
DISTANCE: 25.6-mile loop; add 1.3 miles for side trip into Burt
SURFACE: Paved roads
TERRAIN: Mostly flat with gentle swells, one steep descent and climb
DIFFICULTY: Easy
SERVICES:
    Restrooms: Businesses in Algona, off-route at businesses in Burt, Smith Lake County Park
    Water: Same
    Food: Convenience stores, groceries, restaurants, taverns in Algona; restaurant/tavern off-route in Burt
    Camping: A. A. Call State Park and Smith Lake County Park, Algona
    Lodging: Motels in Algona
    Bike Shop: None nearby
STARTING POINT: Casey's General Store on State Street (U.S. Highway 169) between Wooster and Colby streets in Algona

Algona's POWs

As the tide of World War II turned and Allied forces advanced into Europe, the number of enemy prisoners grew beyond the capacity of English POW camps, so the United States began erecting camps in America. Algona, far from coastal areas and international borders, and devoid of sensitive shipyards, munitions plants, or airplane factories, was chosen as the site of one of the main POW camps.

Camp Algona was established in 1943 on 287 acres of land west of Algona. Eventually, it held 178 buildings, with three prisoner compounds surrounded by two rows of 10-foot-high chain-link fence, topped with barbed wire and studded with guard towers.

The first group of prisoners arrived in March 1944. Over 10,000 prisoners, mostly Germans, passed through Camp Algona, which was the center of a small empire of 34 branch camps spread through the upper Midwest.

With so many of America's young men gone to war, the POWs were an important labor resource. Prisoners helped with spring planting and fall harvesting, detasseled corn, cut timber and pulp, made bricks and tiles. They were paid ten cents an hour, a maximum of eighty cents per day. No prisoner ever worked a job where American labor was available.

The value of their labor has been estimated at over $3.5 million. During the Missouri River floods of 1944, the prisoners saved almost 13,000 acres of cropland and the entire town of Percival, Iowa. They came to Iowa as enemies, but they certainly didn't leave that way.

At war's end, Camp Algona ceased to exist. The buildings were torn down or sold, the fences and guard towers were removed. Today, the land is owned by the City of Algona and occupied by the National Guard Armory and the Municipal Airport.

Here's an easy ride through scenic farm country, with a dip into the East Fork Des Moines River valley to remind you that your bike has more than three gears. The side trip to Burt is worth making just to see what kinds of games are planned for their annual summer celebration.

0.0 miles. Head east on State Street (U.S. Highway 169) from the Casey's store a few blocks east of the main commercial district, and cruise through a quiet residential area to Main Street, where you turn left. Just past the water tower, be careful crossing some rough railroad tracks.

1.6 miles. Turn right onto U.S. Highway 18. This is a busy four-lane road, but you're on it for less than a quarter mile. Pass the Eastland Plaza mini-mall and get into the left lane to turn north onto Plum Creek Road (County Road P54). Almost immediately, you're in farmland. Across the fields on your left, a line of trees marks the rim of the East Fork Des Moines River valley. The road curves through the corn and beans, as devoid of traffic as it is of hills.

6.5 miles. Cross Plum Creek and head up the day's first climb, a gradual, half-mile rise. At the top, you catch sight of Burt's water tower and grain elevator on the northwestern horizon. Now the road straightens into a plumb line across the land's gentle swells. You pass a Century Farm, owned and farmed by the same family for more than a hundred years. Such places are becoming rarer and rarer.

10.8 miles. Turn left at the stop sign onto County Road B19 and cruise west through the Union Slough National Wildlife Refuge, a lovely area of oak savannah and wetlands. You have a good half mile of downhill before crossing the East Fork Des Moines River, then a moderately steep, half-mile climb out of the valley.

12.8 miles. At County Road P44, turn left (south) to continue the loop, or, if you're ready for a break, go straight ahead into the small town of Burt.

In Burt, you'll find Trio's, a bar and grill that offers a chance to find out what's happening at the town's annual celebration. Burt's festivities include some innovative contests, not the least of which is the Shoot the Poop lottery. A 10-by-10-foot section of ground is fenced off and marked into 2.5-foot squares. After the participants put down their money and draw rights to one of those squares, a horse is released into the section. When the horse drops some "road apples," the holder of the square into which they fall collects the money. If the horse fails to "ripen" within a specified time, the winning square is drawn from a hat.

14.4 miles. Heading south on County Road P44, be careful when you cross the railroad tracks—they're rough and set at a wheel-grabbing angle. County Road P44 is straight, smooth, and hardly traveled. The farms along here look prosperous: the buildings sport recent coats of paint, the lawns and gardens are well tended.

17.8 miles. At the T intersection, turn right onto County Road B30. Dip down to cross Black Cat Creek, then climb back up and turn left onto U.S. Highway 169. About a half mile south of Smith Lake County Park, look for two old storage tanks on your left; turn left onto 240th Street to get away from the highway traffic.

20.8 miles. At the stop sign, turn right and head south on River Road. There's a golf course on your left; on the right, cornfields extend to the horizon, broken only by the highway. River Road curves gradually right and gives you a nice downhill.

22.8 miles. Watch out for rumble strips before you intersect with U.S. Highway 169 again—they're hard to spot in the concrete road surface. Turn left on 169.

23.1 miles. At the four-way stop, turn left onto State Highway 18 and cross the Des Moines River again. The outside lane has plenty of room for lane sharing with motor traffic as you climb out of the river valley. After you cross a set of railroad tracks, turn right onto Main Street.

25.0 miles. Turn right onto State Street and follow it back to Casey's General Store.

Ride 21

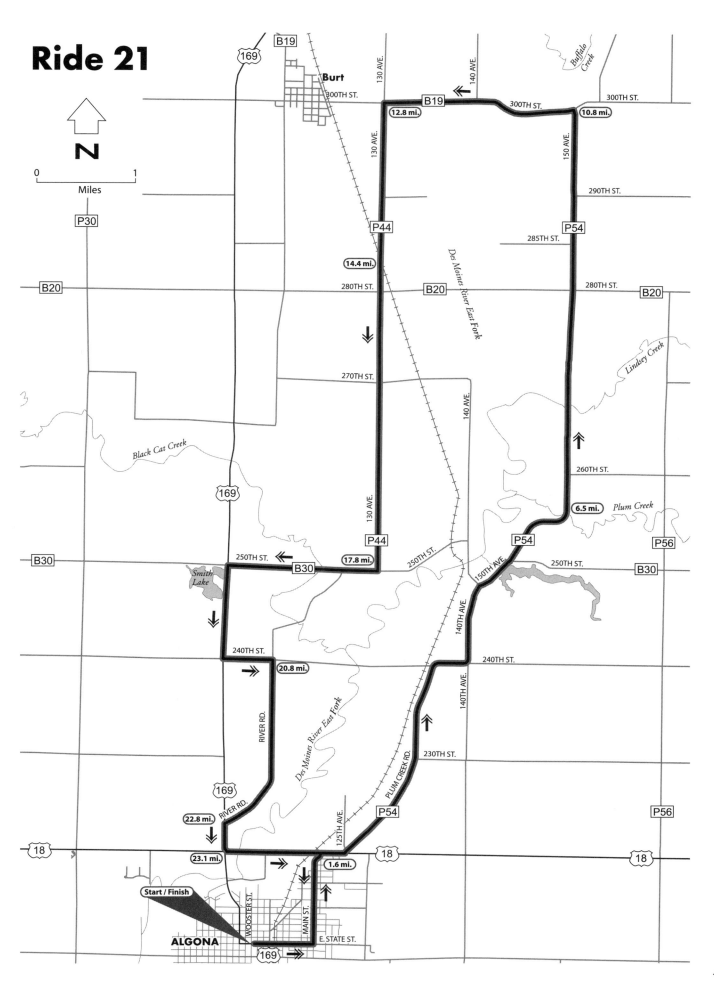

N

0   1

Miles

B19

169

Burt

300TH ST.

130 AVE.

140 AVE.

Buffalo Creek

B19   12.8 mi.

300TH ST.

300TH ST.

10.8 mi.

150 AVE.

P30

P44

290TH ST.

P54

14.4 mi.

Des Moines River East Fork

280TH ST.

B20

285TH ST.

B20

280TH ST.

B20

B20

Lindsey Creek

270TH ST.

140 AVE.

130 AVE.

Black Cat Creek

169

260TH ST.

Plum Creek

6.5 mi.

P54

P56

P44

17.8 mi.

250TH ST.

250TH ST.

250TH ST.

B30

250TH ST.

B30

Smith Lake

B30

150TH AVE.

140TH AVE.

240TH ST.

240TH ST.

240TH ST.

20.8 mi.

RIVER RD.

Des Moines River East Fork

140TH AVE.

230TH ST.

PLUM CREEK RD.

169

22.8 mi.

RIVER RD.

125TH AVE.

P54

P56

18

18

23.1 mi.

18

Start / Finish

1.6 mi.

WOOSTER ST.

MAIN ST.

E. STATE ST.

ALGONA

169

45

RIDE 22
If the Shoe Doesn't Fit Ride

LOCATION: County and state roads between Dolliver Memorial State Park and Otho
DISTANCE: 13.4-mile loop
SURFACE: Paved roads
TERRAIN: Gentle swells, half-mile climb at start, steep descent at finish
DIFFICULTY: easy
SERVICES:
    Restrooms: At start/finish, off-route at convenience store in Otho
    Water: Same
    Food: Off-route at convenience store in Otho
    Camping: Dolliver Memorial State Park, Otho
    Lodging: Hotel, motels, and bed and breakfasts in Fort Dodge
    Bike Shop: The Bike Shop, First Avenue, Fort Dodge
STARTING POINT: Campground entrance at Dolliver Memorial State Park, southeast of Otho

This short, scenic, and easy ride starts next to the Des Moines River and climbs through the cut that waterway has made in the glacial till, makes a loop over land flattened out by the last glacial advance, then drops back past a bluff that reveals a cross-section of Iowa's geologic history.

0.0 miles. Clip into your pedals at the entrance to the Dolliver Memorial State Park campground. Across the road, the Des Moines River chuckles around a shallow curve. Turn left on the park road (County Road D33). Your legs get an immediate wake-up call as you head north, climbing a moderately steep grade out of the river valley.

They get a short rest as you pass Boneyard Hollow, a narrow ravine named by early settlers who found piles of bison bones here. The bones were probably left by Indians, who either drove the bison over the cliffs to their deaths, or into the narrows where they could be easily slaughtered by hunters. Beyond Boneyard Hollow, the hill gets considerably steeper, but the climb is short.

Boneyard Hollow is also the site of an historical hoax. In 1912, a family picnicking nearby found a lead tablet with a Latin inscription saying it had been planted by Father Hennepin, the French-Canadian explorer, in 1701. Hennepin is credited with discovering the Des Moines River. The tablet caused quite a hubbub—Hennepin reported finding the Des Moines River where it empties into the Mississippi, nearly 200 crow-flying miles away, and there's no record of his straying so far from there. As it turns out, he didn't: The tablet was planted by pranksters.

1.0 miles. Leave the park and emerge from the forest. Off to your left, there's a beautifully restored Victorian-era house; there's another one a quarter mile up the road, painted with the same color scheme.

2.2 miles. You're into farmland now as you curve west on County Road D33, with corn and bean fields on both sides of the road. You can't help but notice that the fields are fenced, and that all of the fence posts on your left are topped with . . . shoes. There are work boots, sneakers, loafers, business shoes, high heels, cute little pumps, cowboy boots, children's shoes, snowmobile boots, ice skates, even a pair of flip-flops. Every fence post for more than a half mile sports footwear.

A set of Burma-Shave-style signs (you have to go the opposite direction to read them) says:

> As you travel down the road
> Be sure to check our posts
> Some footwear we put there
> Others by a ghost!

The fenced land belongs to a Lyle Heatherton, whose wife started the collection of shoes when she mounted her baby's outgrown slippers on the first posts. The Heathertons have four sons, who generate a considerable number of outgrown shoes. The adult Heathertons added their own worn-out footwear and the line grew. The idea caught on with neighbors and townsfolk from Otho, and the line of shod fence posts just keeps extending.

5.0 miles. Turn left onto County Road P59. (County Road D33 continues straight into the town of Otho. About four-tenths of a mile from here on County Road D33 is a convenience store with a rudimentary kitchen that serves pizza, hamburgers, and sandwiches.)

As you pedal south on County Road P59, you'll see signs proclaiming it the "Dragoon Trail." The Dragoons were a lightly armed U.S. Army cavalry force that scouted Iowa after it was opened to white settlement. In 1835, they blazed a trail along the Des Moines River, establishing outposts between Des Moines and Fort Dodge.

8.6 miles. Go left with the Dragoon Trail onto County Road D43 (State Highway 50). The road is flat and could've been drawn with a straight edge between the fields of corn and soybeans. There's virtually no traffic. Watercourses meander through the fields, marked by occasional trees. You cross Crooked Creek, a pretty little stream winding beneath black walnut trees on its way to the river.

11.6 miles. Turn left onto Dolliver Park Road (County Road D33). To the right, the road is gravel, signed as Quail Road. As you re-enter the State Park, you'll notice R. L. Antiques on your right, another beautifully restored Victorian-era farmhouse painted in the same color scheme as those you passed at the beginning of the ride.

You have a fast, winding, mile-long descent through the forest as the road follows Prairie Creek's course to the Des Moines River. Hundred-foot cliffs line the creek's far bank: their striations are a 150-million-year geologic history of this area. On the timbered ridge atop those cliffs are three Indian mounds dating back to the Woodland Indian culture of 1100 A.D. The run-out from this descent will carry you back almost to your starting point without your turning a pedal.

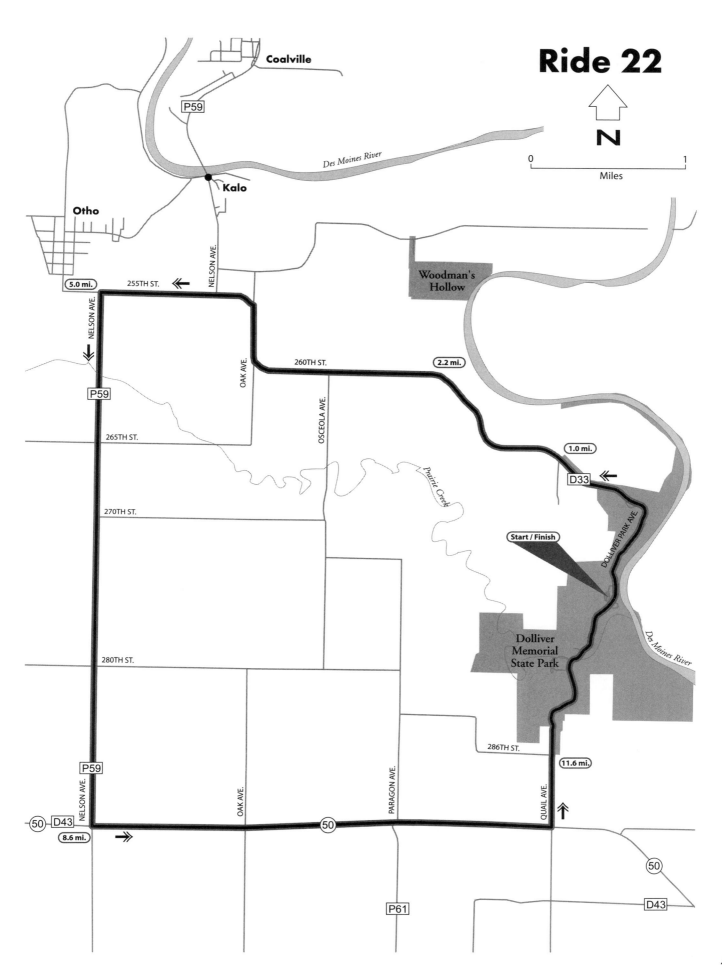

Ride 22

N

0   Miles   1

Coalville

P59

Des Moines River

Kalo

Otho

Woodman's Hollow

255TH ST.

NELSON AVE.

5.0 mi.

P59

OAK AVE.

260TH ST.

2.2 mi.

OSCEOLA AVE.

265TH ST.

Prairie Creek

1.0 mi.

D33

270TH ST.

DOLLIVER PARK AVE.

Start / Finish

Des Moines River

280TH ST.

Dolliver Memorial State Park

P59

NELSON AVE.

OAK AVE.

PARAGON AVE.

286TH ST.

QUAIL AVE.

11.6 mi.

50   D43

50

50

8.6 mi.

D43

P61

RIDE 23
Marsh-mellow Ride

LOCATION: County roads between Marshalltown and Lamoille
DISTANCE: 16.7-mile loop
SURFACE: Paved roads
TERRAIN: Long, rolling hills and twisting creek valley
DIFFICULTY: Moderate
SERVICES:
  Restrooms: Businesses in Marshalltown
  Water: Same
  Food: Restaurants, convenience stores, and grocery in Marshalltown
  Camping: Riverview Park, Marshalltown
  Lodging: Motels in Marshalltown
  Bike Shop: Bikes to You, Southridge Road; Mike's Schwinn Cyclery, Main Street, Marshalltown
STARTING POINT: Northwest corner of Courthouse Square in Marshalltown

The Marshall County Courthouse is the starting point for this ride, which takes you by some impressive 19th-century Main Street homes, over rolling hills above the Iowa River, then through Linn Creek's valley back into town.

0.0 miles. Pedal west on Main Street from the northwest corner of the courthouse square, the intersection of Main and Center streets. The Marshall County Courthouse here was designed by the same architect who designed Iowa's State Capitol building. It was built in 1884-86 and extensively renovated in the mid-1970s. There's a wonderful brick-and-concrete mandala at the starting point, the bricks bearing the names of contributors to Marshalltown's downtown renovations. The outside circle is inscribed with aphorisms: "Pray for a good harvest, but continue to hoe," "Children need more models than critics," "You can't fake listening," and others.

From Main Street Road west of Marshalltown you look across rolling hills to the Iowa River valley.

Main Street has very wide lanes—plenty of room to share with cars. As you ride west, you pass through the business district quickly and Main Street becomes a tree-lined street with lovely old homes interspersed with very attractive contemporary ones. At about a half mile from the start, look on your right for a place with cloyingly cute heart-shaped windows, neighbored by a house that can't decide between Federalist and Hacienda styles.

2.5 miles. You've climbed your first hill of the ride, an easy grade, and now Main Street becomes Main Street Road (County Road E35). Ahead, the road rolls over a series of low hills. On your right is the Iowa River valley, carpeted with corn and hayfields. The views from the hilltops are gorgeous.

4.5 miles. Cross State Highway 330. Traffic is heavy and fast on State Highway 330; just south of here the highway becomes "the Diagonal," the shortest route to Des Moines from the northeast. County Road E35 is smooth concrete and true as a carpenter's rule as you cruise west over the land's rolls.

6.5 miles. Turn left to head south on County Road S70 (Knapp Avenue). The road flattens out a bit, or at least the hills seem lower as you come into the hamlet of Lamoille. This used to be a real town, with a general store and a railroad depot, but nowadays there's not much here but a few homes and a church.

Just past the church, you have a steep downhill on rough pavement. Start braking early—at the bottom of the hill is a set of *very* uneven railroad tracks that you don't want to hit with any speed behind you.

8.9 miles. Turn left onto County Road E41 (235th Street). In a half mile, County Road E41 turns left and becomes Knoll Way—stay on it. You have a great view down into a hollow on your right, where Linn Creek meanders through grasslands. The road winds down to the creek and follows it east and north through a crease in the hills. This is a lovely section with rounded, forested hills rising on both sides.

11.2 miles. County Road E41 intersects with State Highway 330 (Marshalltown Boulevard) and you turn left. This is a busy road: be cautious. After only two-tenths of a mile, you hit a blinking yellow light and State Highway 330 veers off to the left, but you continue east on County Road E41.

The road surface is a bit rough as you cross Linn Creek and start up the steepest climb of the ride, heading back into Marshalltown. This is the truck route into town, but traffic is light to moderate. The road changes names to Lincoln Way (at one time, this was U.S. Highway 30, the Lincoln Highway) on the outskirts of Marshalltown. There are some interesting contemporary homes along here.

15.7 miles. After a fast downhill, bear left onto Madison Street (Lincoln Way continues straight). Be careful crossing the railroad tracks here—the angle is bad, threatening to catch your wheel.

16.1 miles. At the four-way stop, turn left onto Third Street and follow it up to Main Street. Take a right on Main and ride three blocks back to your starting point.

Ride 23

N

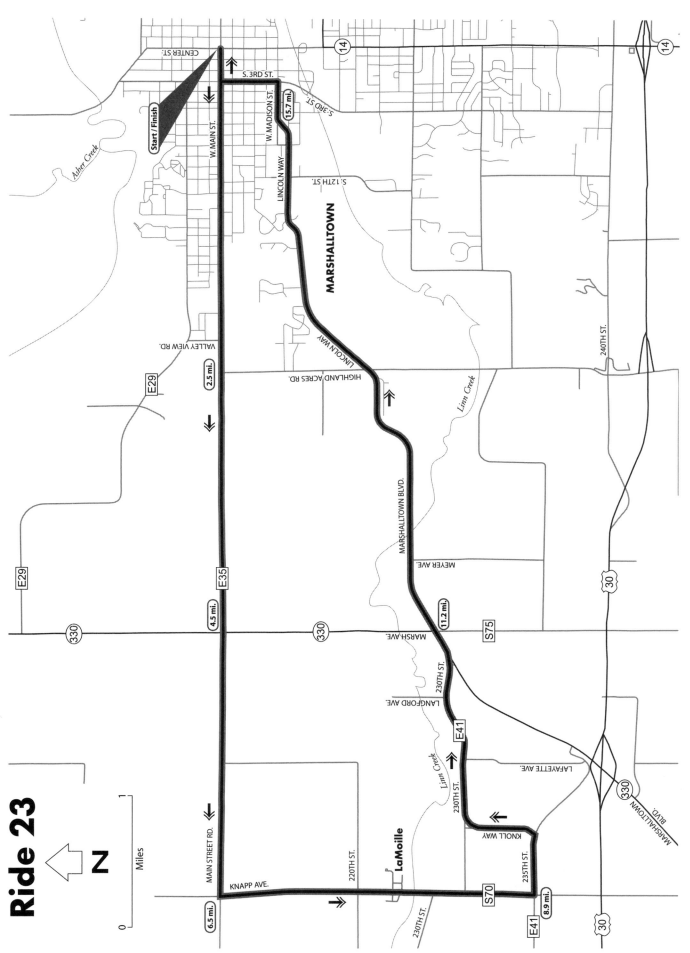

Miles
0   1

MARSHALLTOWN

LaMoille

Start / Finish

CENTER ST.
S. 3RD ST.
W. MAIN ST.
W. MADISON ST.
LINCOLN WAY
S. 12TH ST.
S. 3RD ST.
15.7 mi.

14
14

Asher Creek

VALLEY VIEW RD.
E29
E29
2.5 mi.
E35
4.5 mi.
330
330

HIGHLAND ACRES RD.
LINCOLN WAY
Linn Creek
240TH ST.
30

MARSHALLTOWN BLVD.
MEYER AVE.
S75
11.2 mi.
MARSH AVE.
230TH ST.
LANGFORD AVE.
LAFAYETTE AVE.
330
MARSHALLTOWN BLVD.

Linn Creek
230TH ST.
E41

KNOLL WAY
235TH ST.
S70
E41
8.9 mi.
30

MAIN STREET RD.
KNAPP AVE.
220TH ST.
230TH ST.
6.5 mi.

RIDE 24
Urban Sprawl Ride

LOCATION: Squaw Creek Trail, city and county roads on the northwest side of Ames

DISTANCE: 11-mile loop

SURFACE: Paved trail and roads

TERRAIN: Mostly flat, with a couple of low hills

DIFFICULTY: Moderate

SERVICES:

Restrooms: At start/finish, businesses at mile 8.7 on Stange Road

Water: Same

Food: Café, off-route at mile 8.7 on Northridge Parkway

Camping: Ledges State Park, Boone

Lodging: Motels and bed and breakfasts in Ames

Bike Shop: Skunk River Cycling, Main Street, Ames

STARTING POINT: Brookside Park's parking lot, off Sixth Street in Ames

America's First Land-Grant College

It was a revolutionary idea: The Federal government would help every state establish colleges and make advanced education available to all. Sponsored by Congressman Justin Morrill of Vermont, the Morrill Act of 1862 gave each state 30,000 acres of federal land for each of its senators and representatives in Congress. The land was to be sold and the proceeds were to be put into an endowment fund to support colleges in each state.

The colleges would be open to all, teaching practical subjects such as agricultural science, engineering, and home economics. This was a dramatic shift in educational philosophy, changing the purpose of higher education from classical to applied studies that would prepare students for real work in the real world.

Iowa, the first state to accept the terms of the Morrill Act, quickly established the Iowa State College of Agriculture and Mechanic Arts. It was the first of what quickly became known as the land-grant colleges.

Now Iowa State University, this first land-grant college, has an enrollment of over 27,000 students. Its campus of nearly 2,000 acres in and around Ames holds 160 buildings that house nine colleges, offering more than 100 undergraduate degrees.

Predictably, agricultural studies are a big part of Iowa State. The university has the world's largest concentration of faculty dedicated to sustainable agriculture, and was the first to offer a doctoral program in that field. It has 11 research units concerned with agriculture and animal husbandry.

But it's not all just food crops: ISU is also home to Reiman Gardens, a 14-acre educational display garden. In 2001, Reiman Gardens won the All-American Rose Selections President's Award as the nation's most outstanding public rose garden.

Iowa State gives us bread . . . and it gives us roses too.

Urban sprawl happens everywhere, even in a state as rural as Iowa. This ride begins on a lovely trail through a city park, then works its way to the outskirts of Ames. You escape the city for a nice loop, then come back through developments that are spreading Ames well into the countryside.

0.0 miles. From the southern end of the parking lot off Sixth Street in Brookside Park, turn left onto the Squaw Creek Trail, which parallels the waterway on your right. Brookside Park is shaded by maple, elm, cottonwood, oak, and black walnut trees, and soon you're winding through streamside forest.

0.6 miles. Cross the creek and your streamside idyll ends as the trail becomes a side path along 13th Street. Turn left to head west on the side path, cross Stange Road, then slip under a railroad bridge.

1.8 miles. Hyland Avenue comes in from your left. Thirteenth Street, continuing straight, becomes Ontario Street, and narrows to two lanes. You can stay on the side path, riding against traffic, or move onto Ontario Street—the lanes are comfortably wide. You'll notice bits and pieces of Iowa State University's far-flung campus as you ride. The open fields along here are part of the College of Agriculture, which is all that's saved them from being gobbled up by developments.

3.0 miles. Turn right onto Dakota Avenue. Two-tenths of a mile north, cross a

set of railroad tracks and Dakota instantly becomes a two-lane country road. You've escaped the city for the time being.

So far, the route has been very flat, but as you move north into the countryside you have a nice downhill to Onion Creek, then a pretty stiff climb back up. This is exurbia, a mixture of woods, widely spaced single family homes, an occasional farm building and cornfield. Off in the distance is the Ames water tower; on your left is the ISU Beef Cattle Nutrition Management Research Center.

5.6 miles. At the T intersection, turn right, heading east on Cameron School Road. There's a gradual downhill to cross Squaw Creek, then a long, gradual rise. I once found a lemonade-and-cookies stand run by some young schoolgirls along here. The cookies were chocolate chip, made with real butter, selling at four for a quarter.

6.6 miles. Turn right at the T onto George Washington Carver Avenue. In 1891, Carver became the first African-American to enroll at Iowa State College of Agriculture and Mechanic Arts, which became Iowa State University. His gift for botany and horticulture was quickly recognized, and he was encouraged to stay on as a graduate student, then appointed as Iowa State's first African-American faculty member. Carver moved on to Alabama's Tuskegee Institute, where his work resulted in the creation of 325 products from peanuts, over a hundred products from sweet potatoes, and hundreds of other products from plants native to the south.

Along the street named in Carver's honor, open land begins to give way to impending development. On the right, a soybean field stretches to the tree line along Squaw Creek; on the left, a development of very large garages attached to medium-sized houses is going up, all cheek by jowl and treeless. Mini-mansions are clustered around a pond with a fountain in its middle.

The road curves left and changes names to Bloomington Road. In about a quarter mile, George Washington Carver Avenue curves south again, but you continue east on Bloomington.

8.2 miles. Turn right to go south on Stange Road. There's a median strip with lamp posts between the lanes, and the development is going strong on a planned community. In a half mile, the road widens to four lanes with a grassy median as it passes a blooming retail/commercial center that will soon be surrounded by housing.

9.0 miles. Cross 24th Street and get onto the side path trail along Stange Road. The expansion cracks on this side path are very rough; you may prefer to ride the road if traffic is light.

9.7 miles. Turn left onto the side path along 13th Street. In about a half mile, you cross the creek again and turn right to take the Squaw Creek Trail back to your starting point.

Ride 24

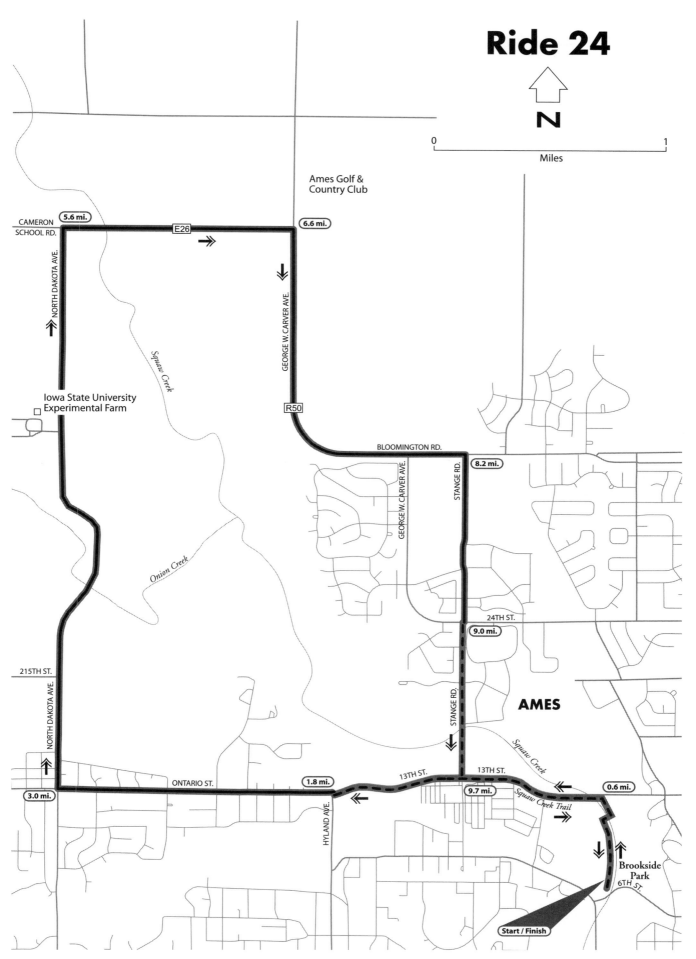

N

0   1
Miles

Ames Golf &
Country Club

CAMERON
SCHOOL RD.
5.6 mi.
E26
6.6 mi.

NORTH DAKOTA AVE.

GEORGE W. CARVER AVE.

Squaw Creek

Iowa State University
Experimental Farm

R50

BLOOMINGTON RD.

GEORGE W. CARVER AVE.

STANGE RD.

8.2 mi.

Onion Creek

24TH ST.
9.0 mi.

215TH ST.

NORTH DAKOTA AVE.

AMES

STANGE RD.

Squaw Creek

ONTARIO ST.
1.8 mi.
13TH ST.
13TH ST.
0.6 mi.
3.0 mi.
9.7 mi.
Squaw Creek Trail

HYLAND AVE.

Brookside
Park
6TH ST.

Start / Finish

51

RIDE 25
Chuggin' Up the Chichaqua

LOCATION: Chichaqua Valley Trail, county and state roads between Baxter and Mingo
DISTANCE: 20.1-mile loop
SURFACE: Paved trail and roads
TERRAIN: Flat trail, moderate hills on roads
DIFFICULTY: Moderate
SERVICES:
  Restrooms: Trailheads in Baxter, Ira, and Mingo
  Water: Same
  Food: Restaurants and convenience stores in Baxter, tavern in Mingo
  Camping: Ashton Wildwood County Park, Mingo
  Lodging: Bed and breakfasts in Baxter, motels in Marshalltown or Newton
    Bike Shop: Bikes to You, Southridge Road; Mike's Schwinn Cyclery, Main Street, Marshalltown
STARTING POINT: Chichaqua Valley Trail head off State Street in Baxter

The Central Iowa Circle of Trails

For decades, bicycling advocates, regional planners, and others have envisioned a system of connected multi-use trails circling Des Moines, mostly on abandoned rail lines. Though the vision is far from realized, several pieces of the circle are in place—and the next five rides will take you over the best parts of them.

Three of the rides use rail-trails. You can look forward to smooth asphalt and negligible grades as you cruise portions of the Chichaqua Valley Trail (Ride 25), the Raccoon River Valley Trail (Ride 28), and the Great Western Trail (Ride 29). But the rides aren't all flat—each is a loop ride, starting out on roads over rolling terrain, then returning via the trails.

Ride 26: Saylorville Lake Swooping, runs along the Neal Smith Trail beside Saylorville Lake. Unlike the rail-trails, this path is deliciously curvaceous and decidedly hilly—your gears will get a workout. You're back on flats, however, along the Clive Greenbelt Trail on Ride 27: Cruisin' in Clive, a beautiful out-and-back sojourn through the woods along Walnut Creek.

Except for the Clive Greenbelt Trail, none of these rides cover the whole length of the trails that are included. You can extend your trips by simply following the trails. Ride 25: Chuggin' Up the Chichaqua, for instance, includes only the eastern half of the Chichaqua Valley Trail. Ride 28: Lots of Loops, uses only 21 of the Raccoon River Valley Trail's 56 miles. The Neal Smith Trail and Great Western Trail, too, extend beyond what's described here.

For complete maps of these trails and information about other trails in the "Great Circle" around Des Moines, contact the Iowa Tourism Department through their Web site at www.iowatourism.com.

This pretty loop takes you over long, rolling hills to the small town of Mingo, then back to Baxter on the hill-free Chichaqua Valley Trail. If you want to avoid the hills, you can simply ride the trail both ways.

0.0 miles. Get on your bike at the Chichaqua Valley Trail head in Baxter and head south on the smooth, paved trail. Baxter's a very prosperous-looking little town with a small but sprightly downtown. Pedal through backyards, cross a couple of residential roads, and pass an attractive development of new homes, then turn right to head west on County Road F17 (State Highway 223). The ditches are awash with Queen Anne's lace and black-eyed Susans.

1.4 miles. Take a left onto County Road S52 and cruise down the slope past a nice oak savannah and pastureland. When you hit the bottom of the hill, you immediately start climbing the next one—there's not much flat between the ups and downs of this land. At a bit over three miles, the Chichaqua Valley Trail angles across the road. The road rises along the side of the hill, affording a beautiful view across the valley carpeted with hayfields and crops.

4.6 miles. Turn right onto County Road F24, heading west again. The land is very rounded here: rolling hills with tree-crowned summits and valleys, the slopes blanketed with crops. The road is lined with chicory, pink clover, and Queen Anne's lace.

6.2 miles. After a long, steep descent, cross Turkey Creek and the Chichaqua Valley Trail again as you enter the hamlet of Ira. There's a nice trailhead park next to the Community Center. Ira's main businesses seem to be the Ira Auto Repair Shop and a huge yard of junked cars, Jack Bucklin Auto and Parts. A sign says there are used cars for sale, but all of the cars in sight are very badly used.

The road runs, straight as a dog heading for a steak, over flats for the next few miles. It's good high-gear cruising through this valley, with softly rounded hills rising on both sides. Someone has planted the outside row of a cornfield with morning glories, and purple flowers twine up the cornstalks.

10.2 miles. Cross Clear Creek, then Indian Creek, and turn right onto State Highway 117. Two-tenths of a mile farther on, bear right onto East Street, following the sign to Mingo.

Mingo is only slightly larger than Ira and bills itself as "A Town for All Seasons." The Chichaqua Valley Trail head here has a roofed pavilion, playground equipment, and a portable toilet. On the western edge of town, surrounded by empty storefronts, is Ozzy's, which serves frozen pizza along with liquid refreshments.

You're through with hills now. Jump on the Chichaqua Valley Trail and turn left, heading east. The trail runs on a rail line abandoned in 1983 by the Chicago & Northwestern Railroad and the grade never exceeds two percent. Intermittent woods line the trail as it weaves between the hills.

14.9 miles. Cross a tiny bridge, then get another look at the junked cars of Ira. (They don't look much better from the trail than they did from the road.) At the trailhead, there's a sign warning, "Some days you are the bug, some days you are the windshield." The trailhead also has a pit toilet and water fountain.

Leaving Ira, the trail runs parallel to Turkey Creek, going slightly uphill through the narrow valley. There's a stretch of marshland and forest along the meandering creek on your right; on the left, grassland rises up the hillside to a forest at the top.

17.6 miles. Cross County Road S52 and the grade becomes slightly more noticeable. There are occasional benches along the trail for rest stops. Trees line the trail now, with only occasional breaks to give you views of the hills. Keep an eye out on the left for llamas—you may see some of them out grazing on the hillside.

19.6 miles. The trail crosses County Road F17 (State Highway 223) and enters Baxter. Another half mile and you're back at the start.

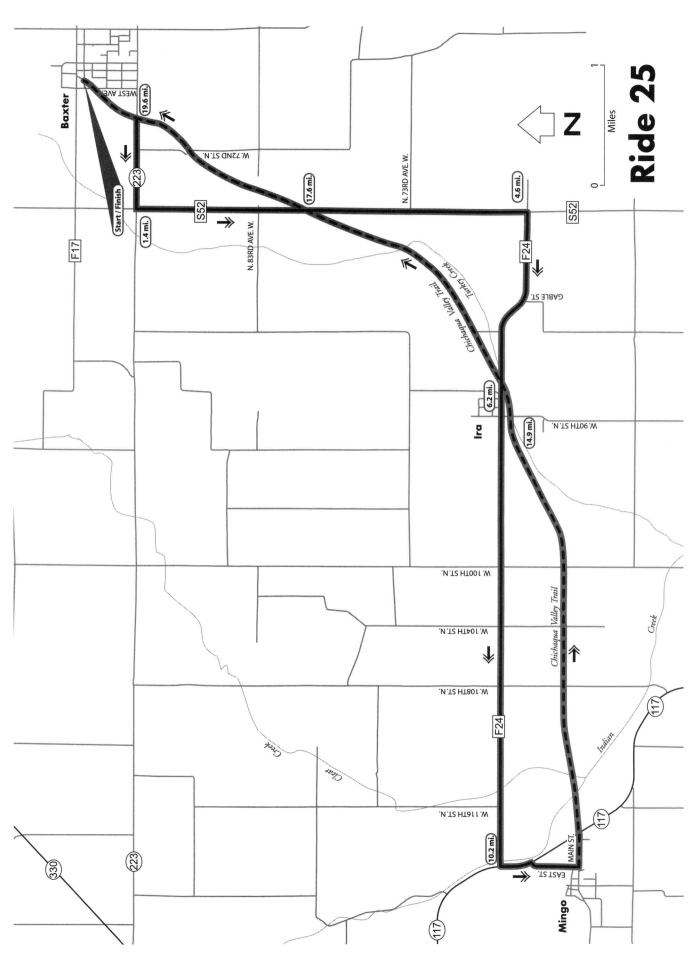

Ride 25

N

Miles

0 1

Baxter

Start / Finish

WEST AVE.

19.6 mi.

223

W. 72ND ST. N.

1.4 mi.

S52

17.6 mi.

N. 73RD AVE. W.

4.6 mi.

S52

N. 83RD AVE. W.

Chichaqua Valley Trail

Turkey Creek

F24

GABLE ST.

6.2 mi.

Ira

14.9 mi.

W. 90TH ST. N.

W. 100TH ST. N.

W. 104TH ST. N.

Chichaqua Valley Trail

W. 108TH ST. N.

F24

Clear

Creek

Indian

Creek

117

117

W. 116TH ST. N.

10.2 mi.

MAIN ST.

EAST ST.

Mingo

117

F17

223

330

RIDE 26
Saylorville Lake Swooping

LOCATION: Neal Smith Trail along the east side of Saylorville Lake
DISTANCE: 14.1 miles one way
SURFACE: Paved trail
TERRAIN: Lots of short hills
DIFFICULTY: Moderate
SERVICES:
  Restrooms: At start, recreation areas and campgrounds along the route, and finish
  Water: Same
  Food: Big Creek Beach concession stand, off-route in Polk City
  Camping: Campgrounds around Saylorville Lake
  Lodging: Motels in Ankeny
  Bike Shop: Polk City Bike Rental, Third Street, Polk City
STARTING POINT: Big Creek Beach at Big Creek State Park, south of Sheldahl

This ride takes you over the tremendously scenic trail above Saylorville Lake, an Army Corps of Engineers flood-control project on the Des Moines River. The ride has lots of short climbs and steep descents to give your gears plenty of use, and lots of twists and turns to test your bike-handling skills.

0.0 miles. Take off from the concession stand at Big Creek Beach, following the 10-foot-wide asphalt trail south. You leave the beach area quickly and travel through a corridor flanked by trees and shrubs. Picnic areas abound on this stretch, each with restrooms, shaded tables, and benches. The winding trail affords lots of views of Big Creek Lake as you pedal over gentle rises and falls, warming up for the hills to come.

You'll pass the Butterfly Garden just before you reach ride's end at the Saylorville Lake Visitor Center.

2.7 miles. The trail merges onto the park road to cross the dam across Big Creek. On the far side, turn right with the trail as it leaves the state park. The trail narrows to 8 feet wide and the surface gets bumpy from frost heaves, underground roots, and the like. This part of the trail was built over 20 years ago and is showing its age. It follows Big Creek to its junction with the Des Moines River, then ducks into the woods.

The trail gets seriously twisty as you cross a series of trestles high above arms of Saylorville Lake. Watch your speed! The hills are steep, the curves are sharp, and the trail is narrow. It's an exhilarating ride, but you have to stay alert.

5.1 miles. As you approach a trail intersection, you can see the Polk City water tower ahead. The intersecting trail goes off to the left to a gravel road. Stay on the main trail to pass a sports complex, then duck through an underpass beneath the road.

6.1 miles. Another spur trail takes off to the left, leading to a small trailhead parking lot and the road into Polk City. In about a half mile, you get your first glimpse of Saylorville Lake through a screen of trees on your right. Enter the Sandpiper Recreation Area, one of many areas set up to take advantage of the recreational opportunities on the lake. There's a swimming beach here if you're ready for a dip.

7.3 miles. The trail emerges from the woods into a boat storage area. Pedal through the marina and turn left, heading out the driveway. In the distance, you can see the Saylorville Lake Dam and, beyond it, the towers of Des Moines. At the triangle, bear left and head for the exit, then turn right at the edge of the parking lot and pick up the trail again.

There's a nice downhill before you cross another arm of the lake and ride past the marina's anchorage. Most of the boats are houseboats and party barges, with a couple of sailboats for variety. The trail surface is very rough through here and you pay for the downhill with a steep climb out of the anchorage.

8.1 miles. After another wooded stretch, the trail comes into the Prairie Flower Recreation Area parking lot. Bear right onto the road, ride past picnic shelters and a children's play area, and turn left at the stop sign to follow the bike route. Prairie flowers are everywhere as you pedal away from the campground.

9.1 miles. At the T intersection, follow the road right as it loops through another campground, then turn right onto the shaded trail once more. Soon you come out into the Oak Grove Recreation Area's parking lot. Continue straight through the lot and along the park road to the campground entrance, then cross the street and turn left onto the trail again. Turn right at the next trail intersection (straight ahead is a dead-end road) and pump uphill to the Red Feather Prairie area, a plateau overlooking the lake. It's a beautiful ride through the tall grasses and flowers as the trail winds around the prairie, then slips back into the shade of the woods.

13.8 miles. Pass the Butterfly Garden, replete with flowers of all colors and descriptions.

14.0 miles. The trail comes up onto the road and you turn right to end the ride at the Saylorville Lake Visitor Center.

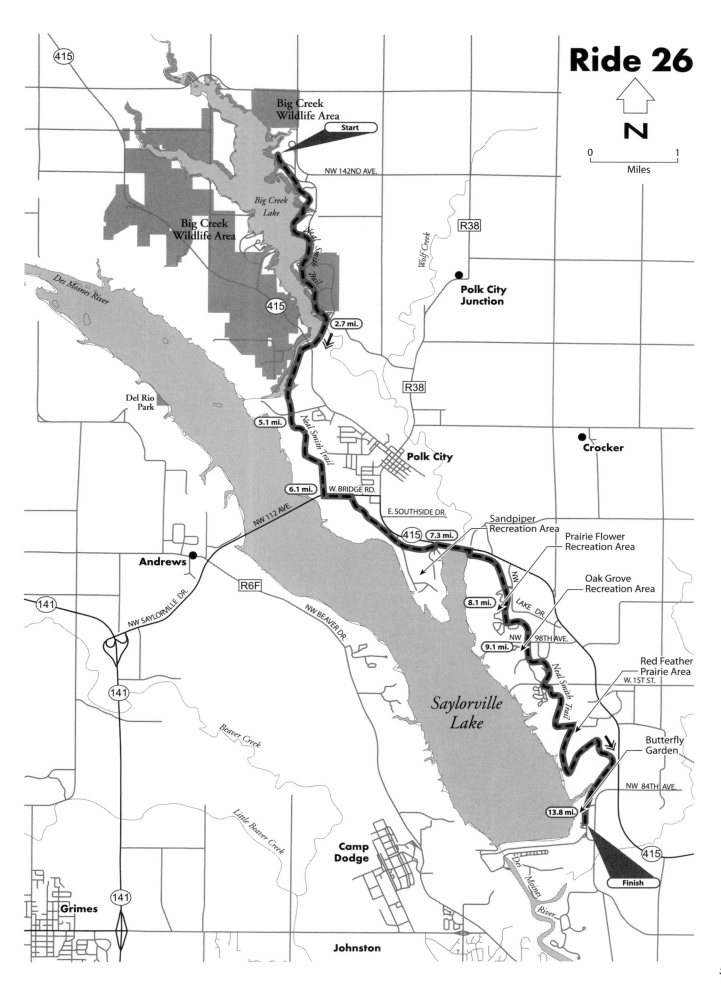

Ride 26

N

0 _____ 1
Miles

Big Creek
Wildlife Area

Start

NW 142ND AVE.

Big Creek Lake

Big Creek
Wildlife Area

Neal Smith Trail

415

2.7 mi.

Wolf Creek

R38

Polk City
Junction

R38

Des Moines River

Del Rio
Park

5.1 mi.

Neal Smith Trail

Polk City

Crocker

6.1 mi. W. BRIDGE RD.

E. SOUTHSIDE DR.

NW 112 AVE.

Sandpiper
Recreation Area

Prairie Flower
Recreation Area

415 7.3 mi.

Andrews

R6F

NW SAYLORVILLE DR.

NW BEAVER DR.

8.1 mi.

NW LAKE DR.

Oak Grove
Recreation Area

141

NW 98TH AVE.

9.1 mi. NW

Red Feather
Prairie Area

W. 1ST ST.

141

Beaver Creek

*Saylorville
Lake*

Neal Smith Trail

Butterfly
Garden

Little Beaver Creek

NW 84TH AVE.

13.8 mi.

Camp
Dodge

Des Moines River

415

Grimes

141

Finish

Johnston

RIDE 27
Cruisin' In Clive

LOCATION: Clive Greenbelt Trail in Clive
DISTANCE: 12.4 miles out and back
SURFACE: Paved trail
TERRAIN: Flat, winding trail through floodplain forest
DIFFICULTY: Child's play
SERVICES:
  Restrooms: At start/finish and along trail
  Water: Same
  Food: At start
  Camping: Walnut Woods State Park, Des Moines
  Lodging: Motels in Urbandale
  Bike Shop: Many in Des Moines
STARTING POINT: Casey's General Store on the southwest corner of the intersection of Woodland Avenue and Hickman Road (U.S. Highway 6) in Clive

Here's a short, gorgeous ride through the woods along Walnut Creek. It's hard to believe you're in the thick of the Des Moines metro area as you cruise the Clive Greenbelt Trail, listening to birds and the soft rush of the creek over shallow ripples.

0.0 miles. From the Casey's General Store at the corner of Woodland Avenue and Hickman Road, turn right (south) on Woodland Avenue and ride into the Woodlands housing development. The road curves right to become Lakeshore Drive, but you continue straight ahead onto the trail that leads out of the curve. Coast down the hill into Walnut Creek's valley.

At the bottom of the hill, turn left at the T intersection and head east along the Clive Greenbelt Trail. There's a beautiful buffer strip of wildflowers between the trail and the backyard of a very large, expensive-looking house. Continue down a slight incline between trees, tall grasses and shrubs. There are lots of raspberries along here for the picking.

0.5 miles. Go straight at the trail intersection; the trail coming in from the left is a connection to the Raccoon River Valley Trail. You'll note some very swanky homes on your right, but the woods quickly block your view of them. Ignore the trail coming in from the right—it goes to that housing development. A short distance later, you cross Walnut Creek for the first time.

The Clive Greenbelt Trail was one of the first trails built in the Des Moines area, and it's showing its age. Frost and underground roots have buckled the trail's surface—keep an eye out for the bumps so you're not bucked off your bike. This is a high-population area and lots of people use this trail. It's not a place for speed—there are many blind curves and you never know when some pedestrians or leashed dogs might be around the next one. Stay alert, be courteous, and be careful, especially if you're riding in the early morning, late afternoon, or on a weekend.

It's easy to see why the trail's so popular: It's a beautiful, winding ride through the forest. The trail is dappled with sun filtered through the trees, which also tend to dampen the sounds of traffic in the distance. It's easy to forget you're in a city.

2.2 miles. Pass a spur trail that goes to 108th Street and Lincoln Avenue, then a second one to the same neighborhood. You skirt a broad meadow, a prairie restoration project, on your left. More than 30 species of native grasses and wildflowers are planted here, filling the area with color.

As you slip back into the woods, a sign says you're entering the Greenbelt Park Forest and Woodlands, a 180-acre area of protected forest with oak, walnut, cottonwood, and box elder trees. The trail winds past a small playground and crosses Walnut Creek again. Walnut Creek is considered a warm, low-water stream. It holds more than 20 species of fish, according to another trailside sign.

2.9 miles. There's a water fountain here where you can refresh yourself without dismounting. It's very handy! Continue east on the trail, passing several intersections with feeder trails; the main trail is obvious. There are lots of curves, making for a fun ride as you slalom through them.

4.2 miles. Pass a small trailhead with picnic benches and playground equipment, but no sign of restrooms or water. You've come out of the woods again, and now some commercial/industrial properties remind you of the surrounding city. The trail crosses the creek yet again, goes under 86th Street, and slips back into the woods. It's not long before you're back in the open, however, passing a group of storage tanks on the left, then riding through the back lots of businesses.

5.4 miles. Cross a small bridge, pass a couple of trailside benches, and go beneath a road lined with commercial establishments, then turn right at the trail intersection to ride down behind the Burger King, still following the creek's course.

5.8 miles. Enter a lovely park area with a playground, picnic benches, restrooms, and a baseball field. The trail is very rough through here. Ignore all the intersecting trails and continue along with Walnut Creek on your right.

6.2 miles. The trail ends abruptly at Center Street, near its junction with 65th Street. Though you probably wish this lovely trail could go on forever, you have to turn around and retrace the route to your starting point.

Watch out for pedestrians and others on this popular trail.

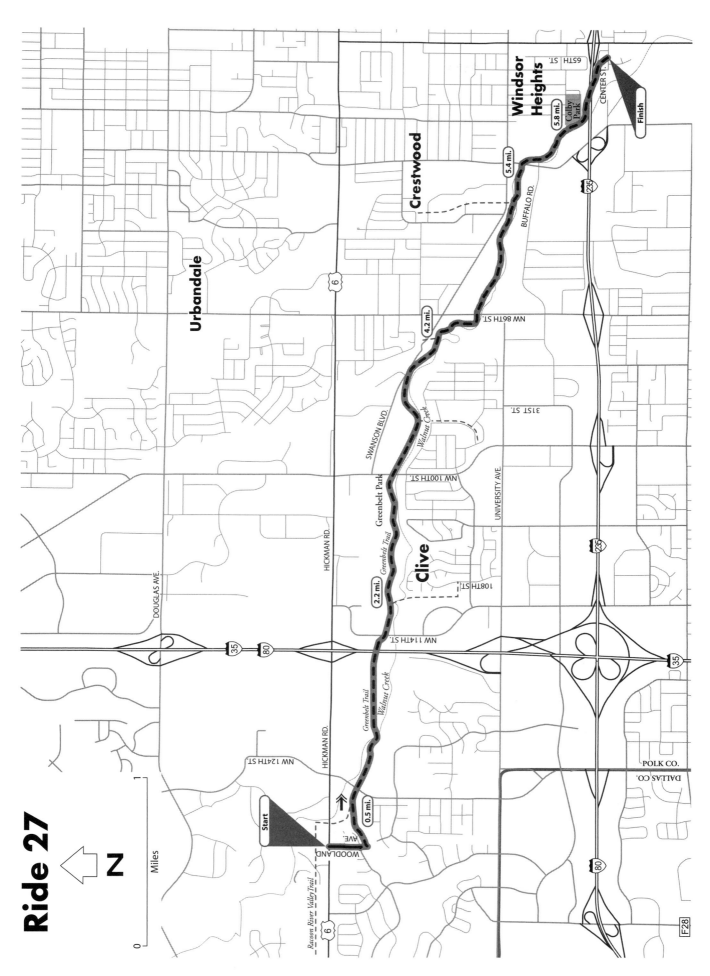

Ride 27

N

Miles
0   1

Racoon River Valley Trail

6

Start

NW 124TH ST.

WOODLAND AVE.

0.5 mi.

Greenbelt Trail

Walnut Creek

HICKMAN RD.

35
80

NW 114TH ST.

Clive

2.2 mi.

Greenbelt Trail

Greenbelt Park

108TH ST.

NW 108TH ST.

NW 100TH ST.

DOUGLAS AVE.

HICKMAN RD.

6

SWANSON BLVD.

Walnut Creek

31ST ST.

UNIVERSITY AVE.

235

35

Urbandale

4.2 mi.

NW 86TH ST.

Crestwood

5.4 mi.

BUFFALO RD.

235

DALLAS CO.
POLK CO.

80

Windsor
Heights

5.8 mi.

Colby
Park

65TH ST.

CENTER ST.

Finish

F28

RIDE 28
Lots of Loops Ride

LOCATION: County roads and the Raccoon River Valley
Trail between Adel and Panora
DISTANCE: 49.4-mile loop; can be cut in half
SURFACE: Paved trail and roads
TERRAIN: Essentially flat on the trail, gentle swells on roads
with some steep descents and climbs at river crossings
DIFFICULTY: Moderate
SERVICES:
    Restrooms: Businesses in Adel, trailhead and businesses
in Redfield, businesses in Panora, trailhead in Linden
    Water: Same
    Food: Restaurants and convenience stores in Adel,
Redfield, and Panora
    Camping: Island Park, Adel; Lennon Mills State Wildlife
Area, Panora
    Lodging: Bed and breakfast in Adel, motels in Waukee
and Urbandale
    Bike Shop: Classic Bicycles, Inc., Sportsmans Club Road,
Adel; several in Des Moines and West Des Moines
STARTING POINT: Subway Restaurant parking lot at the
corner of U.S. Route 6 (Greene Street) and U.S. Highway
169 (South Eighth Street) in Adel

Don't let the mileage deter you from this figure-eight
ride. You can shorten it by doing only the top or bottom loop.
The top loop of the "8"—between Panora and Redfield—
includes the prettiest section of the Raccoon River Valley Trail
and the best ice cream stop of the ride.

0.0 miles. From the back of the parking lot at the
Subway Restaurant in Adel, head west (left) on the Raccoon
River Valley Trail. Turn right onto 11th Street, the third road
from your starting point, ride five blocks, and turn left onto
Grove Street. Pedal another four blocks on Grove and hang a
right onto 15th Street.

A nice downhill speeds you out of town and across
Butler Creek. As you climb up from the creek, 15th Street
bends west and becomes County Road F51. Gentle swells of
land roll off to the horizons, giving a false impression of flat-
ness—you can't see the waterways that have carved deep valleys through here, but you'll encounter some very noticeable
grades as you cross them.

The asphalt-paved road is very smooth, straight as a line
of type, and nearly devoid of traffic. You smile at a couple of
beautiful red-brick farmhouses and a Victorian place that's
downright gorgeous, then frown at a gas pipeline pumping
station that sticks up like a wart on Mother Earth's face.

9.6 miles. Turn left on County Road P46 (El Paso Avenue)
to head south. This turns into First Street and takes you downhill into Redfield. The place was originally called New Ireland,
but a man named James Redfield bought up most of the town
and, in 1860, gave it his name.

12.5 miles. Just past the Dexfield Diner & Pub (good
food there!), turn right onto Thomas Street. Pass the town
park, cross the Raccoon River Valley Trail, and bear left to go
over the Middle Raccoon River. (You can turn left onto the
trail to cut this ride short and head back to Adel; pick up the
narrative at 39.4 miles)

Climb from the river in a series of steps, with respites
between rises—the last quarter mile is the steepest part of the
climb. Thomas Street is now County Road F59 traveling west
over the plateau between the South and Middle branches of
the Raccoon River. The ride is pretty and mostly flat, but the
road's expansion cracks are real butt-bumpers.

19.8 miles. Turn right onto County Road P28 to head
north. There's a spectacular view through a crease between
the hills here. County Road P28 jogs right, then left, then
right, working its way north and west. There are lots of wooded
areas, welcome variations to the corn and bean fields.

26.0 miles. After a long, fast descent, cross the Middle
Raccoon River again, then make another serious climb back to
the plateau. When you crest the hill, you'll see Panora ahead.

28.0 miles. County Road P28 becomes Third Street as
you coast downhill into Panora. Turn right on Clay Street to
reach the Raccoon River Valley Trail at Heritage Park. Turn
right, heading southeast on the trail.

The trail runs behind grain bins and the elevator,
through backyards and across city streets. As you go by TJ's
Sandwich Shop & Ice Cream Parlor (good food, low prices),
stop at the Trail Pass box and fork over two dollars for a day
pass. The money goes directly to trail maintenance.

You ride through a green tunnel of overlapping tree
branches for about two miles, and the shade is welcome. The
trail is basically flat, but beset by poorly sealed cracks and
frost heaves (they *need* your two dollar trail fee!). After about
four miles, you reach a repaved section that's smooth as glass.

33.8 miles. The woods back off as you ride through
Linden, a small town that seems to be getting smaller. The
trailhead here has a portable toilet and picnic tables. There's a
tendency to zone out as you cruise this smooth, straight, flat
trail, but don't fall into it: The shoulders are soft and if you
stray off the trail you're liable to take a serious spill.

38.5 miles. You've been playing leapfrog with a stream,
crossing and recrossing it; now it flows into the Middle
Raccoon River on your right. Just ahead is a good-sized rasp-
berry patch.

39.4 miles. Cross County Road F59 in Redfield. The trail
cuts diagonally through the city blocks, runs by the grain bins
and elevator, then past the old railroad depot that's been
spruced up as a trailhead. There's a snacks-and-soda concession here on weekends.

Coming out of town, the trail passes the Glen-Gery
Brick Plant, revealing why Redfield's downtown has all those
brick buildings. There are tall-grass prairie remnants along
the trail ahead. This type of prairie used to cover hundreds of
thousands of square miles; now there are fewer than 10,000
acres of it in all of Iowa.

43.7 miles. This used to be Kennedy Station, a commercial center that sprang up when the railroad was built. Trains
were the main transportation for goods and people, but as
roads were improved in the 1920s and '30s, Kennedy died out.

48.5 miles. On the outskirts of Adel, you pass an
enormous brickyard with stacks of bricks in all colors. Watch
out for the road crossings as you pedal the last mile to your
starting point: The curb cuts are worse than speed bumps.

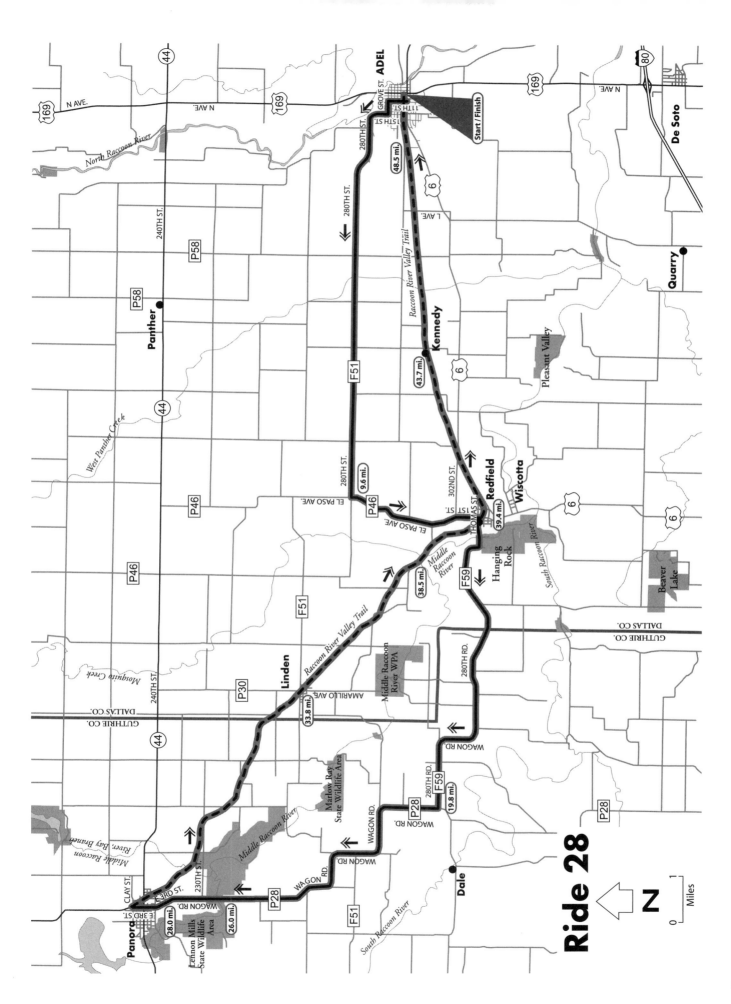

Ride 28

N

0 | 1
Miles

RIDE 29
Ride of the Swans

LOCATION: State and county roads and the Great Western Trail between Martensdale and Cumming
DISTANCE: 21.5-mile loop
SURFACE: Paved trail and roads
TERRAIN: Flat trail, gentle rises on roads
DIFFICULTY: Easy
SERVICES:
> **Restrooms:** At start/finish, convenience store in Norwalk, mile 17.2 on Great Western Trail
> **Water:** At start/finish, convenience store in Norwalk, and trailside rest area at mile 18.0
> **Food:** Convenience store in Norwalk
> **Camping:** Walnut Woods State Park, Des Moines
> **Lodging:** Motels in Des Moines
> **Bike Shop:** Several in Des Moines
> **STARTING POINT:** Great Western Trail head at City Park on Iowa Avenue/Inwood Street in Martensdale

Rails that Became Trails

The Rails-to-Trails movement has certainly benefited from the work of A. B. Stickney of Minnesota, the man who built the Chicago Great Western Railroad. (Stickney's given name was Alpheus Bede; it's little wonder that his initials became his moniker.)

Stickney's first railroad was the Minnesota and Northwestern, built in 1885 to run from Saint Paul, Minnesota, to the Iowa state line. In 1887, Stickney combined that line with another—the Chicago, Saint Paul & Kansas City —and five years later he added another company to create the Chicago Great Western Railroad. By 1903, the Chicago Great Western connected Saint Paul, Chicago, Kansas City, and Omaha. The railroad's three main lines radiated from Oelwein, in northeastern Iowa.

The Chicago Great Western was never a powerhouse in the world of railroads. It was a latecomer to the highly competitive Midwestern region, and was primarily a bridge carrier, transporting freight between gaps in other, larger rail networks. After Stickney's retirement in 1908, its viability spiraled slowly downhill. Threatened with bankruptcy, it merged with the Chicago & North Western Railway in 1968; that company was subsequently swallowed by the Union Pacific Railway in 1995.

Today, more miles of the original Chicago Great Western Railroad's right-of-way have been abandoned and converted to trails than remain in service for the Union Pacific. Five of the trails included in this book are on former Chicago Great Western right-of-way: the Heritage Trail (Ride 3), the Butler County Nature Trail and Rolling Prairie Trail (Ride 5), the Chichaqua Valley Trail (Ride 25), and the Great Western Trail (Ride 29). Another half-dozen trails in Iowa also take advantage of the paths that A. B. Stickney laid down.

The steepest hill on this ride goes down! The loop's first half travels roads with light traffic; the second half is on the Great Western Trail, a smooth rail-trail that sweeps through beautiful farm country south of Des Moines.

0.0 miles. From the Great Western Trail head in Martensdale, turn left onto Inwood Street, which quickly changes its name to Iowa Avenue. Pass through the rather moribund business center of Martensdale—there's a post office housed in a trailer, but not much else—and turn left onto State Highway 28, heading north. You're quickly away from town and cruising over shallow hills, enjoying a bucolic panorama of grazing horses and crops sweeping across the land's swells.

3.0 miles. Cruise through a collection of houses that goes by the name of Prole. There are homes springing up all along this road, harbingers of Des Moines' urban sprawl. The road is smooth and traffic is light as you ride between incipient housing developments and the Rolling Hills Public Golf Course.

6.0 miles. You encounter the steepest grade of the ride, a three-quarter-mile *descent* to cross the North River. You can easily hit 30 mph on this slope, and if you push you might make 40. Best of all, you don't have to make a corresponding climb on the other side of the river!

8.4 miles. At the traffic light as you enter Norwalk, turn left onto North Avenue (County Road G14). The Casey's General Store on the corner is the only food source you'll encounter on this ride. North Avenue rises gradually out of the valley, heading west past fields and widely spaced homes. At the summit, you cross a broad, flat plateau with long views on both sides across corn and bean fields. Wildflowers dot the roadside with color.

11.2 miles. On your right is Cumming Orchard, with rows of fruit trees that almost hide a small pond. A family of swans makes its home here; if you take a break and walk over to the pond, you may be lucky enough to catch the adult swans leading their young ones on a swim. They're magnificent birds and the setting is perfect.

12.8 miles. Go straight through the four-way stop at 43rd Street, into the hamlet of Cumming. There's an impressive 19th-century house on the left; on the right is Sweeney's Skylark Gasoline, an antique gas station with walls sided with old license plates.

The Great Western Trail head in Cumming is just a parking lot beside the trail. Turn left onto the trail, heading south.

The Great Western Trail runs on a rail bed constructed in 1887 by the Chicago, Saint Paul & Kansas City Railway. It traverses several prairie remnants and wetlands, and a number of endangered plant species are found within its right-of-way, but you probably won't notice them. You also won't notice the very shallow grades as you cruise through open land with panoramic views. Intermittent trees and shrubs line the trail but offer little shade in this stretch.

14.1 miles. There's a rest bench with an awning at the trail's side, looking out over a nice view. Past that, you cross Badger Creek and ride into some welcome shade.

16.8 miles. On the road, you had that steep descent to cross the North River, but here on the trail you cross the waterway on a high trestle. Thanks to the shallow grade engineered by the railroad builders, you hardly notice there's a valley involved. Less than a half mile from the river, you pass another rest bench and a small clearing with a pit toilet.

18.0 miles. At an intersection with a gravel road, there's another roofed bench for a rest stop, and, surprisingly, a water fountain. The countryside in this stretch of trail is notably hilly, the glacial soils deeply carved by small waterways. The trail clings to the sides of the hills, staying as level as the railway engineers could make it.

21.4 miles. You come through a cool, shady section and into the trailhead at Martensdale, your starting point.

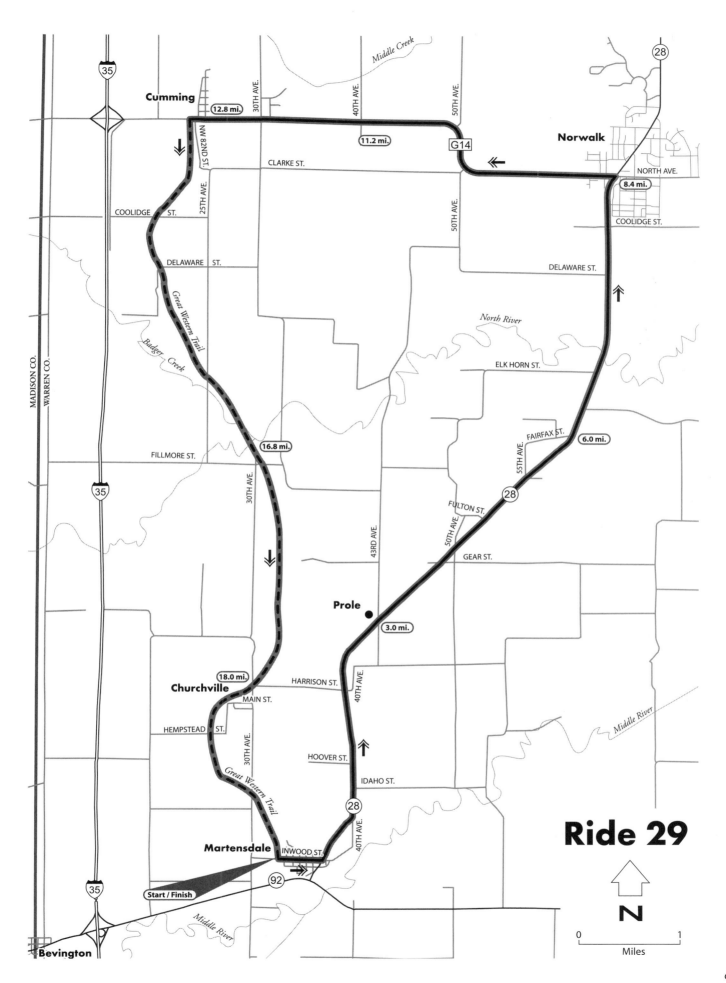

Cumming

12.8 mi.

30TH AVE.

40TH AVE.

50TH AVE.

Middle Creek

28

11.2 mi.

G14

Norwalk

NORTH AVE.

8.4 mi.

CLARKE ST.

NW 82ND ST.

25TH AVE.

COOLIDGE ST.

COOLIDGE ST.

DELAWARE ST.

DELAWARE ST.

Great Western Trail

Badger Creek

North River

50TH AVE.

ELK HORN ST.

FILLMORE ST.

16.8 mi.

30TH AVE.

55TH AVE.

FAIRFAX ST.

6.0 mi.

28

FULTON ST.

50TH AVE.

43RD AVE.

GEAR ST.

Prole

3.0 mi.

MADISON CO.

WARREN CO.

35

35

18.0 mi.

Churchville

HARRISON ST.

40TH AVE.

MAIN ST.

HEMPSTEAD ST.

30TH AVE.

Great Western Trail

HOOVER ST.

IDAHO ST.

28

Middle River

Martensdale

INWOOD ST.

40TH AVE.

92

Start / Finish

Middle River

Bevington

35

Ride 29

N

0   1
Miles

RIDE 30
Lake Red Rock Ramble

LOCATION: Volksweg Trail from Pella to Fifield Recreation Area on Lake Red Rock
DISTANCE: 24.4 miles out and back
SURFACE: Paved city streets and trail
TERRAIN: Many short, steep hills
DIFFICULTY: Moderate
SERVICES:

    Restrooms: At start, businesses in Pella, recreation areas and campgrounds around Red Rock Lake
    Water: Same
    Food: Restaurants, grocery, convenience stores in Pella
    Camping: Several campgrounds around Red Rock Lake
        Lodging: Hotel, motels, and bed and breakfasts in Pella
        Bike Shop: Iowa Bike and Fitness, Main Street, Pella
STARTING POINT: Corner of Main and Franklin streets on the town square in Pella

The Gunfighter from Pella

With its Dutch motif, Pella seems an unlikely hometown for one of the American west's best-known gunfighters. Still, the fact is that Wyatt Earp spent his boyhood there.

The Earp family arrived in Pella when Wyatt was two years old. In addition to farming, Wyatt's father, Nicholas Earp, served as U.S. Provost Marshal of Marion County. Wyatt spent most of his boyhood working on the farm.

When the Civil War began, Wyatt's father and older brothers joined the Union Army, but Wyatt was too young for military duty. He fretted on the family farm until he was fifteen years old, then ran off to join the war. However, the first officer Wyatt encountered when he joined the ranks was his father, who sent him back home to the cornfields.

After the war, Nicholas Earp came home to Pella, sold his farm, organized a wagon train, and took his family west to California. Wyatt returned to the Midwest in 1870, wandering into LaMar, Missouri, where he met and married Urilla Sutherland. In LaMar, he waited tables at his father-in-law's inn and served as constable—the first of many law-enforcement positions he would hold. The tragic death of Urilla within a year of their marriage, however, set Wyatt wandering again.

The line between law breaker and law enforcer was a thin one in the Wild West, and Wyatt spent time on both sides of it as he built his gunfighter's reputation. He eventually settled on the law-enforcement side, and was serving as a U.S. Marshall when he and his brothers, accompanied by the dentist-turned-gunman Doc Holliday, fought their legendary battle at the O.K. Corral in Tombstone, Arizona.

Wyatt Earp died in Los Angeles in 1929. His boyhood home in Pella is now a museum on First Street, a block from the town square.

This out-and-back ride starts from Pella's beautiful town square, which is surrounded by 19th- and early-20th-century storefronts, and follows the Volksweg Trail as it twists and turns, rises and falls through forest and restored prairie along the shore of Lake Red Rock. The climbs will test your thighs—grades range up to seven percent—and the descents will test your brakes.

0.0 miles. From Pella's town square, head south on Main Street. The street is quite wide, and you'll have plenty of room to share with motor traffic. Pella was founded in 1847 by Separatists who emigrated from the Netherlands to escape religious persecution; its Dutch origins are obvious in the windmill on the town square and celebrated each spring in their Tulip Festival.

After about five blocks on Main Street, turn right to go west on University Street. On your right is Central College, founded in 1853; amazingly, there's a working farm on your left, just blocks from downtown!

1.0 miles. The Pella Volksweg Trail begins as a side path on the south side of University at the intersection with Fifth Street. If you decide to ride the side path, use caution: there are lots of driveways crossing the path and you'll be riding against traffic. Watch for cars turning into and exiting the drives. University turns into Idaho Street (County Road T15) as it curves south.

2.9 miles. Bear left onto 198th Place and head downhill. The side path also follows 198th Place and is signed for a 20 mph speed limit: Observe that limit on the trail! There are still a lot of driveways, as well as pedestrians and other cyclists.

A Dutch-style windmill dominates the town square in Pella.

3.9 miles. If you've been riding the road, turn right onto the Volksweg Trail, which crosses here. It curves around the end of a small pond and plunges into the U.S. Army Corps of Engineers management area. The Corps created Lake Red Rock as a flood control project on the Des Moines River. This is the largest body of water in Iowa, and Red Rock Dam controls runoff water from over 12,000 square miles—precipitation in Worthington, Minnesota, ends up coming through this lake.

4.6 miles. After circling the Howell Station Campground, go right at the T to ride along the Des Moines River, heading for the dam. Pass the bridge across the river and when you reach the V in the trail, bear right. (Going left at that V will take you up to the North Tailwater area and the dam's spillway.)

Now the ride turns into a hill climb as you pump up to the level of the lake. You have a little respite, then make another climb to pass the North Overlook Campground and the trail cutoff to Eagle Creek. Sweep through an open area awash in Queen Anne's lace and prairie sunflowers, climb another short rise, then round a curve into a beautiful vista over the lake and dam.

8.0 miles. After more twists, descents, and climbs, you come out of the trees into a tall-grass prairie. The Corps of Engineers maintains approximately 400 acres of tall-grass prairie around the lake. Only 63 acres are native; all the rest is reconstructed.

A seriously steep climb takes you into the Wallushuck Campground. Pass the trail spur into the campground and ride onward to curve around the anchorage in Marina Cove, then through the Marina's parking lot. The road that appears and reappears on your right is County Road G28.

12.2 miles. Trail's end is the Fifield Recreation Area parking lot. There are plans to extend the trail another five miles to the small town of Cordova within the next few years.

You can retrace the route back to Pella or turn right out of this parking lot to get to County Road G28, then turn right and follow that road east to Pella. G28 becomes Washington Street in town. Riding back on the trail, however, is much prettier and much more fun.

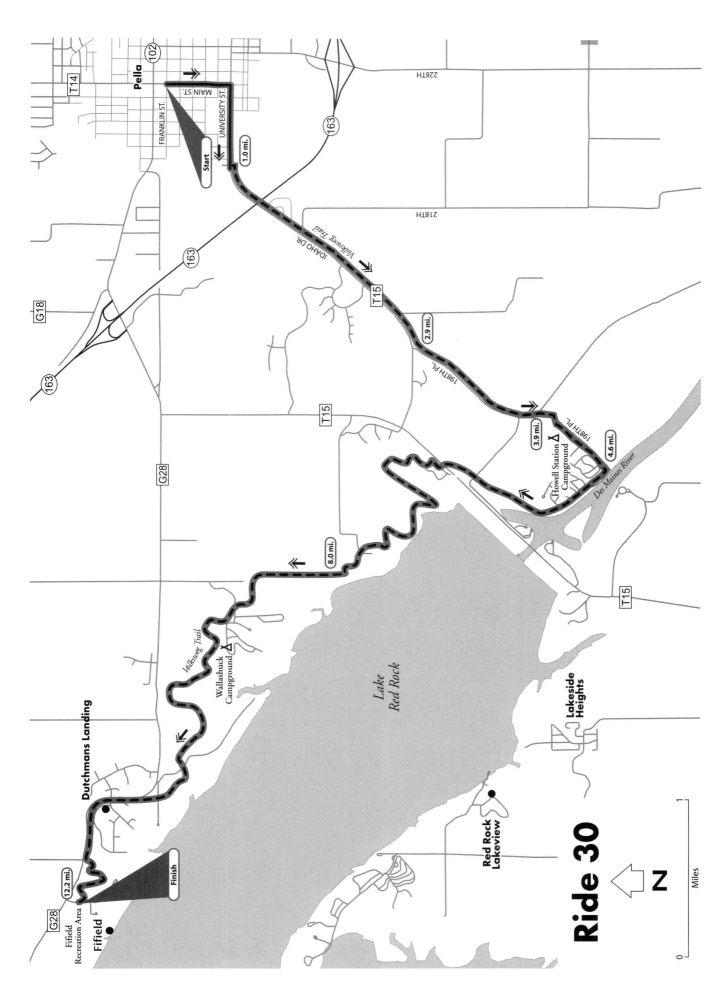

Ride 30

N ←

Miles

RIDE 31
No Bridges Ride

LOCATION: County roads between Winterset and Saint Charles
DISTANCE: 36.5-mile loop
SURFACE: Paved roads
TERRAIN: Hilly, some steep climbs and descents
DIFFICULTY: Moderate to strenuous
SERVICES:
    Restrooms: Businesses in Winterset, outhouse in Peru, convenience stores in Truro and Saint Charles
    Water: Restaurants and convenience stores in Winterset, convenience stores in Truro and Saint Charles
    Food: Restaurants and convenience stores in Winterset, convenience stores in Truro and Saint Charles
    Camping: Pammel State Park, Winterset
    Lodging: Motels and bed and breakfasts in Winterset
    Bike Shop: None nearby
STARTING POINT: Corner of Court Street and John Wayne Drive on the courthouse square in Winterset

The Southern Iowa Drift Plain

The largest landform region in Iowa is the Southern Iowa Drift Plain, which comprises the southern half of the state between the Loess Hills on the west and the Mississippi Alluvial Plain on the east.

Early glaciers swept through here and left behind a thick layer of glacial drift, topped by loess soils. The landscape was similar to that of the Des Moines Lobe—mostly flat with occasional humps of moraines. But in this area, hundreds of thousands of years of erosion and stream development have carved through the soil and drift.

Rivers, streams, and creeks form a pattern of valleys that looks like the branches of a tree. The region is very hilly, but the hills have been created from the top down, by erosion—a giant straightedge placed across the tops of the hills would lie almost flat.

Ride 31: No Bridges Ride, gives you a good sense of this, with long stretches of flat land atop the plateau, punctuated by steep dips into the valleys. On Ride 32: Iowa's First Rail-Trail, you'll follow a grade-free trail through the valleys, then climb over the hills on the way back.

The farther south you go, the deeper the valleys get—and the hillier the ride becomes. Ride 33: Almost Missouri Ride, and Ride 34: Road Apple Ride, will give your legs a serious workout while treating your eyes to outstanding scenery as you pedal across the hills and valleys.

Madison County's covered bridges achieved national attention thanks to Robert Waller's best-seller *The Bridges of Madison County*, and the movie starring Clint Eastwood and Meryl Streep. However, the bridges are all on rough, dusty gravel roads that are poor for biking, so this ride bypasses them in favor of smooth pavement and great scenery.

0.0 miles. Hop on your bike and head south on John Wayne Drive through the business district surrounding the Madison County courthouse square. The Northside Café, where one of the movie scenes was shot, is on the square (Clint Eastwood sat on the fourth stool from the front). You hardly get rolling before you pass a sign that points to John Wayne's birthplace. The Duke grew up in Winterset—his home, now filled with memorabilia, has been turned into a museum.

Bear left at Summit Street and continue south on County Road P71, enjoying the downhill to cross the Middle River. The road name changes to Clark Tower Road and you have about a mile of easy, mostly flat cruising along the river valley. Your first climb will get your heart rate up, but once you've gotten out of the river valley, the land rolls over pleasant, gentle grades. Traffic is very light and very courteous. This whole route is signed with "Shared Roadway" signs bearing the outline of a bicycle—motorists expect to see cyclists here.

6.5 miles. Turn left onto County Road G68 (Peru Road), heading east towards Peru (pronounced PEE-rue). You're on the plateau now, with a stunning panorama of the surrounding farmland.

10.8 miles. Pass the Peru Cemetery on your right. In another quarter-mile, you drop down a seven percent grade for almost a mile before you hit a stop sign in East Peru. There aren't any businesses here, but there *is* a small town park with a unisex outhouse. In 1872, a farmer named Jesse Hiatt discovered an unusual apple tree on his farm north of the village, with fruits of remarkable flavor. He entered the apples in the Missouri State Fair in 1893 and the judge declared it "delicious." The name stuck, and the Delicious apple is now a mainstay on grocery shelves around the country. The original tree is still standing.

County Road G68 becomes Emerson Street and is joined by County Road R21 as you cross Clanton Creek and start on a very steep climb back to the plateau (that seven percent descent you enjoyed demands a price).

13.1 miles. County Road R21 goes straight, but you turn left, following County Road G68 east. Cruise over the gentle curves of the land, enjoying long vistas of hayfields and wooded groves. The corn and soybeans that cover most of Iowa aren't much in evidence here: most of the land is in pasture or hayfields.

16.6 miles. Welcome to Truro, where County Road G68 is named North Street and is joined by County Road G64. There's a convenience store and a consolidated school, but not much else along the road. About a mile outside town, North Street merges with County Road R35 (Truro Road) and turns left.

18.5 miles. Continue north with County Road R35, heading for Saint Charles. The road is mostly flat, flanked by corn and bean fields. You'll see lots of goldfinches darting across the road in bursts of yellow, and you have an expansive view across the hilltops.

23.3 miles. Roll into Saint Charles and up to the stop sign at Main Street. Going to your right takes you into the business district, where there's a convenience store. Your route, however, turns left, heading west on Main Street (County Road G50).

Saint Charles is very small, so you're quickly out of town, cruising downhill to cross Clanton Creek again. The climb from the creek is spread out over two miles in a series of steps. Then County Road G50 becomes Saint Charles Road and leads you over two miles of flats through more lovely country, and ends with a steep descent into the Middle River valley.

34.7 miles. At the stop sign, go right onto Clark Tower Road (County Road P71). The little settlement here is the site of Madison County's first gristmill, built in 1850 and long since fallen to ruin. Climb the hill you came down at the ride's beginning and bear right onto First Street (John Wayne Drive) to get back to the starting point.

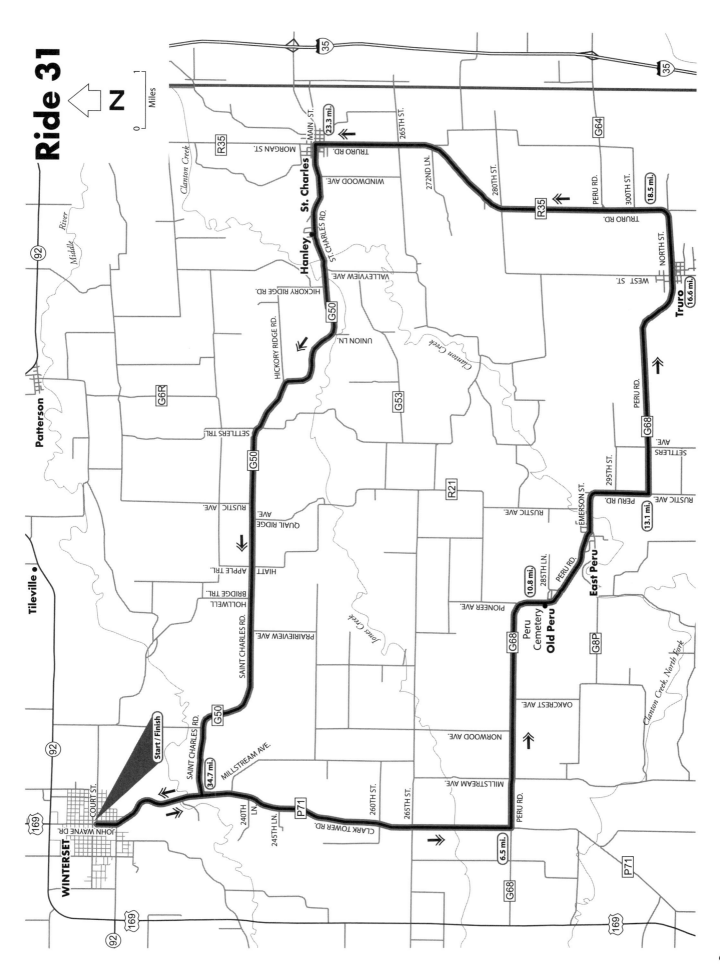

Ride 31

N

0 | | Miles

Patterson

Tileville •

WINTERSET

Start / Finish

Hanley
St. Charles

Truro

Old Peru
East Peru

Peru Cemetery

34.7 mi.

23.3 mi.

18.5 mi.

16.6 mi.

13.1 mi.

10.8 mi.

6.5 mi.

MAIN ST.
MORGAN ST.
WINDWOOD AVE.
TRURO RD.
265TH ST.
272ND LN.
280TH ST.
300TH ST.
PERU RD.
NORTH ST.
WEST ST.
SETTLERS AVE.
RUSTIC AVE.
295TH ST.
EMERSON ST.
PERU RD.
285TH LN.
PIONEER AVE.
OAKCREST AVE.
NORWOOD AVE.
MILLSTREAM AVE.
PERU RD.
265TH ST.
260TH ST.
CLARK TOWER RD.
245TH LN.
240TH LN.
MILLSTREAM AVE.
SAINT CHARLES RD.
PRAIRIEVIEW AVE.
HOLLWELL BRIDGE TRL.
HIATT APPLE TRL.
QUAIL RIDGE AVE.
RUSTIC AVE.
SETTLERS TRL.
HICKORY RIDGE RD.
UNION LN.
VALLEYVIEW AVE.
ST. CHARLES RD.
JOHN WAYNE DR.
COURT ST.

Clanton Creek
Middle River
Jones Creek
Clanton Creek
Clanton Creek, North Fork

R35
G50
G6R
G53
R21
G68
G8P
G64
P71

35
92
169

65

RIDE 32
Iowa's First Rail-Trail

LOCATION: Cinder Path, county, state, and federal roads between Chariton and Derby
DISTANCE: 23.4-mile loop
SURFACE: Crushed-limestone trail, paved roads
TERRAIN: Flat trail, rolling hills with two steep climbs on the road
DIFFICULTY: Moderate
SERVICES:
    Restrooms: Businesses in Chariton, outhouse on Cinder Path at .2 miles.
    Water: Businesses in Chariton
    Food: Restaurants, convenience stores, and grocery in Chariton
    Camping: Red Haw State Park, Chariton
    Lodging: Motels in Chariton
    Bike Shop: Connecticut Yankee Pedaler, Court Street, Chariton
STARTING POINT: The Cinder Path trailhead on the south side of U.S. Business Route 35, on the western outskirts of Chariton

Ghost Towns

State Historical Society records show that there may be as many as 2,000 ghost towns in Iowa. These ghost towns are former hamlets now marked only by a forgotten foundation or a lilac bush and some trees, or once-thriving villages that have melted down to a few houses and boarded-up commercial buildings.

The reasons for their decline and abandonment are many. In some cases, a local industry failed and, with no work, the residents moved on and the business district withered and died. The placement of rail lines in the 19th and early 20th centuries created new towns and doomed those that were bypassed; then, as railroad traffic declined and rail lines were abandoned, many of the "depot towns" also disappeared.

In southern Iowa, more ghost towns are a-making through the consolidation of small farms into huge ones, a lack of diversified industry, and depopulation. The town of Derby, through which Cinder Path travels, once had a fleet of three school buses to gather children for the town's schools. The buses are gone now, along with the schools; even the garage that serviced the buses is abandoned. In another decade, as its aging population dies or moves to retirement venues, Derby may be marked only by a couple of rusting grain bins and a few surviving—but decaying—homes.

The Rails-to-Trails movement was in its infancy when the Cinder Path was developed in the early 1970s. This ride on Iowa's first rail-trail takes you through forests and wetlands along the Chariton River to the fading town of Derby. The return trip travels the roads over rolling hills back to Chariton.

0.0 miles. There's no water source on this route, so fill your water bottles at one of the restaurants or convenience stores on U.S. Business Route 34 before you start. Head southwest on the crushed-limestone Cinder Path, past the Shelton Marsh. You'll be next to this marsh for the next mile, until it drains into the Chariton River.

A short way up the trail is a wayside with a unisex outhouse. Trees shade the trail; through them you catch glimpses of the marsh on your left, farm fields on the right. The trail surface is well drained even in wet weather, but it's rough in places—watch for holes and bumps.

1.2 miles. Cross the first of sixteen wooden trail bridges over small waterways running into the Chariton River, which is hidden by the woods on your left. The trail is slightly uphill, and straight as a two-by-four. Its first noticeable curve is about a half mile away. It's cool here in the riparian woods, and quiet but for the soft crunch of your tires on the trail.

2.7 miles. You have to maneuver around a barrier to cross a dirt road—you can get through on the right. There are wires strung across the trail at just about every road crossing; apparently, there have been some problems keeping motor vehicles off the trail. Soon, on your left, a small bridge crosses the trailside ditch to a bench sheltered by a roof. It looks like an idyllic resting place, as does the octagonal gazebo you pass in another mile.

6.1 miles. Here's a real rarity: a covered bridge on a trail! It's very picturesque, though a bit incongruous out here in the middle of the woods, where only bicycles and pedestrians will cross it.

7.0 miles. You've been riding parallel to the Chariton River and now you cross it, with a nice view to your left of a farm up on the hill. The trail turns south, away from the river, keeping to the woods. About a mile and a quarter farther, after crossing County Road H50, the trail surface deteriorates somewhat. Keep a watchful eye on your path.

9.5 miles. You emerge from the woods onto a gravel road in Derby. If you'd rather not tackle the hilly roads back to Chariton, turn around here and retrace your route. Otherwise, turn right onto the gravel, then go left onto the paved Front Street.

Derby is a dying town. Only the post office remains open amid the boarded-up buildings of its erstwhile business district. Follow Front Street to Broad and turn right, then make another right turn onto Chariton Avenue (County Road H50), and Derby falls behind, continuing its descent to oblivion.

11.0 miles. County Road H50 crosses Cinder Path after a long, shallow downhill, then starts a long, gradual climb. The next two and a half miles of rolling hills give your legs and gears a workout, but then you have four flat miles on top of the plateau. There are a number of Old Order Amish in this area, so keep an eye out for Amish farmers working their fields with horse-drawn machinery.

18.0 miles. At the T, turn left onto State Highway 14. You'll encounter some traffic on State Highway 14, particularly during commute hours, as you climb over more hills. There are expansive views all around of hayfields and croplands. Farm buildings dot the hilltops above wooded valleys.

20.9 miles. Cross the Chariton River on the outskirts of Chariton, then make the ride's steepest climb as you enter town. A curb and gutter widens the lane, so cars have plenty of room to pass you safely. Cross the overpass above U.S. Highway 34, then go through an underpass beneath the railroad. Turn left onto Grand Street to ride past gorgeous 19th-century homes and a very impressive stone Masonic Temple.

22.5 miles. Turn left onto Court Street. Pass the Lucas County Courthouse, then coast downhill to the trailhead where you started. Don't take the descent too fast; a half mile down, there's a Dairy Queen that may have an ice cream sundae with your name on it.

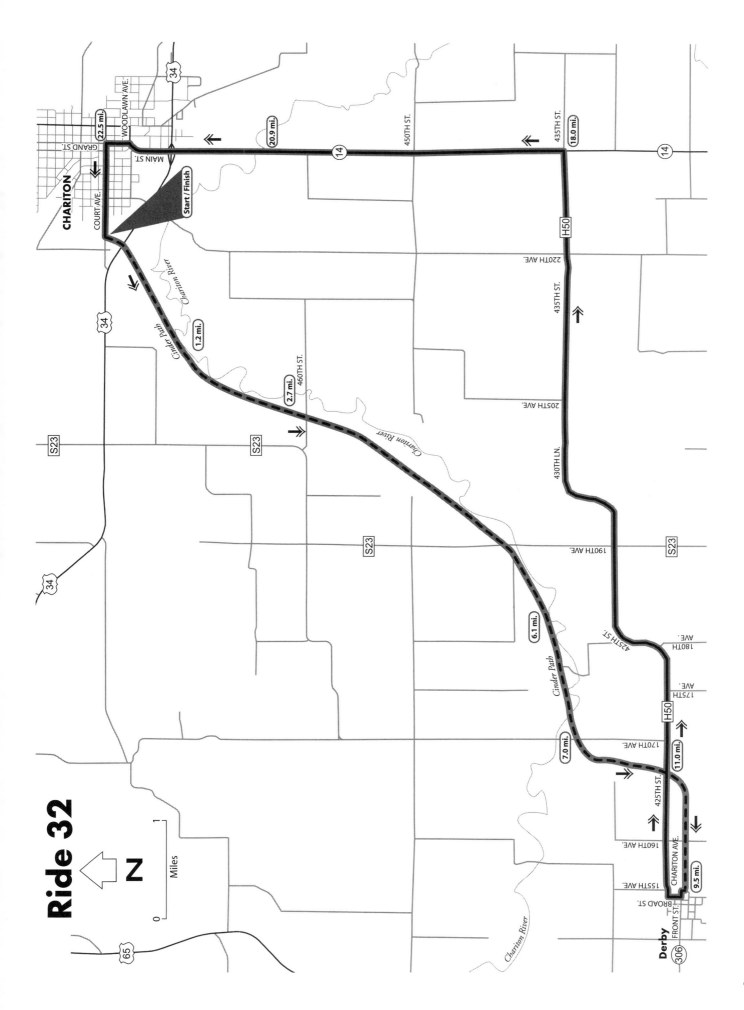

Ride 32

N

Miles

0   1

RIDE 33
Almost Missouri Ride

LOCATION: County and state roads between Leon and Davis City

DISTANCE: 27.7-mile loop

SURFACE: Paved roads

TERRAIN: Lots of hills, with steep climbs and fast descents

DIFFICULTY: Moderate to strenuous

SERVICES:

> **Restrooms:** Businesses in Leon, town park and café in Davis City, Nine Eagles State Park
>
> **Water:** Businesses in Leon, café in Davis City, Nine Eagles State Park
>
> **Food:** Restaurants, convenience stores, and grocery in Leon; café in Davis City
>
> **Camping:** Nine Eagles State Park, Pleasanton; Little River Recreation Area, Leon; Slip Bluff County Park, Davis City
>
> **Lodging:** Motels and bed and breakfasts in Leon
>
> **Bike Shop:** None nearby

STARTING POINT: Decatur County courthouse square in Leon

Hills, wooded valleys, more hills, pasture and prairies, and some more hills greet you on this ride. The views are gorgeous and the roads are little traveled as you skirt along the Missouri state line at the bottom of central Iowa.

0.0 miles. From the Decatur County Courthouse in Leon, head south on Main Street for two blocks, then turn right onto First Street (State Highway 2/U.S. Highway 69). Your first hill comes on the way out of town as you make a short drop to cross railroad tracks and a small waterway, then climb back up and turn left, heading south on U.S. Highway 69.

On the left is the Leon Lanes & Café—if you need fuel

The tiny Davis City Café on U.S. 69 serves an outstanding breakfast.

for the ride, this is the place to get it. The breakfast service is a bit slow, the ambiance is basic bowling alley, but the servings are huge and delicious and the prices are low.

Within a mile and a half, Leon is a distant memory. The country is jumbled hills, but U.S. Highway 69 smooths them out into long down slopes and gradual climbs. The road surface is a bit rough: watch for potholes and uneven expansion cracks. There's hardly any traffic: Interstate 35 to the west has siphoned off most north-south travelers.

5.6 miles. On the left is a farm advertising Registered Texas Longhorns, but no animals are in sight. Most of the roadside is wooded, with occasional breaks through which you have fine views of pastureland, hills, and hollows. You've been losing altitude since you left Leon: This ride to Davis City is basically downhill.

8.0 miles. Glide down a long slope into the flats of the Grand River Valley. On the right is the Davis City Park, where there are odiferous pit toilets, a shelter, and picnic tables. A bit farther along, Davis City's business district consists of several empty brick buildings, a very seedy looking bar and grill, and the tiny Davis City Café, which is locally famous for its breakfasts and John Wayne memorabilia.

8.8 miles. Turn left onto Dale Miller Road (County Road J66). The next four miles are flat and beautiful as you wind south and east through the cornfields that blanket the bottomland. Tree-covered slopes rise on all sides. Cross the Grand River again and enjoy another level mile before you start up from the valley. The steep part of this climb is at the beginning; the grade eases after about a half mile, but the road continues rising for another mile and a half to pass Nine Eagles State Park.

In the past few years, the Iowa Department of Natural Resources has put about $5 million of renovations and improvements into this park. The campground is first-rate, and the swimming and boating area on Nine Eagles Lake is very attractive.

14.9 miles. A sign welcomes you to Pleasanton, but there's not much here except a small playground and some nice-looking homes. At the junction with Old Highway J66 (County Road R46), turn left to head east—straight ahead takes you into Missouri within a few hundred yards.

16.0 miles. Go left with County Road R46, which is now called Pleasanton Road, to start heading north. The hills roll on as you cruise by hayfields, pastures, and fallow land dotted with prairie flowers. You have an exhilarating, 35+ mph descent into the Little River valley, then a pretty mile of flat land before you shift down for a steep half-mile climb back up to the plateau. The next five miles are over a delightful series of dips and rollers until you hit another steep, fast descent to cross McGruder Creek on the outskirts of Leon.

27.0 miles. County Road R46 becomes Main Street as you enter Leon, passing an old railroad depot that's been turned into the Decatur County Engineer's office. Ahead is the steepest climb of the ride, so shift down to your granny gear—the hard part only lasts about a quarter mile, and you'll have a half mile after it to catch your breath before you're back at your starting point.

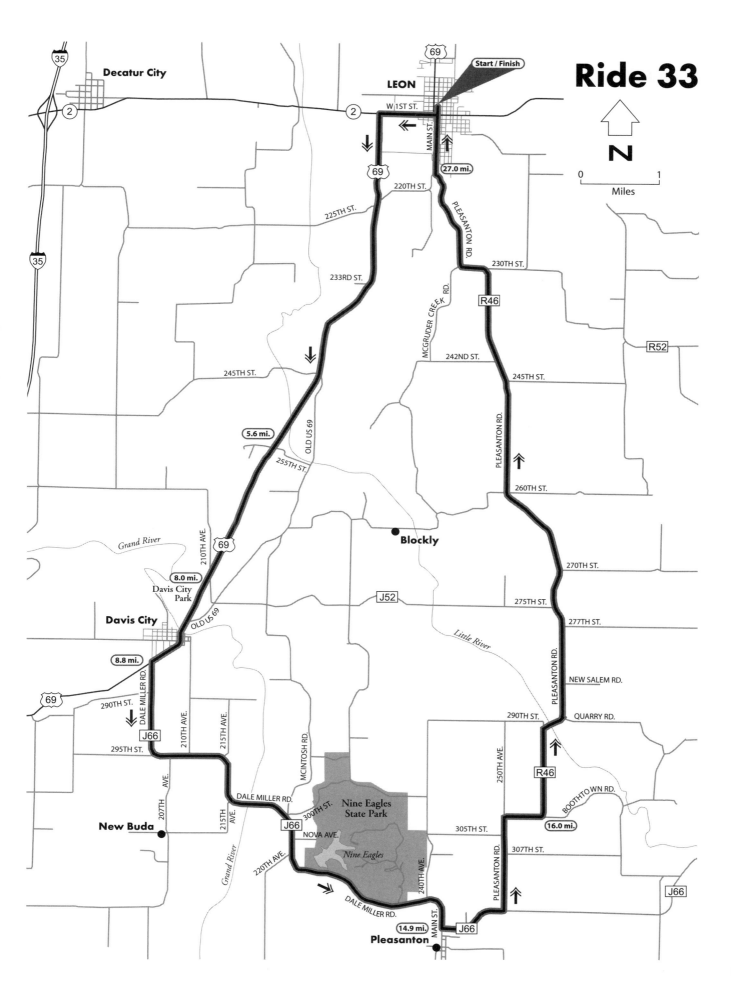

Ride 33

N

0   1
Miles

Decatur City

LEON

Start / Finish

W 1ST ST.

MAIN ST.

27.0 mi.

220TH ST.

225TH ST.

PLEASANTON RD.

230TH ST.

R46

R52

233RD ST.

MCGRUDER CREEK RD.

242ND ST.

245TH ST.

245TH ST.

PLEASANTON RD.

5.6 mi.

OLD US 69

255TH ST.

260TH ST.

210TH AVE.

Grand River

Blockly

270TH ST.

8.0 mi.

Davis City Park

J52

275TH ST.

Little River

277TH ST.

Davis City

OLD US 69

NEW SALEM RD.

8.8 mi.

DALE MILLER RD.

290TH ST.

290TH ST.

QUARRY RD.

PLEASANTON RD.

J66

295TH ST.

210TH AVE.

215TH AVE.

MCINTOSH RD.

250TH AVE.

R46

BOOTHTOWN RD.

207TH AVE.

DALE MILLER RD.

300TH ST.

Nine Eagles State Park

16.0 mi.

New Buda

215TH AVE.

J66

NOVA AVE.

305TH ST.

240TH AVE.

Grand River

Nine Eagles

220TH AVE.

307TH ST.

PLEASANTON RD.

J66

DALE MILLER RD.

14.9 mi.

MAIN ST.

J66

Pleasanton

69

RIDE 34
Road Apple Ride

LOCATION: County roads between Lamoni and Kellerton
DISTANCE: 23.7-mile loop
SURFACE: Paved roads
TERRAIN: Rolling hills with some steep climbs and descents
DIFFICULTY: Moderate
SERVICES:

    Restrooms: At businesses and Community Center in Lamoni, mini-mart in Kellerton
    Water: Same
    Food: Restaurants, taverns, and convenience stores in Lamoni, mini-mart in Kellerton
    Camping: Shade Tree RV Park, Lamoni; Slip Bluff County Park, Davis City; Nine Eagles State Park, Pleasanton
    Lodging: Motels in Lamoni
    Bike Shop: None nearby

The "Grand Old Man" of Horseshoes

The most durable sports champion Iowa has ever fielded was Frank E. Jackson, a farmer from Kellerton, Iowa. His sport was horseshoes, and he dominated it.

Horseshoe pitching started among Greek and Roman cavalrymen, who found the shoes were a good substitute for a discus. Somewhere in the mists of time, someone decided it would be more fun to throw for accuracy instead of distance, and stakes were introduced. The game has been played in America longer than the States have been United: Revolutionary soldiers whiled away idle hours "tossing the Dobbins."

In 1909, a horse show promoter in Bronson, Kansas, decided to hold a World Championship Horseshoe Pitching Tournament as an extra attraction. Frank Jackson, just a month shy of his 39th birthday, stepped up and blew the competition away, then defended his title at the next six World Championships. He held the title for an extra three years because no tournaments were held in 1916-18, then lost it in 1919.

Frank came back, however, and over the years won a total of fifteen World Championships. He claimed his last international title in 1926. At age 62, he was still able to win the 1933 Iowa State Championship.

Horseshoe pitching ran in Frank's family. In 1931, two of his sons, Hansford and Carrol, beat him in the tournament at the State Fair—Hansford had only one loss in the tourney, so he won the Championship that year. The next year, however, Frank came back and clobbered Hansford, as well as two more sons, Carrol and Vyrl, to take back his state title.

Frank quit farming and moved to Florida in 1933, where he operated a motel for a while. He lived to be almost 90.

STARTING POINT: Lamoni Community Center on Main Street, on the west side of Lamoni's business district

You expect hills in southern Iowa, and this ride meets that expectation. The roads in this area have warning signs to watch for horse-drawn carriages used by the local Amish. Horses often leave traces along the roads, of course, which accounts for this ride's name.

0.0 miles. From the Community Center on the west side of Lamoni (pronounced lah-MOAN-eye), turn left (west) on Main Street. You head up a gentle grade, a foretaste of the hills to come, and soon pass Liberty Hall, a lovely, yellow Victorian-style house. This was the home of Joseph Smith III, son of the founder of the Church of Jesus Christ of the Latter Day Saints (the Mormons).

When Brigham Young led the Mormon migration to Utah in the late 1840s, not all of the church members agreed with either his plans or his doctrines. In the 1860s, opposition to Young coalesced around Joseph Smith III and the Reorganized Church of the Latter Day Saints (RLDS) was formed. In 1881, the RLDS purchased over 3,000 acres of land in Iowa, established the town of Lamoni (named for King Lamoni in the Book of Mormon) as its headquarters, and built Liberty Hall to house its leader. The building is now a museum depicting life in the Smith home circa 1900.

Past Liberty Hall, Main Street becomes County Road J55, lined with wildflower-filled ditches. It's as straight as the pinstripe in a banker's suit, and as rolling as that suit when the banker sits down. The countryside is beautiful: pastures, hayfields and crops spreading over undulating hills, with trees marking watercourses that meander through the hollows.

6.1 miles. At the T intersection, turn right and head north on County Road P68, a two-lane hardtop with no shoulder, no centerline, no fog lines, and no traffic. Look back to your right for a postcard-quality view of the hills you've come over.

There's a farm along here with a couple of dogs who will probably come out to let you know you're trespassing. Yell at them and let them know you're fiercer than they are, and they'll back down.

The hills on County Road P68 are steeper but shorter than those on County Road J55. Don't be reluctant to use your granny gear: Better to spin than to strain.

12.2 miles. As you enter Kellerton, the speed limit drops to 25 mph, but there are few moving cars to observe it. Turn right onto Fifth Avenue. You can't help noticing the street signs, which are shaped like horseshoes with ox yokes dangling from the ends, commemorating Frank E. Jackson, 15-time World Horseshoe Pitching Champion. Jackson's family provided the funds to put up the street signs as a town beautification project a decade or so ago.

Ride three blocks on Fifth Avenue and turn right on Decatur Street to go through the one-block business district. There's not much business: The Second Home Bar, some empty storefronts, and a gas station with the Munion Mini Mart. The paved road turns left and becomes Sixth Avenue.

12.8 miles. Turn right at the T and head south on County Road J45. Pass a cemetery on your left, a baseball diamond on your right, and you're out of Kellerton. After about a mile, you have an outstanding view down through a valley—a fine example of southern Iowa's distinctive beauty. Grind up a steep climb, then enjoy several miles of rollers and flats as County Road J45 works its way west and south towards Lamoni.

After passing a farm where all the buildings are painted bright white beneath turquoise blue tin roofs, you'll slip through what used to be the town of Tuskeego, now reduced to a couple of nondescript buildings. The land rolls nicely beneath your wheels as you look out over the rounded landscape.

19.9 miles. Turn right onto County Road R18. From here, the hills are spaced perfectly for cruising—build your speed on the downs, keep it up on the flats, and you'll sweep over the shallow climbs with ease.

22.6 miles. Go left onto County Road J55 (Main Street) and pass Liberty Hall again on the way back to your starting point.

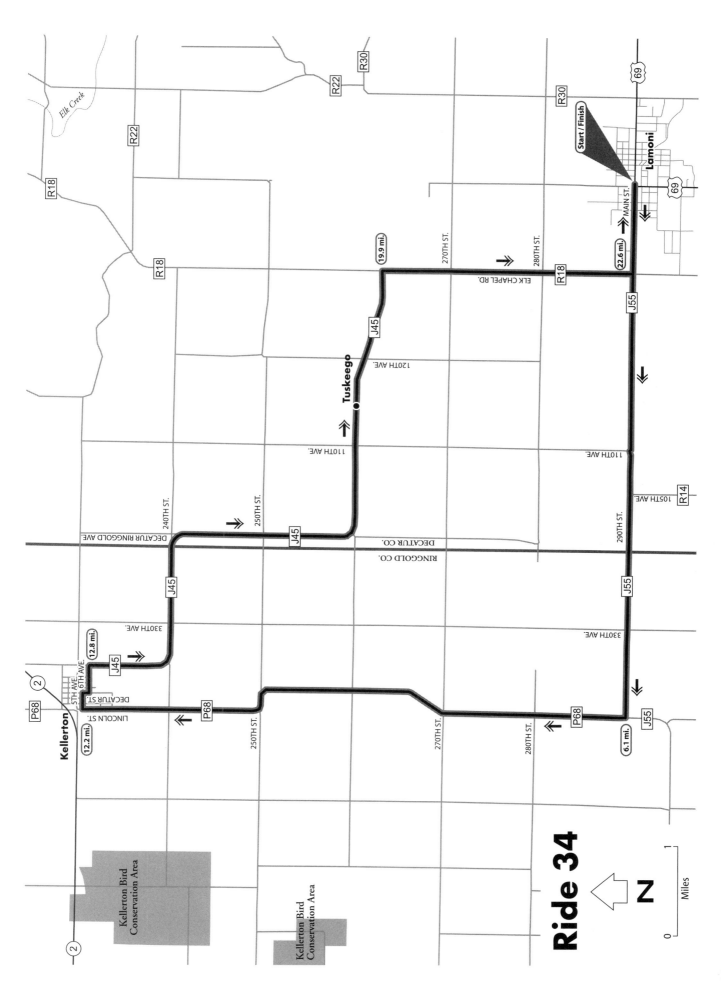

Ride 34

N

Miles
0   1

71

WESTERN IOWA

RIDE 35
Nearly Minnesota Ride

LOCATION: Iowa Great Lakes Trail and county roads around Spirit Lake
DISTANCE: 17.4-mile loop
SURFACE: Paved trail, paved roads
TERRAIN: Mostly flat
DIFFICULTY: Easy
SERVICES:
>**Restrooms:** Family Diner at start/finish, Mini-Wakan State Park, Marble Beach Park
>**Water:** Same
>**Food:** Family Diner at start/finish, tavern at mile 15.5
>**Camping:** Cenla Campground, Spirit Lake; Marble Beach, Spirit Lake
>**Lodging:** Motels and bed and breakfasts in Spirit Lake
>**Bike Shop:** Okoboji Bikes, Milford

STARTING POINT: Family Diner on the northeast corner of the U.S. Highway 7/Peoria Avenue intersection on the western side of the city of Spirit Lake

A paved trail starts you on this gorgeous loop around Spirit Lake, leading away from town and onto county roads. There are plenty of lake views and the countryside is lovely as well. At the northern end of the lake, you actually straddle the Iowa/Minnesota state line.

0.0 miles. From the 1950s-style Family Diner, head north on the Iowa Great Lakes Trail, which is a side path along Peoria Avenue. It crosses a railroad track, turns right along 153rd Street/15th Street, then goes left to cut through a neighborhood and get into a pretty stretch of open land. You catch a glimpse of East Okoboji Lake on your right.

1.9 miles. The trail emerges onto Hill Avenue (State Highway 276). Go left at the T to continue north (a right turn takes you into downtown Spirit Lake). You're between the top of East Lake Okoboji and bottom of Spirit Lake for a pretty ride through the grounds of the Spirit Lake Fish Hatchery.

2.5 miles. The trail crosses the spillway between the lakes and ends momentarily at 252nd Avenue. Turn left to cross the railroad tracks, then get onto the renewed trail along 252nd. It angles away from the road, cuts over to 140th Street and Sunset Drive, and continues north.

3.4 miles. Next to the trail is a concrete patio with benches and a pedestal holding an open book, "In loving Memory of Muriel Smith." The site overlooks a wetland where redwing blackbirds mingle with wood ducks and mallards and match their songs against the croak of frogs and whine of insects.

4.2 miles. At County Road A15 (125th Street), leave the trail and turn right on County Road A15. A bit over a quarter mile ahead, turn left at the stop sign, still following County Road A15, which has now merged with State Highway 327 and County Road M56.

5.7 miles. County Road A15 turns right, but you continue north on County Road M56. Small fields bordered by trees stretch to the lake on your left; on the right, more fields flow over low hills.

7.7 miles. You've turned to the west and the road has become 100th Street; now it intersects with 510th Avenue (County Road 17), which comes in from the right. Ignore the Bike Route sign pointing you up County Road 17 and continue west as the road changes names to County Road 2. The road name confusion stems from the fact that you're straddling the Iowa/Minnesota state line. County Road 2 is in Iowa, but it's a Minnesota road.

Now you have your best view of Spirit Lake so far. According to legend, the lake is named for a pair of lovers. In the distant past, a band of Dakota Sioux Indians brought a captive white woman to this lake, where she caught the eye of a young chief, Star of Day. Star of Day, too, was white, captured years before and adopted into the tribe. He fell in love with the maiden and freed her, then escaped with her across the lake in his canoe. A storm blew up and the lovers drowned, but their spirits live on, under the lake's waters.

10.1 miles. Pass Mini-Wakan State Park, then cross an isthmus with lake on both sides. A flock of white pelicans is likely to be hanging out here, as well as Canada geese, herons, and other wading birds.

10.7 miles. Turn left to head south on State Highway 276 (480th Avenue). Cross another isthmus, this one between Spirit Lake on your left and Little Spirit Lake on your right. Pedal over a series of low hills, accumulations of glacial debris that mark the edge of the ice sheets that advanced and retreated through here 14,000 years ago. From the hilltops, you'll see two wind generators ahead, which provide power for the local elementary and high schools. The smaller of the two was put up in the mid-1990s, paid for itself in four years, and now generates over $20,000 a year for the school district.

15.5 miles. The road has curved east, bringing you to the outskirts of the city of Spirit Lake. Turn right onto Hill Avenue, and immediately cross a set of railroad tracks. Just beyond them is the park area you came through on the trail at the start of the ride. Turn right onto the trail and follow it back to the Family Diner.

White pelicans flock at the northern end of Spirit Lake.

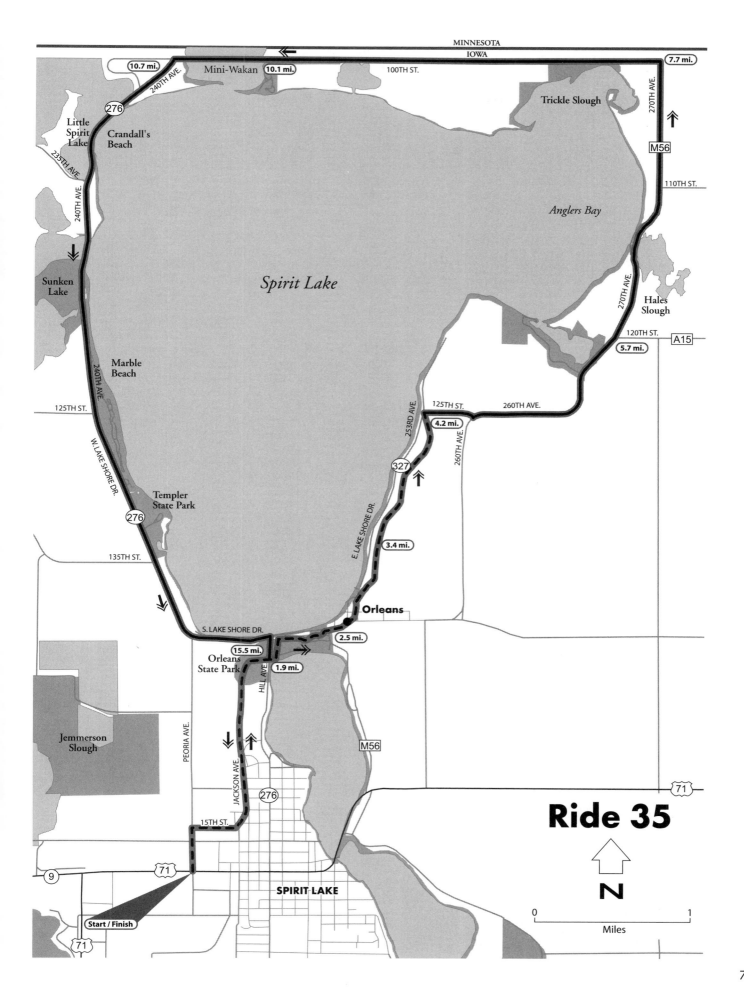

MINNESOTA
IOWA

10.7 mi.
240TH AVE.
Mini-Wakan
10.1 mi.
100TH ST.
7.7 mi.
270TH AVE.
Trickle Slough
276
Little Spirit Lake
Crandall's Beach
M56
235TH AVE.
240TH AVE.
Anglers Bay
110TH ST.
Sunken Lake
270TH AVE.
Hales Slough
Spirit Lake
120TH ST.
A15
5.7 mi.
Marble Beach
240TH AVE.
125TH ST.
125TH ST.
260TH AVE.
253RD AVE.
4.2 mi.
327
260TH AVE.
W. LAKE SHORE DR.
276
Templer State Park
E. LAKE SHORE DR.
3.4 mi.
135TH ST.
Orleans
S. LAKE SHORE DR.
2.5 mi.
15.5 mi.
Orleans State Park
1.9 mi.
HILL AVE.
PEORIA AVE.
JACKSON AVE.
M56
Jemmerson Slough
71
276
15TH ST.
71
9
Ride 35
N
SPIRIT LAKE
71
Start / Finish
0
Miles
1

75

RIDE 36
Bikin' 'Boji

LOCATION: Iowa Great Lakes Trail, Kenue Park Trail and town roads near Arnolds Park

DISTANCE: 10.7-mile loop

SURFACE: Paved trails, paved roads

TERRAIN: Gentle rises and falls on the trails; very short but steep hills on Lakeshore Drive

DIFFICULTY: Moderate

SERVICES:

Restrooms: Businesses in Arnolds Park, Kenue Park

Water: Same

Food: Restaurants and convenience stores in Arnolds Park

Camping: Arnolds Park City Campgrounds, Arnolds Park; Emerson Bay State Park, West Okoboji

Lodging: Motels, resorts, and bed and breakfasts in Arnolds Park and around Lake Okoboji

Bike Shop: Okoboji Bikes, Milford

STARTING POINT: Lower Gar Park access off 202nd Street, south of Arnolds Park

Iowa's First Tourist Attration

Iowa pretty much avoided the Indian wars that accompanied white settlement west of the Mississippi, so it's ironic that the state's first tourist attraction stemmed from an Indian raid known as the Spirit Lake Massacre.

Relations between whites and the Indians of northwestern Iowa were never exactly friendly, but stayed shy of open hostility until the winter of 1856-57. That was a particularly harsh winter, and both the whites and the Dakota Indians suffered from a serious shortage of food. In March of 1857, a band of hungry Dakotas descended on the scattered settlement of white farmers and homesteaders near Spirit Lake and demanded food. Dissatisfied with the whites' response, they killed more than thirty settlers and carried off four women as captives. One of those was 13-year-old Abbie Gardner. After 84 days of captivity, Abbie was ransomed from a band of Yankton Sioux in South Dakota, for goods valued at $1,200.

Abbie wrote a book about her experiences and, in 1891, returned to Arnolds Park and bought the cabin in which her family had lived and died. She opened it to visitors, charging a quarter from anyone who wished to see her displays of Indian artifacts and listen to her story of the massacre and her captivity.

Abbie Gardner-Sharp died in Colfax, Iowa, in 1921. Her heirs sold the cabin to the Iowa Conservation Commission and in 1973 it was entered in the National Register of Historic Places. It's now a museum, with free admission.

The first three-quarters of a mile of this ride is part of what has been called the most beautiful mile of trail in Iowa by "Iowa Boy" Chuck Offenburger, one of the original organizers of the Register's Annual Great Bike Ride Across Iowa (RAGBRAI). The other miles aren't half-bad either!

0.0 miles. From the lower parking lot in Lower Gar Park, go north on the Iowa Great Lakes Trail, riding through the park's beautiful oak savanna. Lower Gar Lake is on your right, visible through the trees. The asphalt trail leads around the lake, then crosses a bridge over the connection between Lower Gar and Lake Minnewashta and passes an historical marker at the site of the Zeta Henderson family's 1864 homestead. It's a wonderful ride through the woods with occasional glimpses of the lakes. The "Iowa Boy" knows how to call 'em.

0.7 miles. The trail emerges from the woods onto Rohr Street and continues straight on that road. Use caution here: The intersection is at a curve, so motorists may not see you. Past the RV parking lot of Camp Winnekawen, cross the outlet stream from East Okoboji Lake and go by Sawmill Park.

1.3 miles. Bike Route signs point out your left turn onto Bascom Street. Pass the Arnolds Park City Campground-

Minnewashta on your left, then climb a short hill to intersect with Okoboji Grove Road (U.S. Highway 71), where the Iowa Great Lakes Trail starts up again as a side path.

U.S. Highway 71 is a heavily used three-lane road with a center turning lane and 30 mph speed limit. The motorists resent cyclists on "their" road when there's a trail right next to it, so it's probably best to ride the side path, but use caution! There are lots of strip malls with driveways crossing the trail —watch for cars turning into or coming out of them.

2.1 miles. The side path diverges from the road and leads to a bicycle/pedestrian bridge across the channel between East and West Okoboji Lakes. Over the bridge, the trail empties onto Depot Street, which runs behind the stores fronting on U.S. Highway 71, then curves left and uphill to connect again with the renewed side path along the highway.

Pedal past more shops and strip malls (this is, after all, a tourist town), then follow the trail as it veers away from the highway and passes the University of Okoboji Foundation Park, a pleasant trailhead with benches and a picnic table. Cross Exchange Road and ride gratefully into the shade as the trail leaves the business district.

3.8 miles. At 175th Street, turn left, following the sign pointing to the Westport School House. This side path along 175th Street is the Kenue Park Trail. It crosses U.S. Highway 71, goes by the Lakes Art Center and turns away from the highway to enter some woods. Enjoy the whimsical sculptures along the trail, then cross a line of massive, old oak trees and ride a pleasant, flower-filled stretch through grasslands.

5.1 miles. There are restrooms and water here at Kenue Park, as well as the Westport Rural School House. This was the last rural schoolhouse in Dickinson County, moved from its original location in 1997. They even brought along the outhouses!

The trail ends at the gravel park road; turn right to leave the park, then go west (left) on County Home Road. This is a nice country road through cornfields, with a pleasant downhill to West Okoboji Lake.

5.6 miles. Turn left onto Lakeshore Drive. Lakeshore has a paved shoulder and traffic is usually light—everyone's out on the water, not driving around on the roads. Check out the attractive summer homes and cottages that line the road and block all but occasional glimpses of the lake.

The road winds for a couple of up-and-down miles along the cottage-lined lakefront, then, at about the eight-mile mark, climbs a hill and curves around an RV sales lot. There's a short, very steep drop to the traffic light at U.S. Highway 71—watch your speed! Across Highway 71, Lakeshore becomes Gordon Drive.

8.5 miles. Turn right off Gordon Drive onto the Iowa Great Lakes Trail, and retrace your route two miles back to your starting point.

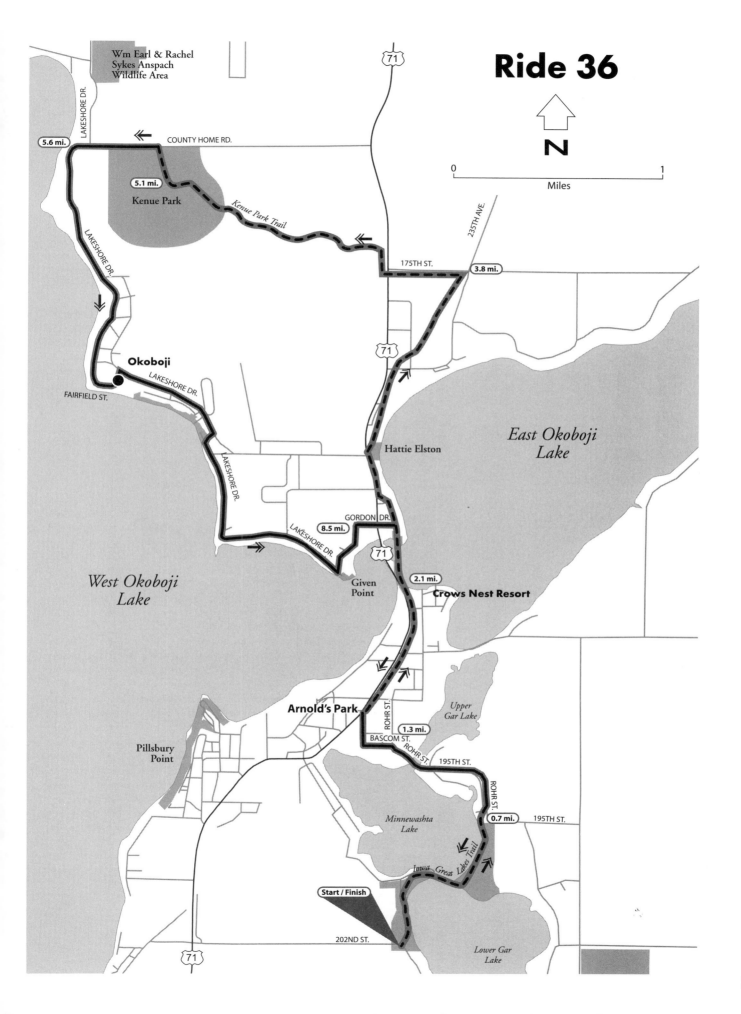

Ride 36

N

0 ——— 1
Miles

Wm Earl & Rachel Sykes Anspach Wildlife Area

LAKESHORE DR.

71

COUNTY HOME RD.

5.6 mi.

5.1 mi.

Kenue Park

Kenue Park Trail

LAKESHORE DR.

235TH AVE.

175TH ST.

3.8 mi.

Okoboji

LAKESHORE DR.

FAIRFIELD ST.

71

LAKESHORE DR.

Hattie Elston

East Okoboji Lake

LAKESHORE DR.

GORDON DR.

8.5 mi.

71

West Okoboji Lake

Given Point

2.1 mi.

Crows Nest Resort

Upper Gar Lake

Arnold's Park

ROHR ST.

1.3 mi.

BASCOM ST.

ROHR ST.

195TH ST.

ROHR ST.

Pillsbury Point

Minnewashta Lake

0.7 mi.

195TH ST.

Iowa Great Lake Trail

Start / Finish

202ND ST.

Lower Gar Lake

71

RIDE 37
Around a Prairie Pothole

LOCATION: County roads between Ruthven and Lost Island Lake
DISTANCE: 11.0-mile loop
SURFACE: Paved roads
TERRAIN: Gentle slopes
DIFFICULTY: Easy
SERVICES:
> **Restrooms:** Businesses in Ruthven, Lost Island Lake County Park, Grandview Park
> **Water:** Same
> **Food:** Restaurant and convenience store in Ruthven, tavern in Grandview Park
> **Camping:** Lost Island Lake County Park
> **Lodging:** Motels in Spencer
> **Bike Shop:** None nearby

STARTING POINT: Joan's Café at the intersection of U.S. Highway 18 and Gowrie Street, on the south side of Ruthven

Prairie Potholes

When the glaciers retreated ten thousand years ago, they left behind a landscape dotted with shallow depressions known as "prairie potholes." These potholes cover millions of acres in the upper Midwest, mostly in the Dakotas, Wisconsin, and Minnesota; northern Iowa is at the southern edge of the pothole region.

The potholes collected moisture and became small lakes, ponds, or marshes, depending on their depth. Some, like Lost Island Lake, are essentially permanent; others go dry during droughts, then reappear during wet periods.

The potholes are critical resting, feeding, and nesting habitat for migratory waterfowl. Beyond that, the pothole wetlands serve a variety of ecological purposes, not the least of which is in improving water quality by filtering and flushing nutrients and organic wastes. However, due to the land's high suitability for agriculture, over half of the prairie potholes in Iowa have been drained and turned into cropland.

For a long time, geologists believed that the prairie potholes in an area were independent of each other, but satellite imagery has revealed that they are interconnected through underground waterways. Lost Island Lake is part of a complex of potholes that includes the Blue Wing Marsh, Barringer Slough, and several other wetlands. The Palo Alto County Conservation Board and Iowa Department of Natural Resources have restored six wetland areas, a welcome reversal of agricultural practices of the last century.

This short, pleasant loop takes you past lots of scenic wetlands and flower-filled prairie. You'll circle Lost Island Lake, Iowa's sixth-largest natural lake, but you won't find an island.

0.0 miles. From Joan's Café in Ruthven, head north on Gowrie Street. Ruthven's a very small town situated atop a low rise in the midst of undulating farmland. You quickly pass through the block-long business district that clusters around the Farmer's Co-op elevator, then make an S turn as Gowrie Street leaves town and becomes County Road M28 (350th Avenue). County Road M28 is a pleasant two-lane road with a good, smooth surface and no traffic to speak of. Coast downhill from Ruthven, then climb a low, gradual rise and look ahead to the tree-encircled blue of Lost Island Lake.

2.1 miles. Turn right on County Road B25 to ride east along the edge of the Huston Prairie, a 53-acre area of restored native grasslands. The tall grasses and prairie flowers wave gracefully in the breeze.

2.6 miles. Take a left onto County Road N20 (355th Avenue) and cruise north through the Blue Wing Marsh Wildlife Refuge. There are six restored wetlands in this area, catering to waterfowl and other wildlife. Keep watch for herons, egrets, and other wading birds. Pedal up a long, shallow

grade, and now, looking across a broad field, you see a line of trees on the Lost Island Lake shoreline.

3.5 miles. Turn left onto 330th Street, heading west through tall prairie grasses to the lake. As you coast downhill, you pass a sign that says "Road Ends." It doesn't: instead, it turns right, entering Lost Island Lake County Park. There are speed bumps in the park road, painted yellow and accompanied by signs that say "Bump" in case you're not paying attention to the road surface. You can get around the bumps on the right.

4.2 miles. Pass the Lost Island Lake Nature Center, an attractive log building with interesting exhibits about prairie wetlands. Outside the building is a colorful wildflower garden and a collection of glacial erratics—boulders brought here by the glaciers, then dropped as the ice receded. Some of these stones originated hundreds of miles to the north, in the far reaches of Minnesota.

The road is pleasantly shady as you pass the campground and come to an inviting beach area. Your ride curves along the shoreline, giving nice lake vistas. Lost Island Lake has a surface area of about 1,266 acres. It's only 14 feet deep at most, with an average depth of 10 feet. It's reputed to be great for bullhead and walleye fishing.

4.9 miles. Exit the park and turn left on 320th Street, which quickly curls back to the lakeshore. There are small summer homes and vacation cottages lining the shore on your left now, and more marshland stretching out on the right.

Pass a roadside park and public access on the lake, then continue past the summer cottages. In the distance across the lake, the Ruthven elevator rises above the land's low rolls.

6.3 miles. Turn left on 335th Avenue and pass the lovely little Holy Cross Resurrection Chapel on your right. You're back into summer cottages now, which block your view of the lake as you approach Grand View Resort, a collection of somewhat shabby buildings and a miniature golf course.

7.0 miles. At the intersection is the Lost Island Corner Store Café, a funky combination of tavern and general store. Bear left onto 340th Avenue to continue circling the lake, then pass Grandview Park and cross a causeway between the lake and one of its arms. On the far side of the causeway is another public access and camping area. You're in the Barringer Slough wetlands now. Keep an eye peeled for the trumpeter swans that were released here in 2004.

8.1 miles. Turn left onto County Road B25 (340th Street). The lake is far away across the grassland on your left. In about three-quarters of a mile, you'll hit County Road N20—watch out for the rumble strips ahead of this intersection, which are well nigh invisible.

8.9 miles. Turn right on County Road N20 (350th Avenue) and you're on your way back to your starting point in Ruthven.

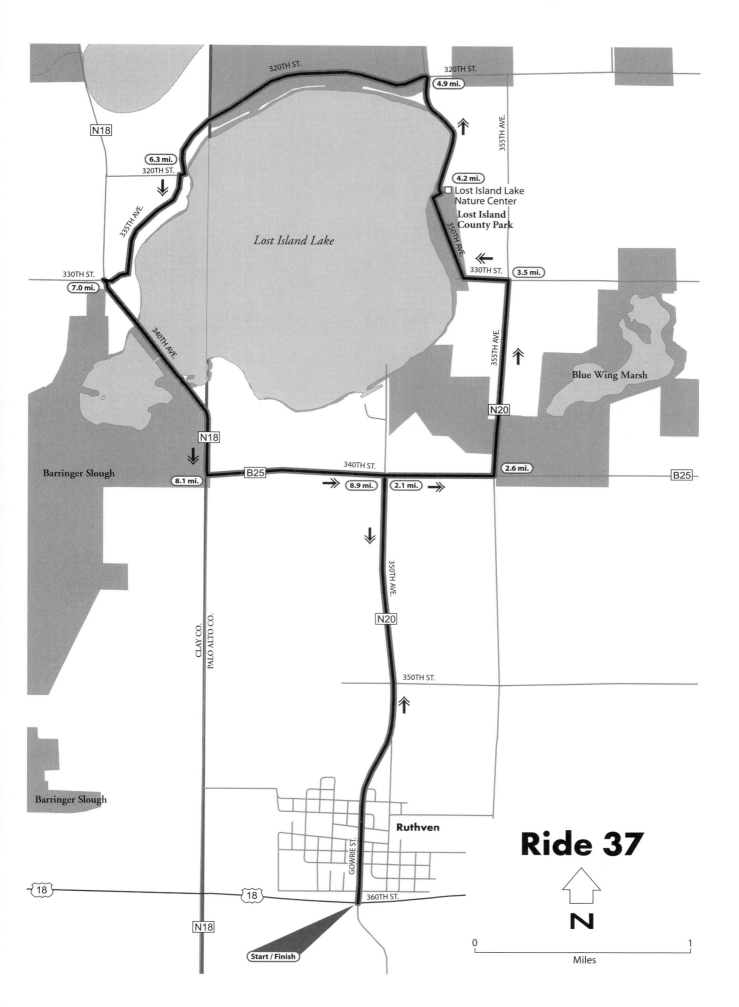

320TH ST.

320TH ST.

N18

4.9 mi.

355TH AVE.

6.3 mi.
320TH ST.

335TH AVE.

4.2 mi.
☐ Lost Island Lake
Nature Center

**Lost Island
County Park**

Lost Island Lake

350TH AVE.

330TH ST. **3.5 mi.**

330TH ST.
7.0 mi.

340TH AVE.

355TH AVE.

Blue Wing Marsh

Barringer Slough

N18

8.1 mi.
B25

340TH ST.
8.9 mi.

2.1 mi.

2.6 mi.
B25

350TH AVE.

N20

CLAY CO.

PALO ALTO CO.

350TH ST.

Barringer Slough

Ruthven

GOWRIE ST.

18

18

360TH ST.

Ride 37

N

Start / Finish

0   Miles   1

N18

N20

RIDE 38
Wind Power Ride

The Storm Lake Wind Farm stretches for miles along County Road C16 south of Peterson.

LOCATION: State and county roads between Peterson and Linn Grove

DISTANCE: 23.0-mile loop

SURFACE: Paved roads

TERRAIN: Mix of hills and flats, steep climbs and descents through the river valley

DIFFICULTY: Moderate

SERVICES:

Restrooms: At start/finish, businesses and Community Center in Linn Grove

Water: Same

Food: Restaurants and convenience stores in Peterson and Linn Grove

Camping: Buena Vista County Park, Peterson; Linn Grove Dam County Conservation Area, Linn Grove (primitive only)

Lodging: Motels in Spencer and Cherokee

Bike Shop: Letsche's Bike Shop, Main Street, Cherokee

STARTING POINT: Jacob Kirchner Memorial Park, off State Highway 10 on the west end of Peterson

Harvesting the Wind

Iowa is the 10th windiest state in the U.S., with over 40 percent of its land suitable for wind generators. The state has the potential to generate 4.8 times its own annual electricity consumption. At present, it's nowhere close to doing that, but it's getting a start.

The Storm Lake Wind Farm in Buena Vista and Cherokee counties, through which you'll pedal on this ride, was developed in 1999 by Enron Wind Corporation. These 257 generators have a 196.5-megawatt capacity—enough to power 72,000 homes.

Each generator requires about a quarter acre of land, including its service road. The land around the generators, of course, is unaffected by them, which makes wind and crop farming perfectly compatible. A farmer can lease land for the generators and still plant crops right up to the tower's base.

Typically, land for the generator is leased at about $750 per year per generator. The landowner also receives a royalty payment on the electricity generated. A farmer can earn as much as $2,000 a year per generator—much more than he'd get from corn or beans on that land.

It takes only an 8-mph wind to make electricity and the generators here seem to be moving constantly. The biggest maintenance problem for these huge structures is lightning—as the tallest, most metallic objects around, they attract a good share of a thunderstorm's attention. You'll probably see a few truncated windmill blades as you make this ride.

Currently, there are four large wind farms in Iowa: this Storm Lake facility, the Top of Iowa Wind Farm near Joice, one near Clear Lake, and the last near Garner. Another 25 generators are scattered around the state. Clearly, wind power has an important role to play in Iowa's future.

Expect some wind on this ride: you're going past one of the world's largest wind farms, and they don't put those things in places that are calm. Windy or not, this is a beautiful ride around the Little Sioux River Valley.

0.0 miles. Clip into your pedals at the Kirchner Memorial Park in Peterson, the site of Clay County's first frame house. The Kirchner home was built in 1867 and stayed in the family until 1971. It was given to Peterson Heritage, Inc., which restored it and furnished it as a turn-of-the-century home. Leaving the park, turn right to head west on State Highway 10. You soon cross the Little Sioux River, then start a mile-long, sometimes-steep climb up the valley's forested side.

0.9 miles. Turn left onto County Road M27 and head south, still climbing up the side of the valley. At the top of the climb, you look across a level plateau to hundreds of wind generators. This is the Storm Lake Wind Farm, and it stretches for miles.

The road is mostly flat and yardstick straight as you approach the wind farm. You can see that the wind generators are big, but it's not until you get right up among them that you realize *how big* they really are: 210 feet tall, with 80-foot blades. You and your bicycle suddenly seem downright tiny, and the "whoosh-whoosh" sound of the blades smothers the sound of your wheels on the pavement.

6.0 miles. Turn left to travel east on County Road C16, still riding through the wind farm. Like County Road M27, this road is devoid of curves as it travels across the gently undulating land. Off to your left is a long view of farms stretching over to the river valley, which is marked by the tree line. On your right, the windmills stand hugely among the soybeans.

9.8 miles. After a steep, fast descent to cross Brooke Creek and a much slower half-mile climb back up to the plateau, you're finally out of the wind farm. Now the view is unobstructed in all directions: farm fields, here and there a forest grove, or single trees marking a waterway.

12.1 miles. Turn left onto County Road M36, heading north. There's a good drop to cross a small waterway, then a longer, gradual climb back up. After about two miles, the road curves right as it merges into County Road C13.

14.4 miles. County Road C13 continues straight, but you turn left with County Road M36, heading north to Linn Grove. Linn Grove's residential area is up on the side of the valley, while the small business district is down by the river. When one of the 211 townspeople says he's "going downtown," he means it literally. It's a precipitous plunge to the few businesses strung out along the road near the river. Stop at The Landing, a canoe rental place and hangout, where you can serve yourself a cup of coffee and join whoever's there in conversation.

15.7 miles. Cross the Little Sioux again and climb the steep, forested valley side back up to the plateau. Locals claim there are mountain lions in this area; the habitat certainly looks good for them, and there are enough deer around here to keep them fat and happy.

17.7 miles. Turn left onto State Highway 10 (500th Street). The highway wends its way west along the edge of the valley, rising and falling slightly. On your left, fields stretch to the tree line along the river, and in the distance on the far side of the valley you can see the wind farm's towers.

A long, curving, very pleasant descent takes you back down into the valley. Your view shortens as you descend, but what it loses in distance it gains in beauty. Crops and grasslands cover the valley floor over to the trees along the river, and you catch occasional glimpses of the sun glinting off the water.

22.1 miles. Pass the sign welcoming you to Peterson; you've only a mile to go to get back to the start point.

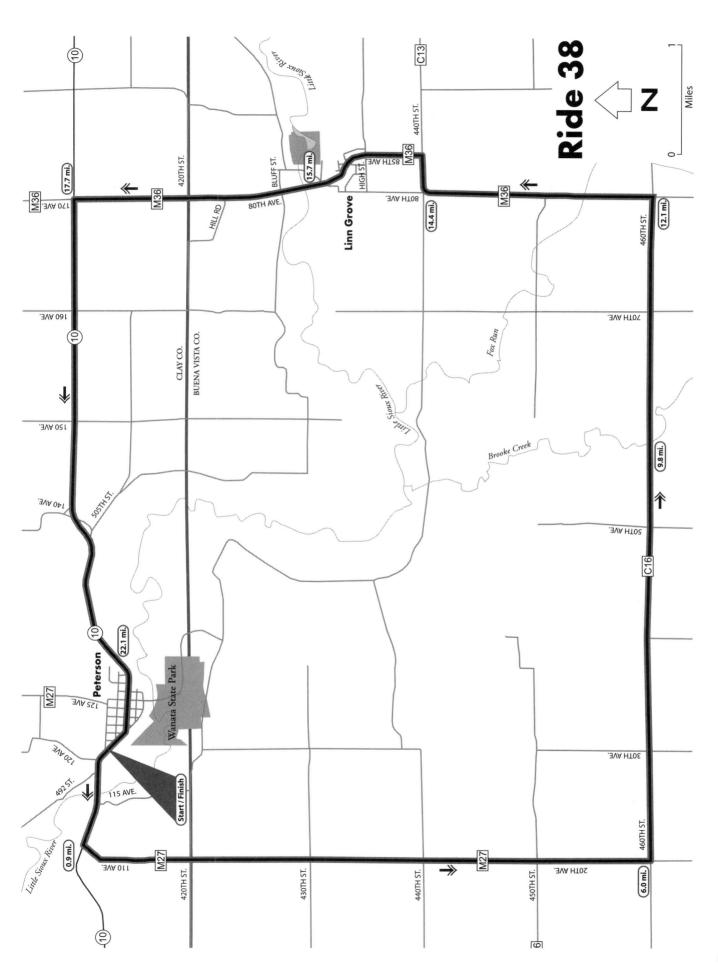

Ride 38

N

0 1 Miles

10

M36 17.7 mi.

170 AVE.

M36

420TH ST.

Little Sioux River

BLUFF ST.

15.7 mi.

HILL RD.

80TH AVE.

Linn Grove

HIGH ST.

85TH AVE.

M36

440TH ST.

C13

80TH AVE.

14.4 mi.

M36

460TH ST.

12.1 mi.

10

160 AVE.

150 AVE.

CLAY CO.

BUENA VISTA CO.

70TH AVE.

Fox Run

Little Sioux River

Brooke Creek

9.8 mi.

140 AVE.

505TH ST.

50TH AVE.

C16

10

22.1 mi.

Peterson

M27

125 AVE.

Wanata State Park

120 AVE.

492 ST.

115 AVE.

Start / Finish

30TH AVE.

460TH ST.

Little Sioux River

0.9 mi.

110 AVE.

M27

420TH ST.

430TH ST.

440TH ST.

450TH ST.

20TH AVE.

M27

6.0 mi.

6

81

RIDE 39
Storm Lake Circle

LOCATION: Lake Trail, city, county, and state roads around Storm Lake

DISTANCE: 12.3-mile loop

SURFACE: Paved trail, paved roads, about one-tenth of a mile of gravel street

TERRAIN: Flat

DIFFICULTY: Easy

SERVICES:

Restrooms: Businesses in Storm Lake, Lake Park in Lakeshore

Water: Same

Food: Restaurants and convenience stores in Storm Lake and Lakeshore

Camping: Sunrise Park, Storm Lake

Lodging: Motels and bed and breakfasts in Storm Lake

Bike Shop: Lakeshore Cyclery and Fitness, Lakeshore Drive, Storm Lake

STARTING POINT: Main Street Park at the intersection of Lake and Railroad streets in Storm Lake

"The Pioneer" looks out across Storm Lake.

Storm Lake (the city) virtually envelops the north shore of Storm Lake (the lake). The city has established over 200 acres of parks next to the water and connected them with a trail. You'll ride that trail as part of this easy, beautiful cruise around the lake.

0.0 miles. Push off from the Main Street Park at the corner of Lake Avenue and Railroad Street and head south on Lake Avenue across the railroad tracks. There are a number of nice old homes along Lake Avenue, including the 1875 Harker House on your right. The street is very wide and bike friendly.

Cross Lakeshore Drive and turn right onto the Lake Trail, heading west through the parklands on the lakeshore. You soon reach the Living Heritage Tree Museum, a collection of trees obtained from historically significant sources. Among these is a sycamore descended from a tree that still grows beside General Washington's headquarters at the 1776 Battle of White Plains, New York. There's also a butternut tree from test pilot Chuck Yeager's farm in Hamlin, West Virginia, and an oak tree descended from Connecticut's Charter Oak.

0.9 miles. After passing the Buena Vista University athletic fields, the trail curves right and becomes a narrow sidewalk along Grand Avenue. Get onto Grand Avenue and follow it through the campus.

1.3 miles. Turn left to head west on Fourth Street, which takes you into a residential district. Fourth Street becomes Shoreway Road as it runs past nice homes with neatly kept lawns, then ends at Angier Drive, where Bike Route signs point you to the right. Go up one block to Fifth Street, turn left, and go over one block to Vista Drive, then turn left again to get back to the lakeshore.

At Rotary Park, the Lake Trail resumes as a side path along State Highway 110. Bear left at the Y to curve around next to the lake in the shade of black walnut, oak, and cottonwood trees, with a wide, long view across the water.

3.2 miles. The trail has come back to parallel State Highway 110 again, and now crosses the inlet waterway that links Little Storm Lake with the larger lake. Over the bridge, the trail empties onto a gravel residential road, but in a few yards you're back on the concrete of North Emerald Drive. At the Y, bear left to stay near the lake; bear left again at the triangle with Kelvin Road.

3.7 miles. Turn right on Parlina Lane, then zigzag through the residential streets: left on Pierce, right on Alvin, left on Kelvin again, which turns into gravel and Ts into Howard Road (also gravel), where you turn right.

4.0 miles. The water tower is directly in front of you as you turn left to head south on State Highway 110. You're quickly away from town, riding up a gradual incline between the cornfields. This is about as much hill as you'll encounter on this ride.

5.6 miles. At the Storm Lake Municipal Airport, turn left onto Airport Road (County Road C65). C65 is a ruled line heading east through the corn. There's a nice view of the lake on your left, with the water tower and grain elevator jutting above the town on the far side.

8.1 miles. Turn left onto 110th Street toward the Bel Air Lake access. The road turns right and becomes first Mallard Avenue and then Lakeshore Drive, then curves east and north along the shoreline. Cross an outlet stream from the lake and ride through a new development of huge garages with attached houses as you come into Lakeshore, "The Best Little City by a Dam Site."

9.7 miles. Pass Lakeside's Lake Street, which comes into Lakeshore Drive from the right. There's a small park on the lake, with a playground and portable toilet. The Lake Trail begins again on the west side of the road. The lake view is beautiful, but don't get too involved with it—there's lots of trail traffic as you pass the Sunnyside Park campground.

10.7 miles. Pass the Pioneer Heritage exhibit near the playground and a swimming pool with a wonderfully whimsical elephant slide. At the Y, stay left to ride at the water's edge. You pass a long, shaped piece of steel—a blade from one of the wind generators in the Storm Lake Wind Farm.

11.3 miles. At Chautauqua Park Drive, leave the trail and turn left on the road for a beautiful stretch along the lake. You pick up the trail again just before it reaches Lake Street, where you turn right to return to your starting point.

Ride 39

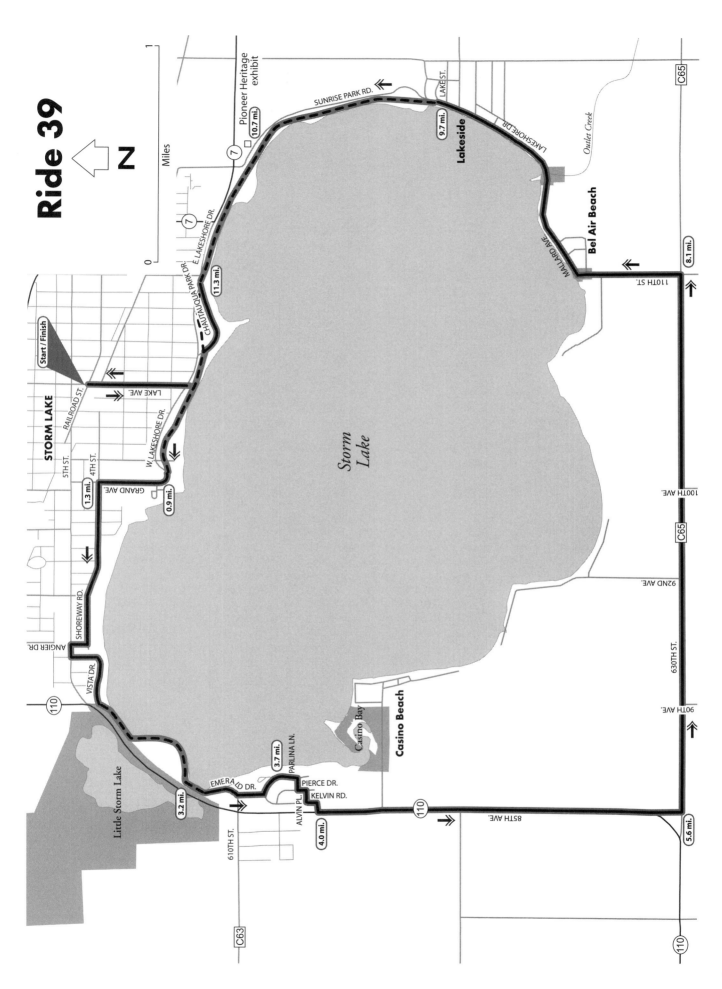

N

Miles

0   1

Start / Finish

STORM LAKE

RAILROAD ST.
5TH ST.
4TH ST.

1.3 mi.

LAKE AVE.

W. LAKESHORE DR.

CHAUTAUQUA PARK DR.

E. LAKESHORE DR.

GRAND AVE.

0.9 mi.

11.3 mi.

Pioneer Heritage exhibit

10.7 mi.

7

7

SUNRISE PARK RD.

LAKE ST.

9.7 mi.

Lakeside

LAKESHORE DR.

Outlet Creek

C65

Storm
Lake

Bel Air Beach

MALLARD AVE.

110TH ST.

8.1 mi.

C65

100TH AVE.

92ND AVE.

630TH ST.

90TH AVE.

5.6 mi.

110

85TH AVE.

110

Casino Beach

Casino Bay

PIERCE DR.
KELVIN RD.
ALVIN PL.

4.0 mi.

PARLINA LN.

3.7 mi.

EMERALD DR.

3.2 mi.

610TH ST.

C63

Little Storm Lake

SHOREWAY RD.

ANGIER DR.

VISTA DR.

110

RIDE 40
The Dutchman's Pizza Ride

LOCATION: County roads and Sioux Center Recreational Bike Trail between Orange City and Sioux Center

DISTANCE: 12.4 miles one way

SURFACE: Paved roads and paved trail

TERRAIN: Gentle rolls, one longish climb and descent on the trail

DIFFICULTY: Easy

SERVICES:

Restrooms: Businesses in Orange City, Sandy Hollow Park, Sioux Center Children's Park, and businesses in Sioux Center

Water: Same

Food: Restaurants and convenience stores in Orange City and Sioux Center

Camping: Alton Roadside Park, Alton; Sandy Hollow Park, Sioux Center

Lodging: Motels and bed and breakfast in Orange City, motels in Sioux Center

Bike Shop: Country Bikes and Produce, Ninth Street SW, Sioux Center

STARTING POINT: Pizza Ranch on Albany Avenue (County Road K64) in Orange City, just south of Second Street NE, on the west side of the street.

You can start and end this ride with a pizza on any day but Sunday. Both Orange City and Sioux Center were settled by Dutch immigrants, and the Dutch Reformed Church influence is still strong. Sunday is a day for church and family—in these towns, an open business on the Christian Sabbath is about as common as hen's teeth.

0.0 miles. From the Pizza Ranch restaurant in Orange City, head north on Albany Avenue (County Road K64). You pass the Century House on your left, a beautiful Victorian built in 1900 by the town's mayor. At 10th Street, a side path starts on the west side of the road and runs for about a half mile before petering out.

You're out of town in just a few minutes, among farm fields stretching to the horizon on both sides of County Road K64. The land rolls very gently, clothed in the greens of corn and beans. The road is smooth asphalt and empty ahead, heading due north. You pedal easily up a slight grade, then drop your chain onto a smaller gear in the rear cluster to take advantage of the downside.

This county is a major livestock-producing area—hogs, beef, dairy, and poultry—and you'd expect the air to smell of manure, but instead it's fresh and clean. A barn on your left has a smiley face painted above its doors; banal or not, it's appropriate to the day.

4.4 miles. Turn left to head west on County Road B40 (400th Street). Atop another rise, you look out over the land undulating beneath its blanket of crops, crossed here and there by fence lines and dotted with small stands of trees. There are occasional houses along the road, and farm silos jut above the horizon.

7.4 miles. A golf course has appeared on your left, and now you turn left into Sandy Hollow Park. Following the signs to the campground, turn right onto a dirt road and circle a small pond. As you pass the campground offices, a family of white ducks greets you, acting as if they own the place. Follow the road through the campground, between rows of RVs and camper-topped pickup trucks.

8.1 miles. Turn left from the campground road onto the asphalt Sioux Center Recreational Bike Trail. The trail winds through tall-grass prairie plantings behind the campground, then heads uphill beneath the power line. Gear down for the hill—it's a half-mile climb and surprisingly steep.

From the top of the hill, the view goes on forever in every direction. Ahead of you to the west is the water tower and elevator of Sioux Center. The trail ambles across the hilltop, then turns right, parallel to a gravel road, and slopes steeply down. Watch your speed here—the trail surface is rough, and at the bottom of the hill there's a sharp turn to cross the road. There are concrete posts at the road crossing that narrow the trail significantly.

After crossing the road, the trail angles past a small shelter and picnic table, then comes out on the south side of County Road B40. There's a well-kept farmhouse here with a great-looking asparagus patch next to the trail.

The trail runs along the ditch next to the road, so your view is constricted as you climb the gradual slope into Sioux Center. When the trail finally gets up to road level, you find yourself next to a development of nice-looking, modest homes, with the water tower dead ahead.

There are a number of driveways crossing the trail: be cautious of turning traffic. County Road B40 becomes Ninth Street SE once you cross Sixth Avenue.

11.2 miles. The roadside trail ends at a four-way stop at Fourth Avenue SE. Continue west on Ninth Street, which has very wide lanes. Be careful of the storm grates—they're wheel-grabbers. The lane is plenty wide enough to stay well to the left of the grates.

At the Health Center attached to the large Christian Reformed Church, turn right onto First Avenue SE, another street with very wide lanes. Sioux Center streets in general are very bike friendly, with extra-wide lanes to facilitate sharing with motor vehicles. Street names are unimaginative numbers—the streets run east–west, the avenues run north–south.

Amble through a very nice residential area, past turn-of-the-century houses with wide front porches, neatly kept lawns, and color-filled gardens, then take a left onto Third Street and go up a block to cross Main Avenue (U.S. Highway 75).

When you cross the highway, you enter the Centre Mall, a 100,000-square-foot enclosed shopping center that takes up an entire block. Rather than do a piecemeal renovation of its downtown, Sioux Center razed the town's central block, moved the few buildings of historical significance out to Historical Village by the fairgrounds, and built Centre Mall.

12.4 miles. End your ride at the Sioux Center Pizza Ranch. The menu's the same as it was in Orange City.

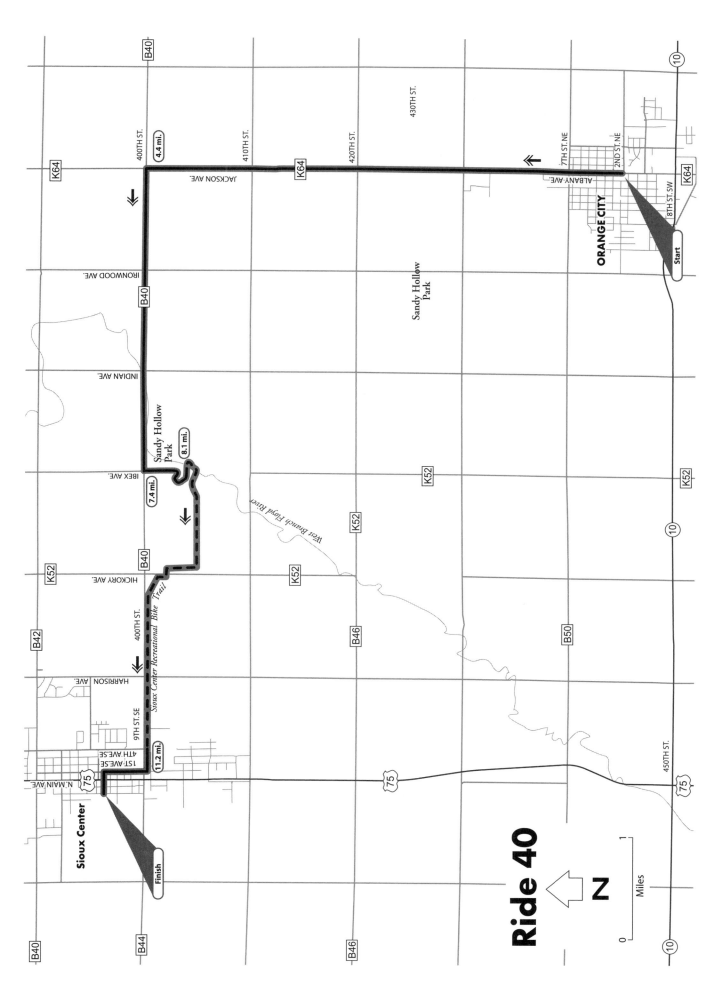

Ride 40

N

Miles

0   1

RIDE 41
Rolling Above the Flats

LOCATION: County and state roads between Akron and Hawarden

DISTANCE: 29.1-mile loop

SURFACE: Paved roads

TERRAIN: Mostly flat along the Big Sioux River, then over rollers for the return trip

DIFFICULTY: Moderate

SERVICES:

> **Restrooms:** At start/finish, businesses in Hawarden
>
> **Water:** Same
>
> **Food:** Restaurants and convenience stores in Akron and Hawarden
>
> **Camping:** Akron City Park, Akron
>
> **Lodging:** Bed and breakfast in Akron, motel in Hawarden
>
> **Bike Shop:** None nearby

STARTING POINT: Akron City Park, on the east side of State Highway 12 at the north end of Akron

The Theft of the County Seat

In 1860, three homesteaders created the settlement of Calliope (pronounced KAL-ee-ope) as the seat of mostly empty Sioux County. Calliope consisted of a log courthouse and three homes, but its ten citizens prospered from the fees paid by settlers who were buying up the surrounding land.

Most of those settlers were Dutch immigrants from Pella, Iowa. They founded Orange City, which quickly outgrew Calliope, whereupon they decided it should be the county seat and, incidentally, collect the land fees (which were, after all, being paid mainly by Dutch settlers). The people of Calliope adamantly disagreed. When Henry Hospers, the patriarch of the Dutch settlement, was elected County Supervisor by a large Dutch majority in 1871, Calliope citizens refused to seat him.

Unwilling to take no for an answer, Hospers called a force of Dutchmen together in January 1872, and crossed the snow-covered hills on horse-drawn sleighs to demand the county land records, money, and County Seal. Calliope residents refused to surrender the keys to the courthouse, so the raiders chopped a hole in its log walls, loaded the safe and the county records onto a sleigh, and hauled them back to Orange City.

From then on, county business was conducted in Orange City. Eventually, a vote was held to decide the matter legally: the Dutch easily won, thanks to their burgeoning population. Calliope was bypassed by the Chicago and Northwestern Railroad and the town of Hawarden sprang up a few miles south, where the railroad was. In 1893, Hawarden annexed the former town.

A replica of the original log courthouse has been erected in Calliope Village, a collection of 14 early homes and stores. A few years ago, the safe stolen by the Dutchmen was returned to that replica, but Orange City is still the Sioux County seat.

The first half of this ride along the Big Sioux River is mostly level, in stark contrast to the second half, which is mostly over hills. The flats are pleasant and easy, and the rollers are fun with an occasional challenge for your thighs.

0.0 miles. Push off from the gazebo in the Akron City Park—there's a swimming pool here, which you'll appreciate at ride's end—and turn north on State Highway 12, heading up a gradual climb. Going up the hill is a paved shoulder, which ends at the crest. The road makes a little dip, then passes the Dunham Prairie Preserve as you go over the next rise.

State Highway 12 flattens out now and you can settle into a good cruising gear. On your left as you head north is a railroad right-of-way; beyond that are fields and a line of trees along the Big Sioux River. The hills beyond the tree line are in South Dakota. To your right, cornfields rise into hills crossed by grass-covered erosion-control terraces. You pass only a few farmhouses, which look long empty and much the worse for wear.

6.2 miles. This is Chatsworth, a cluster of homes that have seen better days. The actual town is a block off the highway to your right; all its storefronts are closed and empty.

Past Chatsworth, the valley narrows and the hills rise directly from the ditch on your right. Grasses stretch to the riverside trees on your left, their seed-topped stalks rippling in the breeze like wavelets on a lake.

8.6 miles. You've climbed a small rise and caught a glimpse of the Big Sioux River on your left; now you reach a Sioux County Historical Site. There's a boulder, mostly obscured by juniper bushes, with a plaque explaining that this was the site of Sioux County's founding in 1860. The plaque is pockmarked by BB gun fire.

There's a nice downhill from Sioux County's origin, then a long flat to run out your momentum. The valley widens again, the hills drawing away on your right and the river meandering behind its tree line on the left.

11.7 miles. Cross First Street of Hawarden, "The Complete Community," then pass Sioux Fertilizer, a long building with a painted mural depicting a river running through farm fields. It's a rather peculiar interpretation of the scene.

12.3 miles. A block past the Fiesta Foods store, turn right on Ninth Street and go three blocks east to Central Avenue, the town's main drag. Turn left on Central, pass Mom's Goodies (with old-fashioned candy and soft-serve frozen yogurt), then turn right, heading east again, on 10th Street (State Highway 10). There's another mural here, this one depicting the Hawarden train depot in a primitivist style of shortened perspective.

It's a bit of a climb out of town on State Highway 10. The lane is nice and wide—plenty of room for sharing—and there are some very attractive old homes along the way.

13.3 miles. Turn right on Buchanan Avenue (County Road K18). The rollers start right away, with gradual slopes and short flats in between them. County Road K18's path is like a goldfinch's flight: a series of swooping up-and-down arcs that head straight south. You speed over a series of rollers heading down to Sixmile Creek, make a stepped climb up the far side of that valley, then run another set of rollers down to Indian Creek and climb another series of steps back up. From the hill crests, look east across roll after roll of the land with rows of corn curving across the slopes; look west to the river valley and the South Dakota hills. It's fast and fun, your legs churning as you shift down your rear cluster to build momentum on the downhills, then shift back up to spin on the climbs.

24.5 miles. At the crest of a steep climb, turn right onto County Road C16, heading west. Off to the left is a wind generator turning sluggishly in the light breeze. After about four more miles of rollers, County Road C16 comes to a T intersection with State Highway 12 and you turn south to head back to Akron.

29.0 miles. Turn left into the Akron City Park. The swimming pool looks particularly inviting right now!

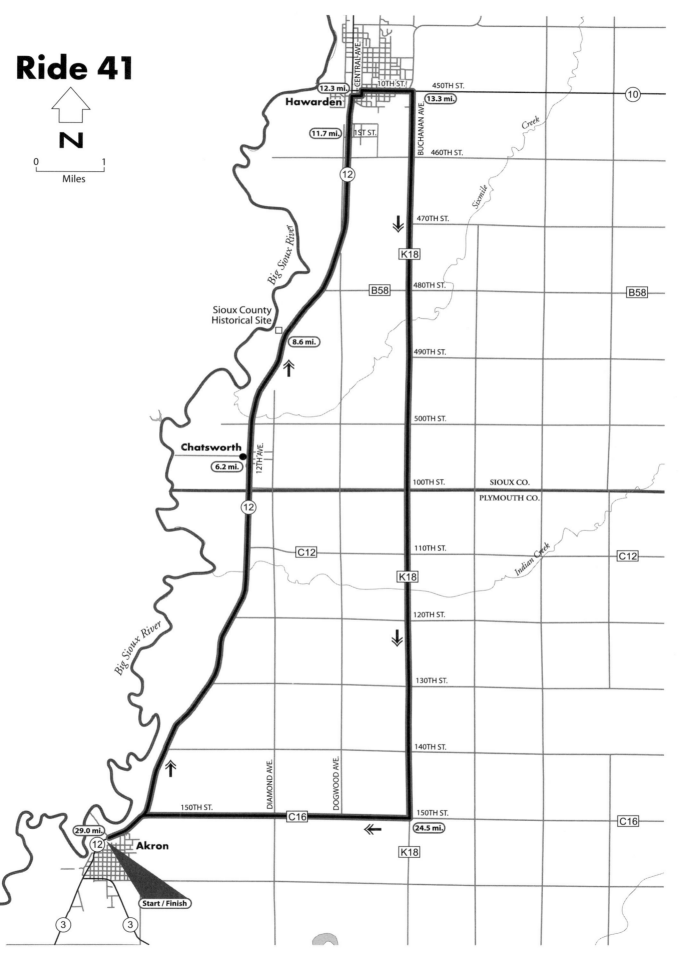

Ride 41

N

0 _____ 1
Miles

12.3 mi.

CENTRAL AVE.

10TH ST.

450TH ST.

10

Hawarden

13.3 mi.

BUCHANAN AVE.

11.7 mi.

1ST ST.

460TH ST.

Creek

12

470TH ST.

Big Sioux River

K18

B58

480TH ST.

B58

Sioux County
Historical Site

8.6 mi.

490TH ST.

500TH ST.

Chatsworth

12TH AVE.

6.2 mi.

100TH ST.

SIOUX CO.

12

PLYMOUTH CO.

C12

110TH ST.

C12

Indian Creek

K18

120TH ST.

130TH ST.

140TH ST.

DIAMOND AVE.

DOGWOOD AVE.

150TH ST.

29.0 mi.

150TH ST.

C16

150TH ST.

C16

12

Akron

24.5 mi.

K18

3

3

Start / Finish

RIDE 42
Following Lewis and Clark

Lewis, Clark, and Seaman stand before the Lewis and Clark Interpretive Center.

LOCATION: Lewis and Clark Trail in Sioux City
DISTANCE: 7.0 miles out and back
SURFACE: Paved trail
TERRAIN: Flat trail along the river
DIFFICULTY: Child's play
SERVICES:
>   **Restrooms:** At start/finish and in Riverside Park
>   **Water:** Same
>   **Food:** Off-route in Sioux City
>   **Camping:** Stone State Park, Sioux City
>   **Lodging:** Hotels, motels, and bed and breakfast in Sioux City
>   **Bike Shop:** Albrecht Cycle Shop, Fifth Street, Sioux City

STARTING POINT: Lewis and Clark Interpretive Center in Larson Park

The Oft Buried Body

Some people just can't stay put, even after they're dead. Such was the case of Sergeant Charles Floyd.

A relative of Captain William Clark's, the 21-year-old Floyd joined the Lewis and Clark expedition when its leaders, on their way to assemble their Corps of Discovery, stopped near his hometown of Louisville, Kentucky. He showed his mettle during the winter of 1803, which the Corps spent training on the Mississippi River, and was approved as a sergeant in command of the second squad in April 1804.

What dreams must have gone through young Sergeant Floyd's mind as the expedition set out into the wilderness! Unfortunately, those dreams never had a chance to come to fruition.

On August 5, 1804, as the Corps labored upriver from Council Bluffs, where they'd met with leaders of the Sioux and other Indian tribes, Sergeant Floyd fell ill. He died two weeks later—the only casualty of the expedition. Historians now believe his illness was a ruptured appendix.

His saddened comrades buried Sergeant Floyd at the top of a high, round hill overlooking the river, near what is now the town of Sergeant Bluff. A cedar post with his name and the date was left to mark his grave.

But Floyd did not rest easily. By 1857, the river had eroded and undermined the bluff where he lay, causing it to slide into the river. People from Sioux City retrieved the Sergeant's skull and some bones that were found scattered on the riverbank, and reburied them about 200 yards east of the original grave.

In 1894, Sergeant Floyd's journal from the Lewis and Clark trip was discovered and published, arousing renewed interest in the young man. Again, his grave was opened. The remains were identified, placed in a sturdy urn, buried once more (with appropriate fanfare), and marked with a marble slab.

But Sergeant Floyd still wasn't at rest. At the turn of the century, Sioux City's citizenry decided to build a monument to the Corps of Discovery's only casualty. The cornerstone was laid on August 20, 1900, the anniversary of his death, and Floyd's much-moved remains were entombed in its concrete core. The monument was dedicated on Memorial Day of 1901 and still stands atop the hill overlooking the river south of Sioux City. Sergeant Floyd hasn't moved since.

Two hundred years ago, Lewis and Clark's Corps of Discovery had to battle the Missouri River current and struggle past the sandbar at the mouth of the Big Sioux River to move through this area. You get to cover the same ground, but you're riding a bike on a gorgeous paved trail. Life's a lot more fun now than it was in 1804, eh?

0.0 miles. Saddle up at the Lewis and Clark Interpretive Center in Sioux City's Larson Park. Check out the larger-than-life statue of Lewis, Clark, and Lewis' dog, Seaman, at the entrance; if you're not in a rush to ride, go into the center and enjoy the interpretive displays.

Like the Corps of Discovery, you head upriver. Your movement is much easier than theirs, of course, as you follow the curving path from the pavilion next to the Interpretive Center and turn right onto the Lewis and Clark Trail to pass the M.V. (Motor Vessel) Sergeant Floyd, built by the U.S. Army Corps of Engineers in 1932 as an inspection boat. The boat is now a museum of the region's maritime history.

The trail winds past parking lots and through the park. At the Y intersection by the park entrance, bear left to follow the path closest to the river. Interstate 29 is on your right and its traffic is noisy and constant; on your left the Missouri River sweeps past much more peacefully. The trail is shaded by silver maples and mulberry trees as you ride easily through the park. You come into a densely wooded section, then emerge to a beautiful view of the river.

1.3 miles. Here on your left is the junction of the Big Sioux River with the Missouri. Lewis and Clark followed the Missouri—your trail turns from their route and goes up the Big Sioux. You notice that you've been climbing: There's a good drop down to the water now. A wooden rail fence separates you from that drop.

You're riding between the Interstate and the river, through intermittent shade from the mulberry trees along here. In early June, this trail is stained purple from the berries crushed beneath bicycle tires and cottonwood fluff drifts in the air like mid-summer snow.

Across the river is the Pointe Nature Preserve in South Dakota, clothed in grasses and trees. In the woods beside the trail, the birds sing loudly enough to overcome the incessant hum of the Interstate's traffic.

3.2 miles. You come into an open area of grassland, pass a sandy beach area on the river, and cross beneath the I-29 entrance ramps. The trail turns and circles, bringing you into Riverside Park. You pass a marina on the river side of the park, soccer fields on your right.

3.5 miles. The trail ends at the parking lot of Riverside Park, near the Bruguier Cabin, home of Sioux City's first white settler, Theophile Bruguier. Bruguier was a French-Canadian fur trader who came to this area in 1849 and wed two daughters of War Eagle, the chief of the Yankton Sioux, the dominant tribe in the area.

Turn around here and retrace your route back to the Lewis and Clark Interpretive Center. And pick some mulberries on your way back—they're delicious.

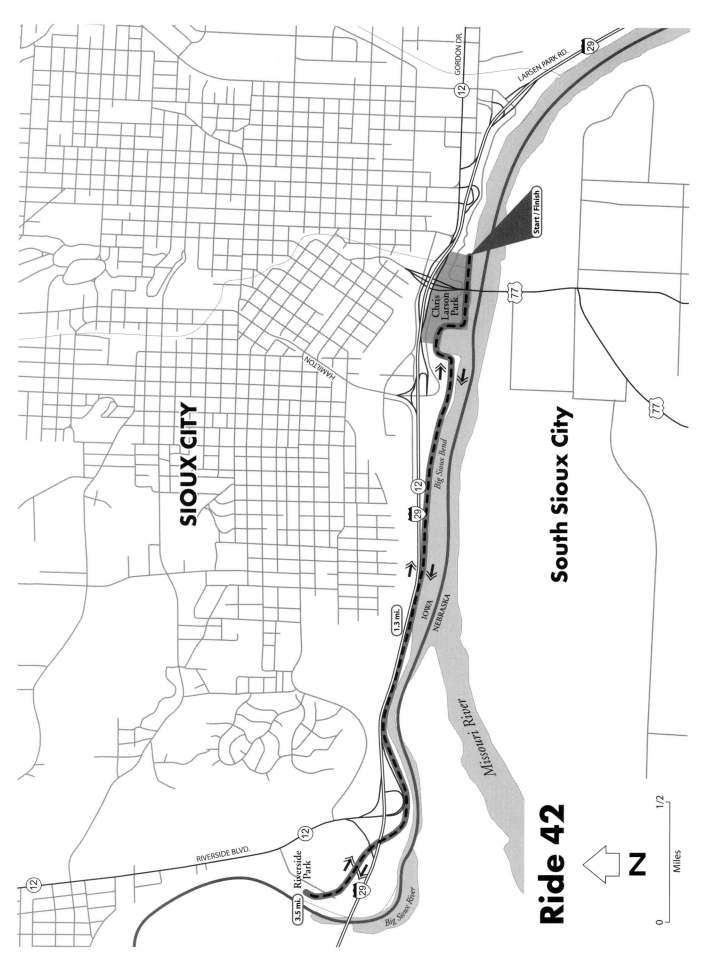

Ride 42

SIOUX CITY

South Sioux City

GORDON DR.

LARSEN PARK RD.

29

12

Start / Finish

77

77

Chris Larson Park

HAMILTON

Big Sioux Bend

12

29

IOWA

NEBRASKA

1.3 mi.

Missouri River

12

RIVERSIDE BLVD.

12

Riverside Park

29

3.5 mi.

Big Sioux River

N

0   1/2

Miles

RIDE 43

Where have All the Bluebirds Gone?

LOCATION: Sauk Rail Trail from Carroll to Lakeview
DISTANCE: 31.7 miles one way
SURFACE: Paved and crushed-limestone trails, paved town and county roads, about 50 yards of gravel road
TERRAIN: Short, steep hills around Swan Lake, then flat rail-trail and roads around Black Hawk Lake
DIFFICULTY: Mostly easy, moderate on trail around Swan Lake
SERVICES:
    Restrooms: At start and finish, trailheads in Breda and Carnarvon
    Water: Same
    Food: Restaurants and convenience stores in Carroll, Breda, Carnarvon, and Lake View
    Camping: Swan Lake State Park, Carroll; Black Hawk State Park and Crescent Park, Lakeview
    Lodging: Motels and bed and breakfasts in Carroll; bed and breakfasts in Lakeview
    Bike Shop: Sun Sport, Fifth Street, Carroll
STARTING POINT: Next to the campground showers in Swan Lake State Park, southeast of Carroll

The start of this ride is serious fun—a twisting, up-and-down trail through Swan Lake State Park—followed by a wonderful rail-trail that follows watercourses through the hills and gives you a hint of what Iowa was like as a true prairie state.

0.0 miles. After getting your trail pass (one dollar for the day) from the park office, head downhill on the park road from the parking lot next to the campground showers. Turn right on the asphalt trail, which leads into the trees and immediately up a short hill. The trail twists and turns past prairie remnants, through woods and savannahs, up and down sharp, short climbs and descents.

2.6 miles. Cross the park road and, at the T in the trail, go right to head northwest. After a short but steep climb, you see Carroll's water tower across the valley. Follow the trail as it winds through the southwest corner of town into Rolling Hills Park.

4.6 miles. The trail Ts into a sidewalk; turn right to cross the bridge, then cross the road to get back onto the trail, which follows the Middle Raccoon River through more parklands. Bear left at the Y by the small trailhead, and now you're on the Sauk Rail Trail.

Carroll falls behind as you follow the river northwest. There are lots of bluebird houses on fence posts, and signs proclaiming the Sauk Bluebird Trail. You'll see redwing blackbirds, an occasional purple martin, robins, orioles, red-tail hawks, goldfinches, even an indigo bunting—but no bluebirds.

8.3 miles. The trail intersects Jade Avenue, a gravel road, and an arrow directs you to the right to cross a set of railroad tracks. Twenty yards up the road, the trail goes off again to the left, parallel to the tracks.

9.4 miles. Enter the hamlet of Maple River. You go left on the road, then right onto the trail again. The asphalt ends and the trail now has a crushed-limestone surface—it's fine for your road tires—as it heads north along the river valley between crop-covered hills. Though it seems utterly flat, you've been rising steadily since leaving Carroll.

When the Middle Raccoon River veers west, the trail continues north along a stream, passing through the Hazelbrush Wildlife Area. Here, crops give way to grasslands and prairie flowers paint the hills with colors. It's a glimpse into Iowa's past, before the prairie was turned into farms.

The rise in the trail becomes more noticeable as the trail twists through this shallow valley, playing leapfrog with the stream. Trees are scarce and when you pass through a small wooded section, the shade is welcome.

15.3 miles. The trail emerges from the grasslands at the intersection of 130th Street and Granite Avenue outside Breda. If you look back, there's a smiley face mowed on a hillside, and a greeting of "HI."

16.6 miles. Cross Breda's main street and pass the old railroad depot at the trailhead next to the grain elevator. The town's small business district, with a tavern and convenience store, is up that road to the left.

This is the height of land: leaving Breda, the trail enters another shallow valley and follows a meandering stream that flows north. The down slope is noticeable only because the pedaling seems easier. Swallows swoop over the stream and redwing blackbirds trill as you pass.

22.3 miles. Cross the road as you enter Carnarvon, and the trail is paved again. The ride through Carnarvon is a bit dreary: you're behind grain bins, which is apparently the dumping ground for rusting-out farm machinery.

23.0 miles. The trail merges onto a gravel road and an arrow points right, under the railroad tracks. Ride the gravel for about 50 yards, then turn onto the trail again. Now you're entering the Black Hawk Wildlife Area. On your left is the railroad embankment; on the right are marshlands and prairie grasses. After you curve past a pond, the trail makes a sharp right to parallel Perkins Avenue (County Road M54). You get some shade going by Black Hawk Marsh, then emerge into a residential neighborhood in Lakeview.

26.9 miles. When the trail intersects with Harrison and Vine streets, continue straight along Vine. Turn right onto First Street, then follow the trail left to its end at McClure Street. Turn right onto Third Street, then go left at Lake Street to begin your circle around Black Hawk Lake.

27.5 miles. Pass a statue of Chief Black Hawk at the entrance to Camp Crescent and turn right onto Crescent Park Drive. You pass some modest summer camps along the lakeshore, catching glimpses of the water between them. Turn left at County Road, then right onto Lakewood Cutoff. The road draws ever closer to the lake, finally running right along its edge.

29.7 miles. Turn right onto East Shore Drive, still following the lakeshore. Fields stretch out on the left, and the lake is a broad expanse of blue on your right.

31.4 miles. At the T intersection, turn right on Quincy Avenue, which takes you to the ride's end at Black Hawk State Park.

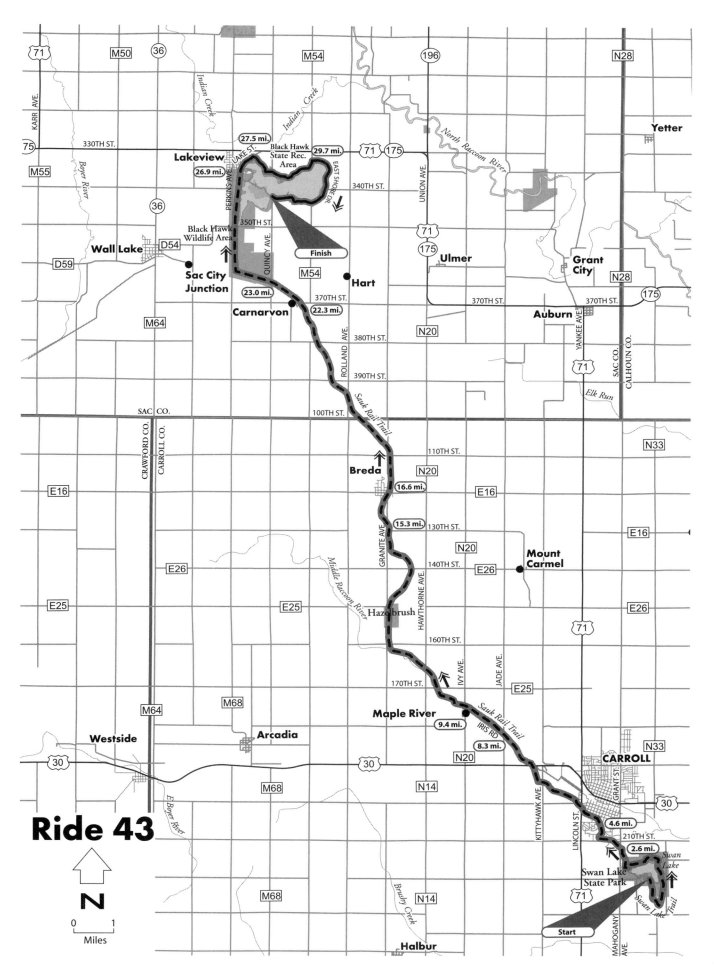

Ride 43

N

0 — 1
Miles

RIDE 44
The Lesser Hills

LOCATION: County, state, and federal roads between Woodbine and Portsmouth
DISTANCE: 32.2-mile loop
SURFACE: Paved county, state and federal roads
TERRAIN: Lots of hills, with steep climbs and descents
DIFFICULTY: Strenuous
SERVICES:
    Restrooms: At businesses in Woodbine and Portsmouth
    Water: Same
    Food: Restaurants and convenience stores in Woodbine and Portsmouth
    Camping: Willow Lake Recreation Area, Woodbine
    Lodging: Motel in Woodbine
    Bike Shop: None nearby
STARTING POINT: LJ's Café on the corner of Fifth and Walker streets in Woodbine

Behind the Loess Hills that line Iowa's western border are more hills, which you'll explore on this ride. The climbs and descents are shorter and not quite as steep as in the Loess Hills, but they'll still test your legs. And you'll have magnificent views to admire while you're pumping up these "lesser" hills.

0.0 miles. Grab a bite at LJ's Café on the corner of Fifth and Walker streets in Woodbine, then head south on Walker and turn right on Fourth Street. Go up a block and turn left on Lincoln Way. This was part of the original Lincoln Highway, the first coast-to-coast national route, and still has the original brick paving laid in the early 1900s. The bricks are a nice historical touch, but not so nice to ride over; fortunately, you're not on them for long. Watch yourself crossing the railroad tracks—they're apt to grab your tire—then bear right onto U.S. Highway 30. Highway 30 is an east–west road, but here it takes you across the Boyer River and heads south.

The road is flat for the first two miles, then starts to rise. There's a narrow paved shoulder outside the fog line that you can ride to give the motorists more room to pass as the road works its way up the side of the Boyer River valley. The slope is pretty easy and the view to your right is gorgeous. You can trace the river's course by the line of riverside trees meandering through the valley.

5.0 miles. Turn left to go east on State Highway 44. There's a bit more hill to climb, then you coast down into Six Mile Creek's valley. The creek is on your right, behind the line of trees; beyond it, crops rise up the terraced hillside. You have a couple of miles of flats before the valley starts to narrow and the road rises in a series of gradual steps.

8.5 miles. On the roadside is a cross planted in memory of Herb Tillitson, who was struck and killed by lightning near here in 1945. Check the sky: any thunderheads in sight?

A series of steep climbs is next; fortunately, there are little dips between them to give your legs a rest. From the crests of the hills, the views are beautiful across the terraced land.

14.7 miles. Welcome to Shelby County. From here, you have two downhill miles through a series of rollers. Turn left onto State Highway 191, then bear left onto Second Street at the welcoming sign to Portsmouth, the "Biggest Little Town in the U.S."

Portsmouth owes its existence to the Chicago, Milwaukee and Saint Paul Railroad, which came through in 1882 and platted the town. The town boasts all of 225 people, most of whom either go to lunch or order it to go from the Club 191 on Main Street, a block to your right. A hamburger, beer, and tip for the hard-working waitress will set you back a mere five dollars.

Second Street becomes Cedar Road after climbing through Portsmouth, heading north. You have about a mile of gradual climbing, then a fast descent before you hit a seriously steep hill. At the crest, the views east and west are tremendous: Tree lines and hilltops define the horizon, and in between are endless rolls with terraces in various shades of green.

21.7 miles. After a stretch of great rollers—you hit 30+ mph easily on the downsides—you turn left to head west on County Road F32. There's a panoramic view to your left as you make a steep descent to cross Pigeon Creek.

23.4 miles. On your right is a house with an incredible collection of funky lawn ornaments. A short distance past it, you're back in Harrison County. Celebrate the change of counties with a very steep climb, then enjoy several miles of fun rollers as the road arrows west over the hills. At the bottom of each dip, the embankments beside the road fall away to give you pretty views down the hollows between the hills.

31.5 miles. You're back to Woodbine—turn right onto U.S. Highway 30, than make an immediate left onto Lincoln Way. This is a nasty intersection: you turn onto Lincoln Way at a curve with bad sightlines, cross two sets of railroad tracks at a wheel-catching angle, then climb a hill to hit another two sets of bad-angle tracks. Take it carefully.

32.1 miles. Turn right onto Fourth Street, then left on Walker, and you're back to your starting point.

Cedar Road arrows across rolling hills north of Portsmouth.

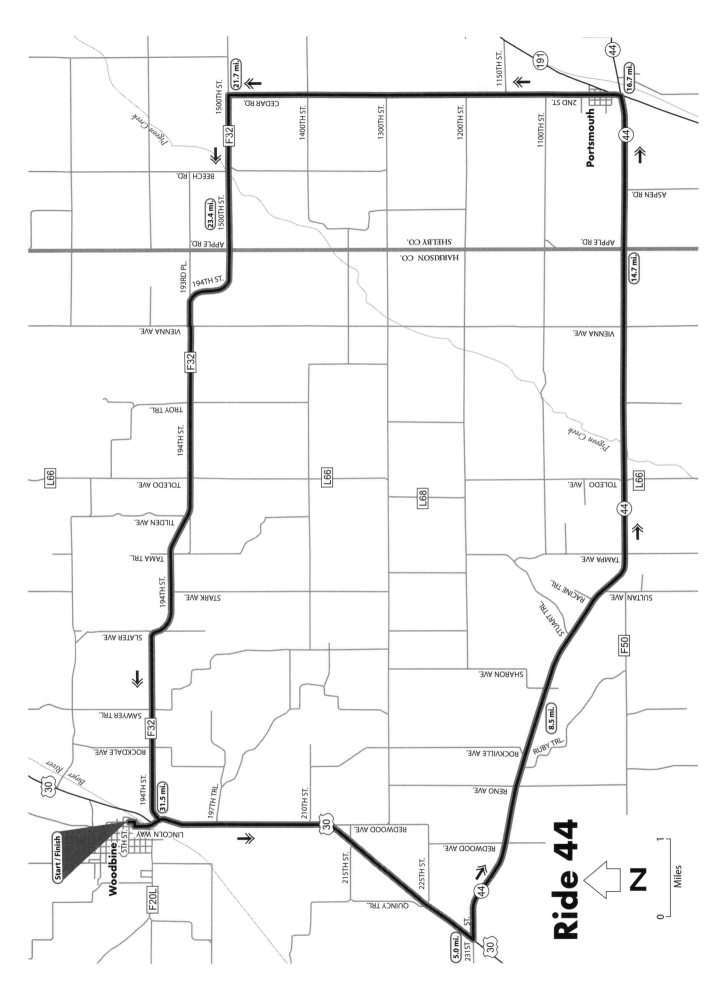

Ride 44

N

Miles
0   1

RIDE 45
The Heart of the Loess Hills

LOCATION: County roads between Magnolia and Pisgah
DISTANCE: 27.2-mile loop
SURFACE: Paved county and state roads
TERRAIN: Very steep hills and a long stretch of flat land
DIFFICULTY: Strenuous
SERVICES:
  Restrooms: Businesses in Magnolia and Pisgah
  Water: Same
  Food: Restaurants in Magnolia and Pisgah, convenience store in Pisgah, Small's Fruit Farm on State Highway 127
  Camping: Wilson Island Recreational Area, Missouri Valley; Town Park, Pisgah
  Lodging: Motels and bed and breakfasts in Missouri Valley
  Bike Shop: None nearby
STARTING POINT: The Country Inn at the corner of Main and Magnolia streets in Magnolia

The Loess Hills

Running in a 200-mile-long line along Iowa's western border, the Loess (pronounced "luss") Hills are astonishing for their beauty and ecological rarity. Their mix of dry soil, exposed slopes, and moisture-holding hollows allow a unique mixture of western and eastern species of plants and animals; their rugged topography is a startling anomaly when compared to most of Iowa's landscape of rounded hills and long slopes.

As the Ice Age glaciers advanced and retreated, they ground the underlying rock into powder-like sediment, which washed down the Missouri River and settled on the floodplain in miles-wide mud flats. The mud dried and the wind picked up the fine-grained particles, carrying them eastward. The heavier grains dropped closest to the Missouri River source, forming high, sharp bluffs on the western edge of the hills; the finer-grained silt flew farther east, tapering the eastern slopes. Repeated over thousands of years, the process built the hills layer by layer.

Originally, the hills were as smooth as a sand dune, but wind and water have carved their highly erodible soil into today's jagged shapes. They were grass-covered, too, described as "bald-pated" by Lewis and Clark in 1804. Fire suppression by farmers for the last century has allowed trees to grow—today the Loess Hills are largely wooded.

It all makes for challenging and beautiful bicycling country. Ride 45: The Heart of the Loess Hills, gives you a somewhat gentle introduction, with some valley roads to cushion the strenuous climbs. On Ride 48: The Taco Ride, you'll see the hills' beauty from the easy grades of a rail-trail. Ride 49: The Hidden Valley, is an unabashed hill fest, with 4 mph climbs and 40 mph descents, and Ride 50: Southern Loess Hills Loop, takes you through the gentler slopes and broad valleys on the eastern side of the hills.

The Loess Hills are decidedly steep, but not too high—they top out at about 250 feet above the Missouri River valley. They'll challenge you going up, reward you with the rugged beauty of their crests, then thrill you going down.

0.0 miles. Step on your pedal at the Country Inn, a tavern/restaurant in the middle of tiny Magnolia, and head north on Magnolia Street. Two blocks later, turn left on Second Street (State Highway 127), pass the town's park, and head downhill. Watch your speed—you want to turn right to continue north on Laredo Avenue (County Road L23), following the Scenic Byway sign to the Orchard Ridge Loop, and the turn comes up fast.

Laredo Avenue travels on a ridgeline, with mild ups and downs. On the left, look into a narrow, pretty valley; on your right are high bluff walls dotted with holes occupied by swallows. Descend gradually to follow a stream through the valley. Steep hills rise on both sides of the road, their slopes covered with prairie grasses.

Your first climb comes at just shy of five miles, when the road diverges from the stream's path and starts a mile-long climb that will put you in your granny gear. At the top of the climb, the view across these rugged, tree-topped hills and valleys is breathtaking. Now the road winds through the hills, climbing and falling, seeking passes from one valley to the next.

8.9 miles. At the bottom of a long descent, turn left onto Easton Road (County Road F20L). The bullfrogs in the pond at this intersection bid you a deep-throated greeting as you head west through Cobb Creek's valley between terraced hillsides. The riding's easy through the bottomland.

11.7 miles. County Road F20L becomes Main Street as you enter Pisgah, "The Heart of the Loess Hills." Pisgah would be more aptly called the "Gateway to the Loess Hills"—it sits on the Soldier River, a natural avenue into the hills. The town looks a bit the worse for wear, but there are restaurants, taverns, and a convenience store here amid the closed-down storefronts.

12.3 miles. Turn left to head south on State Highway 183 (First Street), following the Soldier River as it travels a man-altered course between levees at the bottom of the valley. There's a solid wall of trees on your left, occasionally giving way to hillside hayfields. Traffic is very light and the road surface is very smooth as you cruise over low rises, enjoying downs that are longer than the ups.

At about the 18-mile mark, you emerge from the mouth of the valley into the Missouri River's table-flat floodplain. Continue south over low swells that hardly call for gear changes. The Loess Hills rise straight up from the road on your left; the broad plain of cropland extends on your right to a horizon defined by the line of trees along the Missouri.

21.7 miles. Highway 183 T-bones State Highway 127 and you turn left on the combined 183/127, still heading south along the base of the hills. In about a mile, you'll pass Small's Fruit Farm at the intersection with County Road F32. Small's sells fruit pies in season—the Pie Parlor is definitely worth a stop. Go for the strawberry-rhubarb pie in early summer.

23.1 miles. Follow State Highway 127 as it turns east, and shift down for a long, steep climb. Highway 127 makes no bones about heading back into the hills: It's as straight as the flight of an arrow shot into the sky, and almost as steep.

You top out of the climb after a mile, then have a screaming-fast descent and a couple of rollers that'll hardly slow you down. You have plenty of momentum to cruise across Allen Creek's pretty valley. Keep an eye out for a house on your left with an outstanding rock garden.

Just shy of the 26-mile mark, you start your last climb. It's a bit over a mile long and starts gradually, then quickly becomes very steep. Your thighs will be burning by the time you roll past the Magnolia town park.

27.0 miles. Turn right onto Magnolia Street and grind up the final quarter mile to your starting point.

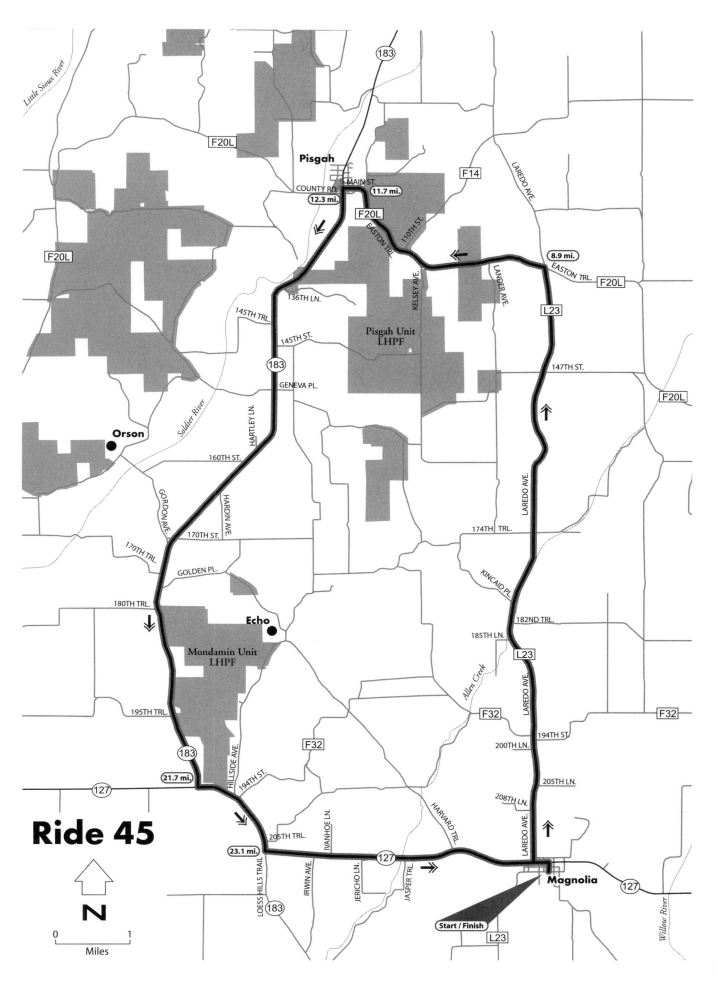

Little Sioux River

F20L

Pisgah

COUNTY RD.   MAIN ST.   11.7 mi.
12.3 mi.

F20L

F14

LAREDO AVE.

F20L

EASTON TRL.

110TH ST.

KELSEY AVE.

8.9 mi.

EASTON TRL.   F20L

136TH LN.

LANDER AVE.

L23

145TH TRL.

145TH ST.

183

GENEVA PL.

Pisgah Unit
LHPF

147TH ST.

Soldier River

HARTLEY LN.

Orson

160TH ST.

GORDON AVE.

HARDIN AVE.

170TH ST.

LAREDO AVE.

174TH TRL.

170TH TRL.

GOLDEN PL.

KINCAID PL.

180TH TRL.

Echo

182ND TRL.

Mondamin Unit
LHPF

185TH LN.

L23

LAREDO AVE.

Allen Creek

195TH TRL.

F32

F32

183

HILLSIDE AVE.

194TH ST.

F32

194TH ST.

200TH LN.

21.7 mi.

127

205TH LN.

205TH TRL.

HARVARD TRL.

208TH LN.

LAREDO AVE.

Ride 45

23.1 mi.

IRWIN AVE.

IVANHOE LN.

JERICHO LN.

JASPER TRL.

127

Magnolia

127

N

Start / Finish

L23

Willow River

LOESS HILLS TRAIL

183

0   1
Miles

RIDE 46
Actually Nebraska Ride

LOCATION: Park road through DeSoto National Wildlife Refuge

DISTANCE: 9.5-mile loop

SURFACE: Paved and gravel park road

TERRAIN: Dead flat

DIFFICULTY: Child's play

SERVICES:

Restrooms: At start/finish; hiking trailhead at 2.5 miles

Water: Wilson Island State Park

Food: None

Camping: Wilson Island State Park, Missouri Valley

Lodging: Motels and bed and breakfasts in Missouri Valley

Bike Shop: None nearby

STARTING POINT: Wilson Island State Park entrance to the De Soto National Wildlife Refuge, west of Missouri Valley

The Invisible Artifact

You can't visit the DeSoto National Wildlife Refuge without becoming aware of the Steamboat Bertrand. The Bertrand was a 161-foot cargo craft bound up the Missouri River to the frontier when it struck a snag and sank in 1865, one of over 400 steamboats to meet such a fate on the Missouri during the steamboat era. What makes the Bertrand special is that it was found and dug up a century later. The river had changed its course—also not a rare occurrence—and the Bertrand's remains were found a half mile from the river.

Several signs on the park road point you to the site of the excavation. At the parking lot, an information kiosk gives a rough outline of the boat's history and salvage—enough to whet your curiosity and induce you to stroll up the walkway to the excavation site.

At the end of the walkway, another kiosk gives you more details. The boat's salvage in 1968 was actually a treasure hunt—the salvagers hoped to find gold, a huge and valuable supply of mercury (used to separate gold from rock), and tons of incidental artifacts of historical interest, not to mention a trove of hundred-plus-year-old whiskey (used to separate gold from miners).

The displays are artfully done and very informative, and by the time you've finished reading them, you can't wait to see this wonderful artifact, so painstakingly retrieved from the mud of the river's former bed.

So you walk the final few yards up a boardwalk and when you get to the end of the walkway, all you see is a pond. There are a lot of turtles in the pond. It's not exactly what you were hoping for, but, as they say, life is full of little disappointments. After the salvagers removed the Bertrand's cargo they reburied the boat in order to preserve it.

If you're disappointed about not seeing the boat, put yourself in the salvager's place: there was no gold, only a few canisters of mercury, and no whiskey on board.

Short and sweet, this ride is best done during the fall waterfowl migration season, when the area attracts hundreds of thousands of birds. Part of the ride is on gravel, but your road tires can handle it. It's not a ride you want to speed through, anyway.

0.0 miles. Swing your leg over the bike at the Wilson Island State Park campground's entrance to the De Soto National Wildlife Refuge, and kick off onto the park road, turning left to head west into the refuge.

Rivers are natural boundary lines, which is why so many states, counties, cities, and towns use them as such. However, rivers also change their courses. The Iowa/Nebraska state line is supposedly the middle of the Missouri River, but right here it's the middle of what *used to be* the Missouri River and is now DeSoto Lake, an oxbow lake left behind when the Missouri moved itself west. One end of the lake is on your right—as soon as you pass the middle of it, you're in Nebraska. So this ride is not really in Iowa at all. (Actually, this land is owned by the federal government, so who cares what state it's in?)

The two-lane park road is pool-table flat as you glide around its curves, and plenty wide enough for comfort, considering the number of cars on it (that number is

probably zero). On your left is the Missouri River, discernible only by a line of bushes and a noticeably wide gap to the forest on the river's western bank. On your right are small cornfields. The National Park Service grows that corn for the birds that travel the Missouri Valley Flyway in their annual migrations.

2.1 miles. A road turns off to the right, leading to the Steamboat Bertrand, and you turn with it. (If you continue straight on the park road, you'll re-enter Iowa and eventually get to the Visitor Center.) The turnoff for the Steamboat Bertrand display is about a half mile up—if you decide to visit it, watch out for the expansion cracks in the pavement. They're almost bad enough to pass for speed bumps.

Past the boat exhibit are long fields of grass surrounded by forest, with small islands of trees in the grassy areas. The Cottonwood and Prairie Grass trails—hiking paths—are on your left, leading into the prairie. There are restrooms and picnic tables at the trailhead.

4.6 miles. This is the Bob Star Wildlife Overlook. A wooden wall has been erected with viewing ports overlooking DeSoto Lake. It's a great place to see the migrating waterfowl. The pavement ends without warning at the Wildlife Overlook, and now you're on gravel. The tire tracks from motor traffic are your best line through the gravel; the cars have pretty much swept all the stones off them. Passing cars raise a considerable amount of dust, however; fortunately, there are very few passing cars.

You're making a loop around the inside of DeSoto Lake's oxbow; you catch glimpses of the water through the screen of trees on your left. There's lots of wildlife here—you can pretty much take it for granted that you'll see deer. During the migration seasons, particularly the fall, when waterfowl come through here by the tens of thousands, their quacks, squawks, honks, and general flutter is a constant background noise.

There are several gravel roads leading off to the left, going through the woods to lake access points. At about six miles, you pass one end of Lakeview Drive; you pass the other end a half mile farther.

7.1 miles. The Wood Duck Nature Trail, another hiking trail, leads off to your left, going to a small pond that's a favorite spot for the local ducks. On your right, the breeze makes the tall grasses sway. They glint in the sunlight like riffles on a lake.

9.1 miles. You reconnect with the hardtop park road and turn left, pass the sign that says you're entering Iowa, and leave De Soto National Wildlife Refuge. In about a quarter mile, you're back to your starting point at the entrance to Wilson Island State Park's campground.

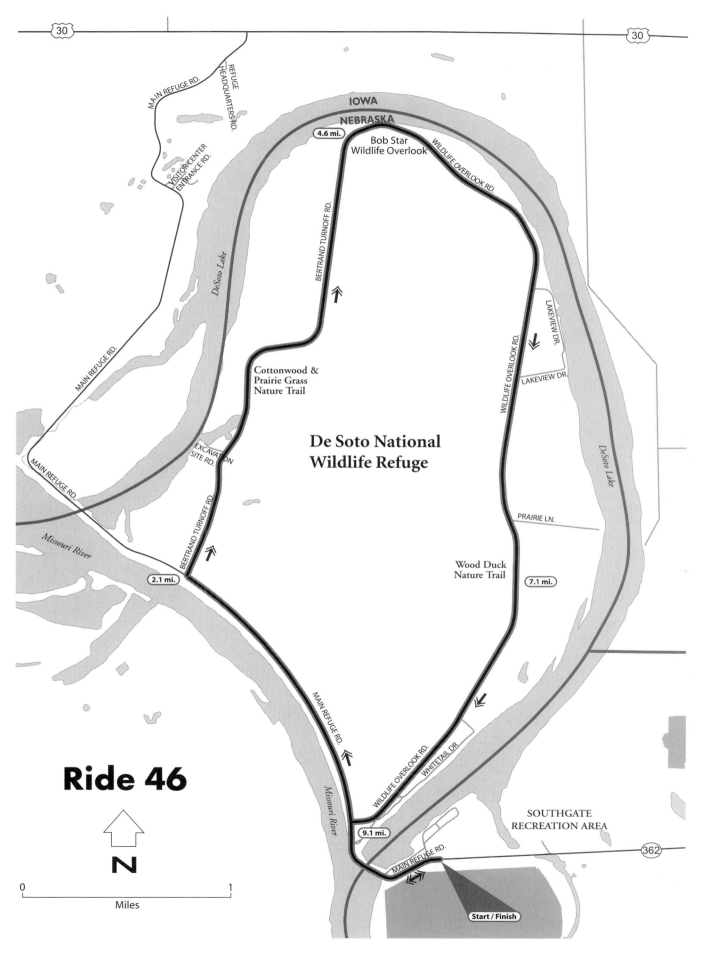

30 30

MAIN REFUGE RD.
REFUGE HEADQUARTERS RD.

IOWA
NEBRASKA

4.6 mi.

Bob Star
Wildlife Overlook

WILDLIFE OVERLOOK RD.

VISITOR CENTER ENTRANCE RD.

BERTRAND TURNOFF RD.

DeSoto Lake

LAKEVIEW DR.

LAKEVIEW DR.

WILDLIFE OVERLOOK RD.

Cottonwood &
Prairie Grass
Nature Trail

MAIN REFUGE RD.

EXCAVATION SITE RD.

De Soto National
Wildlife Refuge

DeSoto Lake

MAIN REFUGE RD.

BERTRAND TURNOFF RD.

PRAIRIE LN.

Missouri River

Wood Duck
Nature Trail

7.1 mi.

2.1 mi.

MAIN REFUGE RD.

Ride 46

⬆
N

0   1
Miles

Missouri River

WILDLIFE OVERLOOK RD.

WHITETAIL DR.

9.1 mi.

SOUTHGATE
RECREATION AREA

MAIN REFUGE RD.

362

Start / Finish

RIDE 47
An Old-Time Coca-Cola Ride

LOCATION: State and county roads between Walnut and Atlantic
DISTANCE: 30.8-mile loop
SURFACE: Paved city, county, and state roads
TERRAIN: Good rollers and some short, steep climbs and descents
DIFFICULTY: Moderate
SERVICES:
    Restrooms: Businesses in Walnut, Marne, and Atlantic
    Water: Same
    Food: Restaurants in Walnut and Atlantic, tavern in Marne
    Camping: Sunnyside Park, Atlantic; Cold Springs County Park, Lewis
    Lodging: Motels and bed and breakfasts in Atlantic, bed and breakfast in Walnut
    Bike Shop: Western Auto, Chestnut Street, Atlantic
STARTING POINT: Aunt B's Kitchen on Antique City Drive (State Highway 83/County Road M47) in downtown Walnut

Some steep hills, fun rollers, wide-open vistas, and interesting towns make this ride both challenging and entertaining. You start and end in "The Antique City," and "The Coca-Cola Capital" of Iowa is the midpoint; hence the ride's name.

0.0 miles. Aunt B's Kitchen is a small restaurant nestled among the antiques shops along Antique City Drive (State Highway 83/County Road M47) in the center of Walnut's business district. It's a good place to fuel up with a piece of pie and cup of coffee before your ride. Saddle up and head south on the Drive, with a short downhill to start you off.

As you leave town, you'll pass an attractive farmyard with a barn built in 1887, just ten years after the city of Walnut was chartered. Past there, you climb your first hill of the ride. As you reach its crest, check out the antique merry-go-round horse pulling an old sleigh in front of the house on your right. Note the deer antlers on the horse's head.

1.9 miles. Turn left with State Highway 83 to head east. You're on high ground, with an all-around view of open corn and soybean fields covering long, low hills. The road surface is good, traffic is light to none, and every once in a while you'll hear the squawk of a pheasant. The next few miles have some great rollers, with 30+-mph descents that give you enough momentum to make the climbs easy.

7.7 miles. Enter Marne: "From a Proud Past to a Promising Future," its optimistic sign reads. There's a tavern up to your left on Marne Road (County Road M56); it and an auto-body shop are the only apparent enterprises upon which Marne promises to build the future.

Marne's in a valley, so the climbs get serious as you leave the small town behind. State Highway 83 seems to go either up or down, with nary a flat in between. At about the 10-mile mark, you gain the summit of all the climbs; now you have about a mile and a half of downhill as you drop into the East Nishnabotna River valley.

13.1 miles. Enter Atlantic and cross the East Nishnabotna. A sign lists 15 churches that welcome you as the highway becomes Second Street. Continue east with Second Street as State Highway 83 turns south.

14.2 miles. At the blinking red light, turn right onto Chestnut Street, Atlantic's main drag. The lanes are quite wide enough to share and traffic moves slowly as you pedal through the prosperous-looking business district. There are plenty of places to stop for food and drink, and an espresso bar, the Latte Loft, above the Pretty Woman clothing shop. Atlantic is home to Iowa's largest Coca-Cola bottling plant, and takes great pride in that fact. If you stop for refreshment, don't ask for a Pepsi.

Turn right onto Sixth Street and pass the town park. The park has a log cabin that was built in 1863—five years before Atlantic was even a town. The Rotary Club and Boy Scouts dismantled and moved the cabin, numbering each log for the reconstruction. The Atlantic Soroptomists have furnished it as it would have been in the 1800s.

Continue west on Sixth Street as it leaves town and becomes County Road G30. Cross the river again and make the gradual climb up from the valley. The land is wide open—you can see just about forever—and the sky is huge. You're back into rollers again, but now you're climbing more than descending; the land generally rises going west. The county road doesn't level the hills as much as State Highway 83 did, so the grades are steeper. The pavement is very smooth and the farmland is beautiful under its varicolored green blanket of crops. The road's as straight as an evil-doer's path to Hell.

25.4 miles. Turn right onto County Road M47. About a half mile north on M47 are some railroad tracks you cross on a downhill—slow down for them, they're very rough.

28.9 miles. County Road M47 merges with State Highway 83 and you continue straight ahead. It's less than two miles back to Walnut and your starting point.

Antique stores are ubiquitous in Walnut, the "Antique City."

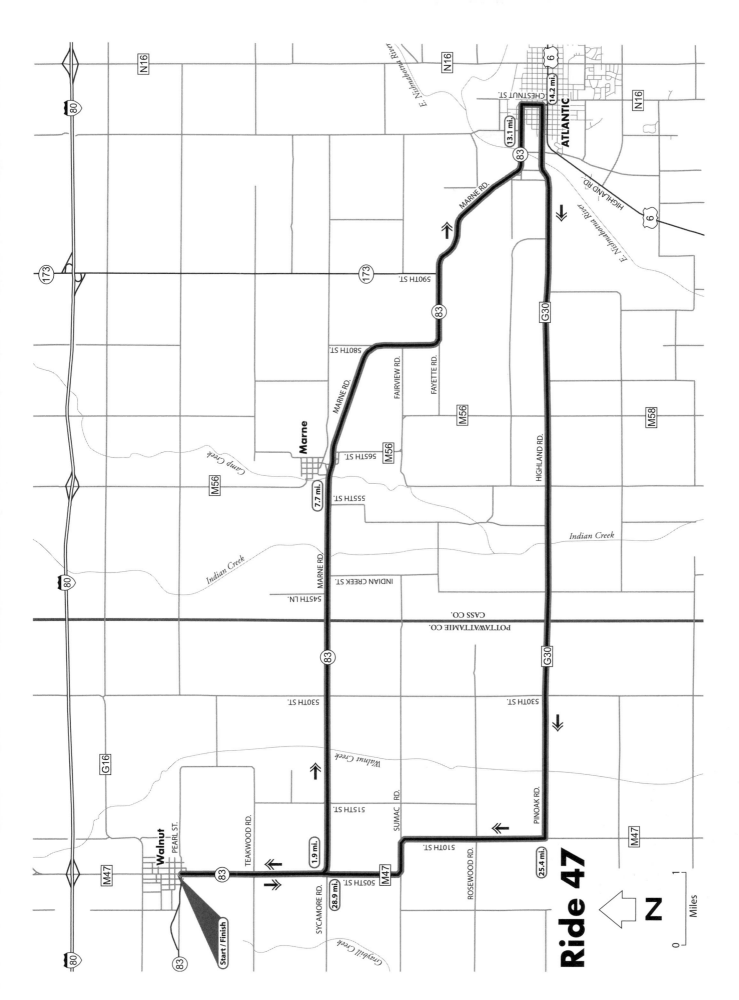

Ride 47

N

0 — 1

Miles

RIDE 48
The Taco Ride

LOCATION: Wabash Trace Nature Trail between Council Bluffs and Mineola

DISTANCE: 19.2 miles out and back

SURFACE: Crushed-limestone rail-trail

TERRAIN: Almost-imperceptible grades

DIFFICULTY: Easy

SERVICES:

   Restrooms: Wabash Trace trailhead in Council Bluffs, businesses in Mineola

   Water: Same

   Food: Restaurant and convenience store in Mineola

   Camping: Lake Manawa State Park, Council Bluffs

   Lodging: Motels, hotels, and bed and breakfasts in Council Bluffs

   Bike Shop: DDs Bike Shop, Third Avenue, and Endless Trail Bike Shop, South Main Street, Council Bluffs

STARTING POINT: Wabash Trace Nature Trail head at the corner of U.S. Highway 275 and East South Omaha Bridge Road, south of the Iowa School for the Deaf in Council Bluffs

The Mormon Battalion

Across the highway from the Wabash Trace trailhead is the site of the Grand Encampment, where Brigham Young and his followers from the Church of Jesus Christ of the Latter Day Saints (the Mormons) paused after their trek across Iowa in 1846. Twelve days after the Mormons set up their camp—which eventually extended nine miles to the east—Captain James Allen of the United States Army arrived, seeking 500 volunteers to fight the war with Mexico.

Brigham Young weighed the request. On the one hand, the loss of 500 able-bodied men would cripple his chances of reaching the Rocky Mountains that year and place a huge burden on those left behind to care for the men's families. On the other hand, however, their service would put the government in the Mormons' debt, and the wages paid to the men by the Army would help resupply the caravan. And, as an added benefit, Captain Allen would give the Mormons the United States Government's permission to settle temporarily on the Indian lands on the western bank of the Missouri.

So Brigham asked for volunteers. Only a handful of men stood up. Brigham announced that if enough young men didn't step forward, he'd draft the old men, then fill the ranks with women. The young men saw the light, stepped forward, and the Mormon Battalion was formed.

They marched out of the Grand Encampment in late July, heading for Fort Leavenworth, Kansas, where they would be mustered into the army. Theirs became the longest sustained march in U.S. Army history. The Mormon Battalion marched more than 2,000 miles, all over the southwest and into California. They never fired a shot in the Mexican War.

Cyclists cross a bridge on the Wabash Trace south of Council Bluffs.

The Wabash Trace Nature Trail was opened in 1988 on former right-of-way of the Wabash Railroad. Every Thursday night in the summer months, hundreds of cyclists ride this route to Mineola for Taco Night at the Mineola Steak House, stuff themselves silly, and ride back to Council Bluffs. Even if it's not Thursday, it's a great ride.

0.0 miles. From the trailhead south of the Iowa School for the Deaf, pedal south on the crushed-limestone Wabash Trace, which runs parallel to U.S. Highway 275. The trail quickly drops below the road's embankment, and is sheltered by trees on the west side.

In a short time you come to an open space where you can see the line of the Loess Hills stretching in front of you. You'll be cutting through those hills, but you'll hardly notice the climb: the railroad cut and filled its way to a nearly flat right-of-way.

2.7 miles. There's a short, sharp descent to cross Bluebird Lane—be careful here: Resist the urge to shoot through this blind intersection.

The trail surface is no problem for your skinny road tires, and trees on both sides keep you in the shade as you ride. There are lots of benches along the trail, inviting rest stops. There's a barely noticeable rise to the trail as it makes its way through the hills, but not enough to get you out of your cruising gear.

5.0 miles. Here's a bench with an open-lattice roof overlooking a beautiful vista across a narrow valley. A small creek winds through a crease between hills, and cattle graze peacefully in the long grass. A quarter mile farther, however, is a much less pleasant scene: a feedlot where the cattle have turned a hillside into an open sore, entirely denuded of grass and slashed with erosion gullies. Manure runoff has killed the trees at the bottom of the hill as well.

In another mile, you ride through a cut and notice that the pedaling is getting easier: You're heading downhill. The slight slope flattens out to cross a trestle over a waterway: Be careful on this, as it has some ruts that can catch a tire. There are lots of mulberry trees through this stretch—in season, the fallen berries are so thick on the trail that they splash your legs as your wheels crush them.

There are many cyclists on this trail, and for good reason: It's a lovely ride. Birds sing in the trailside trees, squirrels and rabbits dart across the path before you. The shade is cool and you're protected from the wind as you ride, and the glimpses you catch of the hilly countryside are entrancing.

7.9 miles. You're coming into one of the trail's most scenic sections now. Through breaks in the trees, you can see the hills rising, with terraces built across their slopes to control erosion. On your right are the rugged Loess Hills; on the left, the hills are lower and more rounded. The mix of woodland, crops, and pastures is ever-changing.

9.6 miles. You reach the trailhead at Mineola, where there's a shelter with a picnic table. Don't ride down the board ramp from the trail—the cracks between the boards can catch your tires. Take the grass-and-gravel path down from the trail into the trailhead.

To reach the Mineola Steak House, turn right onto Railroad Street. There are rumble strips in the shoulder, so you have to ride in the lane. Take a left on Main Street; the Steak House is up two blocks. It's open for lunch from 11:00 to 1:30 on weekdays, for dinner after 5:00 Wednesday through Saturday.

When you've eaten your fill of tacos (if it's Thursday night), turn your bike around and head back north to the Council Bluffs trailhead.

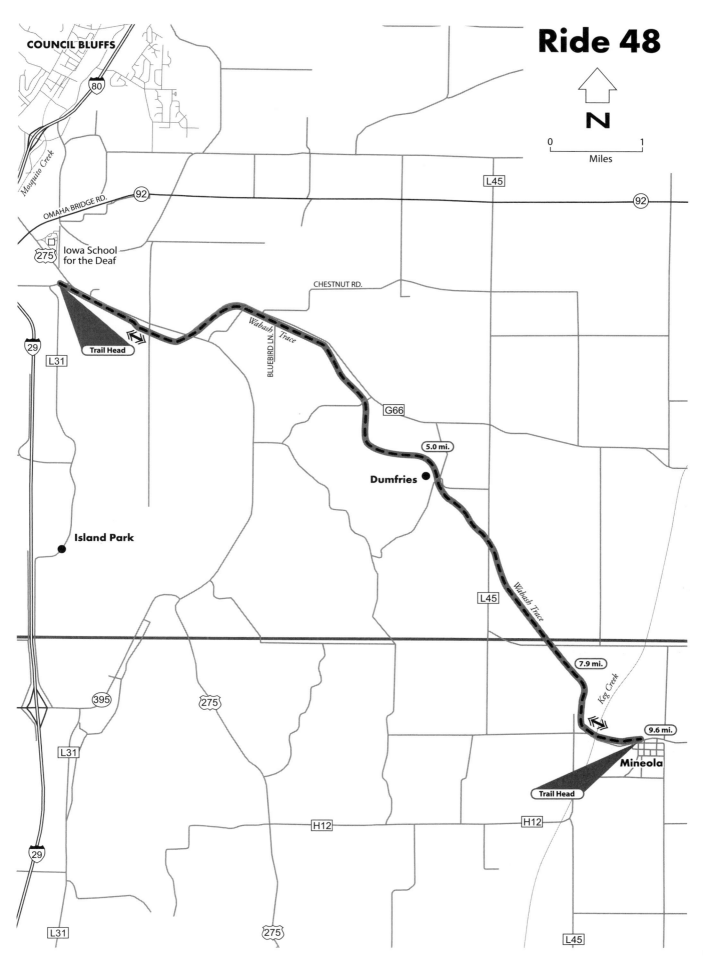

Ride 48

N

0   1
Miles

COUNCIL BLUFFS

Mosquito Creek

80

92

L45

92

OMAHA BRIDGE RD.

275

Iowa School
for the Deaf

CHESTNUT RD.

Wabash Trace

BLUEBIRD LN.

29

L31

Trail Head

G66

5.0 mi.

Dumfries

Island Park

L45

Wabash Trace

395

275

Keg Creek

7.9 mi.

L31

9.6 mi.

Mineola

29

Trail Head

H12

H12

L31

275

L45

RIDE 49
The Hidden Valley

LOCATION: Federal, state, and county roads between Thurman and Tabor
DISTANCE: 18.4-mile loop
SURFACE: Paved county, state, and federal roads
TERRAIN: Short but steep climbs and descents, some rolling hills and flats
DIFFICULTY: Moderate to strenuous
SERVICES:
    Restrooms: At start/finish, businesses in Tabor
    Water: Same
    Food: Convenience store and café in Tabor
    Camping: Waubonsie State Park, Hamburg
    Lodging: Bed and breakfasts in Thurman and Tabor, motels and bed and breakfasts in Shenandoah
    Bike Shop: Kirby's Sales and Service, Rye Street, Shenandoah
STARTING POINT: Thurman City Park on Fletcher Street

An old windmill stands in the Missouri River flood plain at the foot of the Loess Hills.

You'll skirt the western edge of the Loess Hills to start this ride, then climb into them to visit a town that was a hotbed of anti-slavery activity in the mid-1800s. The return trip is along Plum Creek through one of the prettiest valleys in the Loess Hills.

0.0 miles. Kick off from the town park in Thurman, a tiny town with a business district consisting of one empty storefront and one active automotive repair shop, and head north on Fletcher Street. At the four-way stop about 500 feet up the road, Fletcher becomes County Road L44 and takes you out of town.

On your right, the Loess Hills shoot up steeply; on the left, you look across the pancake-flat Missouri River floodplain. The road is smooth, level, and empty as you cruise in your middle gears. You pass some limestone outcroppings after a couple of miles, the bedrock upon which the loess soil was piled to form the hills, then go by a lake and wildlife management area on your left. Ahead, you can see the line of the hills curving slightly east.

4.6 miles. Turn right onto County Road J10 (Waubonsie Avenue) and start a gradual climb into the hills. Catch your breath on a flat stretch after three-quarters of an uphill mile, then shift into your granny gear for a seriously steep mile-and-a-half grind that brings you to the crest. The view is magnificent: rugged lines of tree-topped hills extending for miles. Enjoy that view as you cruise north and east along the ridgeline.

Pass a small pond on your right that cries out for a fly rod—the fish are leaping clear out of the water to catch insects. A quarter mile farther, there's a steep drop into a stream valley, then a tough half-mile climb to Tabor.

9.6 miles. Turn right to head south on U.S. Highway 275, and cruise through Tabor's business district. This town was founded in 1852 by Congregationalist settlers from Oberlin, Ohio. Their first choice for a town site was down in the flats of the Missouri floodplain, but mosquitoes and sickness drove them up into the hills.

Tabor was a hotbed of abolitionist activity in its early years. John Brown used the town as a staging area for his raid into Missouri, where he forcibly freed a handful of slaves and killed one slave owner. Though they were virulently anti-slavery, the citizens of Tabor objected strongly to murder and told Brown he was no longer welcome. They were even more upset when they learned he'd been stockpiling weapons in their town—weapons he used in his notorious raid on the federal arsenal in Harper's Ferry, Virginia.

Tabor was also the starting point for the Tabor & Northern Railroad, proclaimed by *Ripley's Believe It or Not* to be the world's shortest standard-gauge railroad. The line ran all of 8.79 miles to Malvern, where it connected with the Burlington Railroad's tracks. The first train on the line left Tabor on January 1, 1890, and trains continued to operate for 39 years, until paved highways changed people's transportation preferences.

11.6 miles. Turn right and head west on County Road J18 (120th Street). The road rises for the next half mile to a crest where you have a great view of terraced fields and wooded hills. Once over the crest, enjoy a mile-long descent into Plum Creek's valley.

County Road J18 is now Plum Creek Road, as lovely a ride as anyone could ask for. The pavement is smooth, the traffic all but nonexistent as you cruise through this jewel of a valley. Plum Creek meanders through the fields, lined with wide buffer strips of tall grasses and small trees. The hillsides are shaped to control erosion, with as many as five terraces rising up the valley sides. You pass a couple of beautiful old farmhouses, homesteads nestled into hollows between the hills. Keep an eye out for a Victorian-era house on the right, with its garage dug right into the side of the hill.

17.8 miles. Turn right onto East Street (State Highway 145/County Road J24) to come back into Thurman. There are some lovely old Victorian homes along this street; Thurman has a kind of decaying charm to it, hints of a past that was considerably more prosperous than its present.

18.3 miles. Follow County Road J24 as it turns right and takes you back to your starting point at the Thurman City Park.

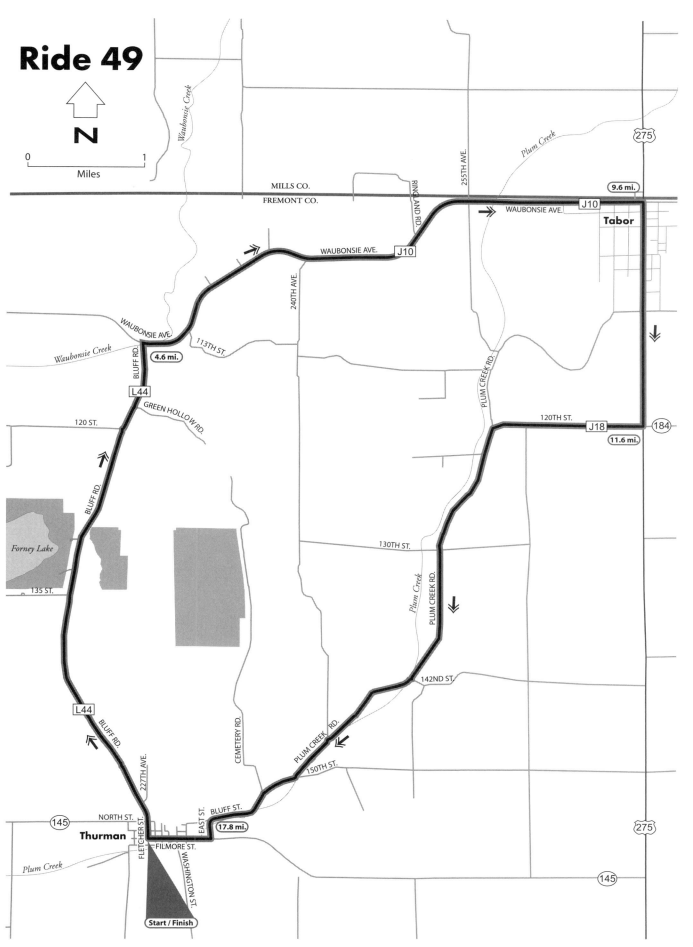

Ride 49

N

0   1
Miles

Waubonsie Creek

US 275

MILLS CO.
FREMONT CO.

RINGLAND RD.

255TH AVE.

Plum Creek

9.6 mi.

J10

WAUBONSIE AVE.

Tabor

WAUBONSIE AVE.

J10

240TH AVE.

WAUBONSIE AVE.

Waubonsie Creek

BLUFF RD.

113TH ST.

4.6 mi.

L44

GREEN HOLLOW RD.

120 ST.

PLUM CREEK RD.

120TH ST.

J18

184

11.6 mi.

BLUFF RD.

Forney Lake

135 ST.

130TH ST.

Plum Creek

PLUM CREEK RD.

142ND ST.

L44

BLUFF RD.

227TH AVE.

CEMETERY RD.

PLUM CREEK RD.

150TH ST.

145

NORTH ST.

FLETCHER ST.

EAST ST.

BLUFF ST.

17.8 mi.

275

Thurman

FILMORE ST.

WASHINGTON ST.

Plum Creek

145

Start / Finish

RIDE 50
Southern Loess Hills Loop

LOCATION: County and state roads between Waubonsie State Park, Riverton, and Sidney

DISTANCE: 25.6-mile loop

SURFACE: Paved city, county, and state roads

TERRAIN: Mostly rollers and flats, but there are a number of short, very steep climbs

DIFFICULTY: Strenuous

SERVICES:

  Restrooms: At start/finish, businesses in Sidney and Riverton

  Water: Same

  Food: Restaurants, taverns, and convenience stores in Sidney and Riverton

  Camping: Waubonsie State Park, Hamburg

  Lodging: Motels and bed and breakfasts in Shenandoah, Iowa, and Nebraska City, Nebraska

  Bike Shop: Kirby's Sales and Service, Rye Street, Shenandoah

STARTING POINT: Campground entrance in Waubonsie State Park on State Highway 2 north of Hamburg

Here at their southern end, the Loess Hills are a single north-south ridge that you'll cross twice. Between those climbs, you'll cruise the West Nishnabotna River valley, run some great rollers, and have a panoramic, postcard-quality view of the Loess Hills from their eastern side.

0.0 miles. Step on your pedals at the entrance to the campground in Waubonsie State Park. From hilltops in this park, you can see into four states: Iowa, Missouri, Nebraska, and Kansas. Head north on the park road (County Road L48/State Highway 239) and bear right as you come up the hill, then coast down to State Highway 2, where you turn right to ride east. You quickly pass the Equestrian Campground and head into a stretch of rollers that'll put all your gears to use.

2.6 miles. Watch out for the rumble strips as you approach the intersection with State Highway 275—they're cut deeply enough to bounce you off your bike. Across State Highway 275, your road becomes County Road J46 (State Highway 42)—State Highway 2 turned north, joining State Highway 275. There's an impressive view of hills stretching into the distance, carpeted with green crops and punctuated by stands of trees. A steep descent gets your speed up close to 40 mph, and you need every bit of that momentum to climb the next hill.

You drop into the valley of the West Nishnabotna River for a flat stretch. At the bridge over the river, signs warn of a flood area—one reads, "Impassible During High Water." If you look closely, you'll see high water marks on roadside utility poles: The marks are higher than the tops of your wheels.

6.5 miles. Pass Riverton's welcoming sign and climb into town past some nice old buildings. Riverton is home to Iowa's oldest Chautauqua Pavilion, which is listed on the National Register of Historic Places.

7.1 miles. Turn left onto County Road L68 and head north. The road drops a bit and crosses the East Nishnabotna River (East joins West Nishnabotna a few miles southwest of Riverton). In the valley on your left lie the Riverton Marsh and the Riverton Wildlife Management Area. This is a stop on the Missouri River flyway—during the migration season, thousands of snow geese descend on the marsh.

Climb a very steep grade to reach the top of the ridge. As you ride north, the Loess Hills are an irregular line of tree-capped slopes across the valley to your left. To your right is a very pretty view across the river valley. Traffic is light and the road is smooth, so you can enjoy the view fully as you cruise this flat stretch.

11.7 miles. Turn left to head west on State Highway 2. There's more motor traffic on this road than you've seen so far, and it's moving fast; however, the drivers are mindful of your presence and give you plenty of room as they pass. There are some downhill rollers to run, then a steep descent back into the West Nishnabotna River valley. The road's embankment is high enough to avoid flooding, apparently: there are no warning signs as you cross the valley. The bridge over the river is very long, however, over a very narrow river.

A steep half-mile climb, then a welcome downhill bring you to the outskirts of Sidney, the Fremont county seat. The Sidney Rodeo, a four-day event that has been nominated for five consecutive years as the PRCA Small Outdoor Rodeo of the Year, is Iowa's oldest outdoor rodeo. It's happened in Sidney every summer since 1923. Another steep climb brings you into the business district.

16.5 miles. State Highway 2 joins State Highway 275 and both turn left to go around Sidney's courthouse square. The Fremont County Courthouse is the third courthouse to occupy this site. The first one was dynamited by unknown parties during the Civil War; the second was set afire by an unknown arsonist in 1888. The current courthouse has survived long enough to get on the National Register of Historic Places.

As you follow State Highway 2 (Illinois Street) past the courthouse, take note of Penn Drug Company on your right, the oldest family-owned drugstore in Iowa. Opened in 1863 by Dr. J. N. Penn, it's now operated by the family's fifth generation. On your birthday, you can get a free soda at the soda fountain that was installed in 1899.

16.9 miles. Hang a right onto County Road J34 (Knox Road) and shift into your granny gear for a climb over the Loess Hills. A half mile past the high school, you'll see a sign that says the pavement ends—it doesn't, though the painted centerline disappears. The descent on the other side of the hill is a screamer, and you have a long flat stretch to run out your momentum.

20.3 miles. Bear left to head south on Bluff Road (County Road L44), curving along the base of the hills as they make a long arc to the southeast. On your left, crops grow plentifully in the Missouri River's floodplain, while on your right the hills rise from the far side of the ditch.

23.9 miles. Turn left onto State Highway 2 again—you've certainly seen enough of *this* road by now—and head east into the hills for one last climb. It's only a half mile to the crest, where you turn right onto State Highway 239/County Road L48 to get back to your starting point in Waubonsie State Park.

Ride 50

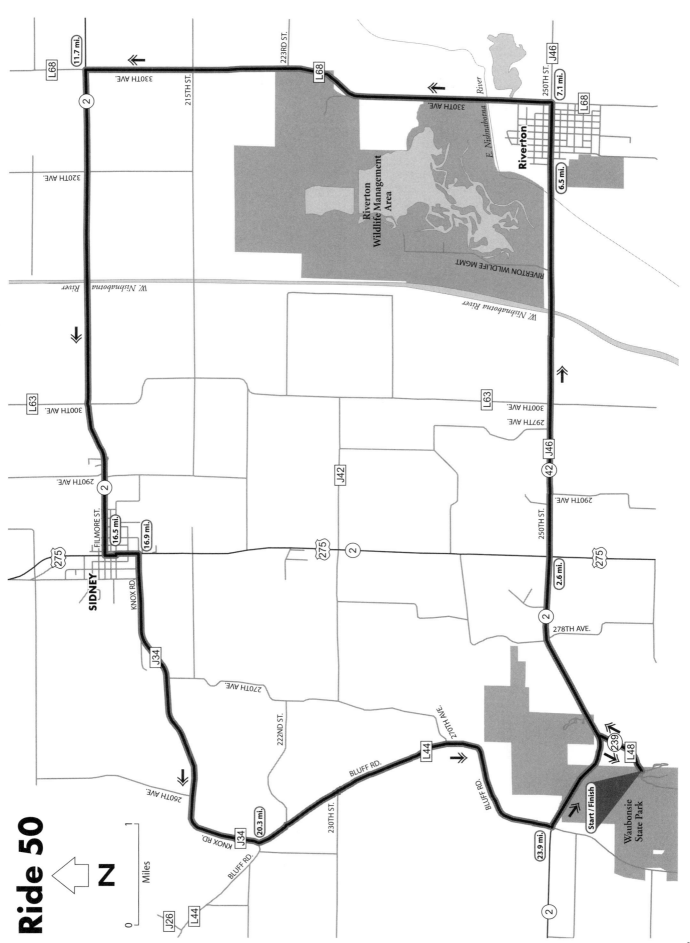

N

Miles
0   1

L68   **11.7 mi.**
330TH AVE.
223RD ST.
215TH ST.
L68
L68   **7.1 mi.**
250TH ST.   J46
River
Riverton
6.5 mi.

320TH AVE.
E. Nishnabotna

Riverton
Wildlife Management
Area

RIVERTON WILDLIFE MGMT.

W. Nishnabotna River
W. Nishnabotna River

300TH AVE.   L63
L63   300TH AVE.
297TH AVE.
290TH AVE.

L63
290TH AVE.

J46
42   J46

J42

SIDNEY
FILMORE ST.
16.5 mi.
16.9 mi.
275
275
2
2   **2.6 mi.**
250TH ST.
275

KNOX RD.
2
278TH AVE.

J34
270TH AVE.
222ND ST.
230TH ST.
BLUFF RD.
L44
270TH AVE.

20.3 mi.   J34
KNOX RD.
260TH AVE.
BLUFF RD.
BLUFF RD.

239   L48
Start / Finish
Waubonsie
State Park
23.9 mi.

J26
L44
2

APPENDIX A

LINKING THE RIDES

The routes in this book are relatively short; most of them can be ridden in just a couple of hours or less. For those who'd like longer rides, including multi-day tours, here are some suggestions for linking the short routes into longer explorations of Iowa's countryside.

EASTERN IOWA

Cedar Valley Century

Rides 4, 5, and 6 (Smell the Chocolate Ride, Finding the Lost County Seat, and Say "Hi" to Chuck Ride) can be linked into a very nice century-plus ride, combining roads and trails. Total distance is approximately 105 miles. You can also make this a pleasant two-day excursion by overnighting at Wilder County Park in Allison, Heery Woods State Park in Clarksville, or a motel in Waverly.

Begin at Cup of Joe in Cedar Falls, the starting point for Ride 6: Say "Hi" to Chuck Ride. Follow the Ride 6 route through New Hartford to Union Road. At Ride 6's mile 24.8, instead of turning right on Cedar-Wapsi Road (County Road C57), turn left to head west. Follow the paved road as it turns north and ride through the tiny town of Finchford. Beyond Finchford, the pavement turns west as County Road C55, then, after a few more miles, turns north as County Road T63.

County Road T63 joins the route of Ride 5: Finding the Lost County Seat, just south of Shell Rock at Ride 5's mile 28.2, the junction with County Road C45. Turn left and head west on County Road C45, and take Ride 5's route in reverse to Allison, where you pick up the Rolling Prairie Trail to Clarksville.

After riding through Clarksville (you're still following Ride 5's route in reverse), you have a choice to make. You can turn into the Schmadeke's driveway about 1.1 miles from where you turned onto County Road C33 from Clarksville's Main Street (Ride 5's mile 5.5) and take the Butler County Nature Trail to the trailhead at Shell Rock, or you can continue straight east on County Road C33. Continuing east on C33 saves you a few miles. If you take the Nature Trail, when you reach the trailhead, turn left (north) on County Road T63 and it will take you up to County Road C33, where you'll turn east.

Follow County Road C33 east to County Road V14, where you turn right to head south into Waverly. County Road V14 becomes Horton Road, and connects you to the route of Ride 4: Smell the Chocolate Ride, at the intersection of Cedar Lane Road, Ride 4's mile 10.3. Follow the Ride 4 route to the Waverly Rail Trail and the Jefferson City Trail to Denver.

At the end of the Ride 4 route, Forrest Avenue Park on the north side of Denver, continue south on State Street into town and turn right to head west on West Fayette Street (County Road C50). County Road C50 turns south, merging with County Road V19 for a couple of miles, then cuts west again to take you to Janesville. Cross U.S. Highway 218, pass the Janesville High School, and turn left onto Main Street. Ride through Janesville's rapidly fading business district and turn left onto County Road V14 (Waverly Road or, to locals, "old Highway 218") to head south to Cedar Falls.

You'll rejoin the Ride 6 route at the junction with County Road C57 (Cedar-Wapsi Road) at Ride 6's mile 27.5. Follow the Ride 6 route description back to your starting point.

Cedar Valley Nature Trail

The Cedar Valley Trail System in Cedar Falls/Waterloo, featured in Ride 7: Tour de Parks, links up with the Cedar Valley Nature Trail, featured in Ride 8: Over the Burned Bridge, providing a 70-mile route from Cedar Falls to Hiawatha, a few miles north of Cedar Rapids. You can start at either end of this great trail system for an out-and-back two-day tour. (Campgrounds are near the Cedar Falls end of the trail; motels are convenient to both ends.) While back-to-back 70-mile days may seem daunting, the route is basically flat and almost entirely shaded, with conveniently-spaced towns for rest-and-refreshment stops, so the miles pass easily.

For trail maps of both the Cedar Trails System and the Cedar Valley Nature Trail, contact the Black Hawk County Conservation Board, 2410 Lone Tree Road, Cedar Falls, IA 50613; (319) 266-6813.

Coralville Lake-Amana Colonies

Ride 11: Sugar Bottom Sojourn, and Ride 12: Around the Amanas, can be linked into a day of extremely varied terrain, with hills and curving roads around Coralville Lake (Ride 11) and the flatter river valley ride through the Amana Colonies. Total distance is approximately 80 miles.

With all the shops, bed and breakfast inns, and good restaurants to explore in the Amanas, however, you might want to start in North Liberty with Ride 11, then ride the link to Amana for some sightseeing and an overnight. Take Ride 12 around the Amana Colonies on the next day, then pedal back to your starting point in North Liberty.

To get from North Liberty to Amana, turn right on Penn Avenue at Ride 11's mile 17.8 and head west. Penn Avenue becomes County Road F28 and crosses Interstate 380, jogs north, then west again. Turn left to go south on County Road W38, then make a right turn onto Upper Old Highway 6 Road NW. That curves around to run into U.S. Highway 6. Turn right onto U.S. Highway 6 and ride west. You'll join the route of Ride 12: Around the Amanas, in Homestead, at the junction of U.S. Highways 6 and 151, a little beyond Ride 12's mile 23.5 Turn right on U.S. Highway 151 and follow the Ride 12 route to Amana. The distance from North Liberty to Homestead is approximately 17 miles.

Mississippi River Ride

For a full day along the Mississippi River, link Ride 14: Mississippi River Trail Ride, and Ride 15: Riding the River Road, into a route from Davenport to Muscatine and back. The out-and-back trip will be about 65 miles long.

Start with Ride 14, from the water Taxi parking lot in Lindsay Park in East Davenport, and follow the route down to Credit Island. Make the circle through Credit Island Park and when you exit the park, turn left onto U.S. Highway 61, heading southwest. This is a four-lane with considerable traffic, but you're on it for less than a mile before you turn left onto Concord Street, which takes you down close to the river again.

Enjoy a nice ride past riverfront cottages, summer homes, and fishing shacks, then turn right onto Utah Street, which takes you to State Highway 22, the Great River Road. Turn left to head southwest on State Highway 22 into Buffalo. At the Clark's Landing restaurant, you're at Ride 15's mile 16.6. Follow the route for Ride 15 in reverse to Muscatine.

CENTRAL IOWA
Two Lakes in One Ride

Ride 19: Rice Lake Roundabout, and Ride 20: Who Named This Lake?, can be linked into a beautiful day's ride over the mostly flat terrain of north-central Iowa. The total length is approximately 65 miles.

Begin your ride from Clear Lake, following the route for Ride 20. At Ventura, Ride 20's mile 8.8, instead of turning right onto Lake Street, continue straight north on County Road S14 to Joice, about 18 miles distant. County Road S14 becomes Western Avenue in Joice, putting you at the beginning of Ride 19's route description.

Follow Ride 19 around Rice Lake and back to Joice. At the intersection with Main Street (Ride 19's mile 14.8), continue straight south on County Road S14. Turn left on County Road A38 and ride east for about a half mile, then turn south again on County Road S18 to head back to Clear Lake.

As you approach Clear Lake, County Road S18 becomes Eagle Avenue/North 16th Street. Cross U.S. Highway 18 and the railroad tracks, and turn left on West Seventh Avenue N, which runs into North Shore Drive around Clear Lake. Bear left on North Shore Drive and you're back on the Ride 20 route. In about three-quarters of a mile, you'll pass the Surf Ballroom, Ride 20's mile 13.9

Raccoon River Valley Trail

Ride 28: Lots of Loops, features a portion of the Raccoon River Valley Trail. This lovely rail-trail begins in Jefferson and runs 56 miles to Clive, where it connects with the Clive Greenbelt Trail described in Ride 27: Cruisin' in Clive. For an excellent two-day tour, start at either end of the trail (overnight and restaurant accommodations are more numerous at the Clive end of the trail than in Jefferson).

For a trail map of the Raccoon River Valley Trail, contact the Greene County Conservation Board, 507 Lincolnway, Jefferson, IA 50129; (515) 386-5674.

Southern Iowa Tour

For a challenging day of riding the southern Iowa hills, link Ride 33: Almost Missouri Ride, with Ride 34: Road Apple Ride. This is about a 70-mile ride; at its end, your legs will definitely be tired.

Start in Leon, following the route for Ride 33 to Davis City (**Ride 33's mile 8.0**). After you pass the Davis City Café, look for a right turn onto County Road J52 (Clark Street). Follow County Road J52 west, crossing Interstate 35, and turn left to go south on County Road R30 (South Smith Street). Turn west again on U.S. Highway 69 (East Main Street) in Lamoni, which takes you to the starting point for Ride 34.

Enjoy the Road Apple Ride and, at its end point,

continue straight on Main Street, retracing your route through Lamoni. Continue east on U.S. Highway 69, which takes you back to Davis City. Before you get into Davis City's business district, turn right onto Dale Miller Road (County Road J66) at Ride 33's mile 8.8, then follow the Ride 33 route back to your starting point.

WESTERN IOWA
Iowa Great Lakes Trail

The Iowa Great Lakes Trail, featured in Ride 35: Nearly Minnesota Ride, and Ride 36: Bikin' 'Boji, begins south of Arnolds Park, in Milford. For a great ride of about 30 miles, you can link Rides 35 and 36 together.

Start at the Milford end of the Iowa Great Lakes Trail and ride the trail north through Arnold's Park to Spirit Lake. Follow the Ride 35 route around Spirit Lake, and return south on the trail. When you reach 175th Street and the sign pointing west to the Westport School House, turn right onto the Kenue Park Trail, the side path to 175th Street, and follow the Ride 36 route from Ride 36's mile 3.8. At the end of that ride's route, continue on the Iowa Great Lakes Trail to get back to your starting point in Milford.

Loess and Lesser Hills

Challenge your legs and lungs by combining Ride 44: The Lesser Hills, with Ride 45: The Heart of the Loess Hills, into a gorgeous and very hilly loop of about 72 miles.

From the starting point for Ride 45 in Magnolia, ride north on Magnolia Street and turn right to head east on State Highway 127. In less than seven miles, you'll reach Logan, where you turn onto U.S. Highway 30 east (though it actually is heading north). Follow U.S. Highway 30 for about four miles, then turn right to head east on State Highway 44, which is Ride 44's mile 5.0. Follow the Ride 44 route to Woodbine.

At Ride 44's mile 31.5, turn right onto U.S. Highway 30 and make the immediate left onto Lincoln Way, but instead of following Lincoln Way, bear left on First Street (County Road F32), heading west. The road forks after about a mile; bear right onto County Road F20L, which climbs back into the Loess Hills.

After about 12 miles of beautiful, hilly road, you'll reach the intersection with County Road L23 (Laredo Avenue). This is Ride 45's mile 8.9; County Road F20L is Easton Road. Follow the Ride 45 route through Pisgah and back to your starting point in Magnolia.

Wabash Trace

A portion of the Wabash Trace is featured in Ride 48: The Taco Ride. This trail runs southeast from Council Bluffs to Blanchard, on the Missouri/Iowa border, a total of 64 miles. To make an out and back two-day tour on the Trace, start at the trailhead in Council Bluffs and ride south. Overnight accommodations and restaurants are available in Shenandoah, about 17 miles from trail's end in Blanchard. You can find a map of the Wabash Trace online at http://wabashtrace.connections.net.

Southern Loess Hills

Linking Ride 49: The Hidden Valley, and Ride 50: The Southern Loess Hills Loop gives you a superb day of cycling. You'll have some challenging climbs and zooming descents, a section of fun rollers, and some nice flat stretches, all in an outstandingly scenic area. This figure-eight ride is a bit over 57 miles.

Start in Thurman and make the Ride 49 loop. After you turn west on East Street (State Highway 145/County Road J24) to come back into Thurman (Ride 49's mile 17.8), turn left onto Washington Street (County Road L44) and head south along the edge of the Loess Hills. The road's name changes to Bluff Road and, in a little over seven miles, it merges with County Road J34, which comes in from your right. A bit farther on, County Road J34 turns left (it's named Knox Road here): this is Ride 50's mile 20.3. Follow the Ride 50 route to the entrance to Waubonsie State Park, then east on State Highway 2, following the Ride 50 route to Riverton and Sidney.

In Sidney, at Ride 50's mile 16.5, instead of turning left with State Highway 2 and U.S. Highway 275, turn right on 275, heading north. After about six miles, turn left to head west on County Road J24 (State Highway 145), climbing over the Loess Hills again to return to Thurman and your starting point.

APPENDIX B

MORE GREAT BIKE RIDES IN IOWA

As I wrote at the beginning of this book, the rides I've documented here just scratch the surface of bicycling pleasures in Iowa. Bicycle advocates in this state estimate that there are about 384,000 active cyclists in Iowa (just over 13% of the population). All of those pedal pushers, I'm sure, have some favorite routes that aren't included in these pages.

A good number of those routes, however, show up in the organized bike rides that occur virtually every week of the year (yes, even in December, January, and February!). During the warm-weather months, you can find lots of great rides with convivial company every weekend.

RAGBRAI

No book about cycling in Iowa would be complete without mention of RAGBRAI, the (Des Moines) Register's Annual Great Bike Ride Across Iowa. During the last week of July, 8,500 registered cyclists and up to 15,000 day-riders and hangers-on cycle from the Missouri River to the Mississippi in the longest-running and largest cross-state bicycle ride in the United States.

I admit that I've never done RAGBRAI. In various years, I've ridden with the RAGBRAI crowd for a day; I've worked as a volunteer direction-pointer/question-answerer when the ride came through my town; I've served breakfast pancakes and sausages to RAGBRAI riders to raise money for a nonprofit organization. But I haven't actually spent a whole week of July biking across Iowa in the company of thousands of other cyclists. It just isn't my kind of bike ride.

That said, I direct you to www.ragbrai.org, the ride's official Web site. If you enter "RAGBRAI" into your search engine, you'll find tens of thousands of sites, and much more information than anyone could ever absorb about the ride.

Cedar Trails Festival

For my money, the Cedar Trails Festival may well offer the best-organized trail rides in Iowa. And that's not just because they're free.

The festival occurs on the second weekend of August in the Waterloo/Cedar Falls metropolitan area, and features several bike rides through the 70-plus miles of the Cedar Trails System. The showcase event is the "Light Up the Night Ride" on Saturday night. A loop of more than ten miles of paved trails along the Cedar River is lined with thousands of luminaries and the ride begins just after sunset. Between the candles' light and the moonlight, the effect is almost magical, especially if you make a second circuit after most of the other riders have finished and gone home.

For details about the festival, contact the Cedar Falls Visitors and Tourism Bureau, 6510 Hudson Road, Cedar Falls, IA 50613; (319)268-4266, (800)845-1955; www.cedarfallstourism.org.

Bike Iowa

For a listing of nearly all the organized rides that happen in Iowa—and there are hundreds and hundreds of them—go to www.bikeiowa.com. The site lists rides, bike shops in the state, news, bike clubs, and just about everything else related to cycling in Iowa.

APPENDIX C

TOWN INDEX

COUNTY INDEX